Forgetting Ourselves

Innovations in the Study of World Politics

Series Editor
Zeev Maoz, Tel-Aviv University

Advisory Board

Michael Barnett, University of Wisconsin, Madison
Deborah Larson, UCLA
Jack Levy, Rutgers University

This series provides a forum for the publication of original theoretical, empirical, and conceptual studies that seek to chart new frontiers in the field of international relations. The key emphasis is on innovation and change. Books in the series will offer insights on and approaches to a broad range of issues facing the modern world, in an effort to revolutionize how contemporary world politics are studied, taught, and practiced.

Forgetting Ourselves: Secession and the (Im)possibility of Territorial Identity, by Linda S. Bishai

Forgetting Ourselves

Secession and the (Im)possibility of Territorial Identity

Linda S. Bishai

LEXINGTON BOOKS
Lanham • Boulder • New York • Toronto • Oxford

LEXINGTON BOOKS

Published in the United States of America
by Lexington Books
An imprint of The Rowman & Littlefield Publishing Group, Inc.
4501 Forbes Boulevard, Suite 200, Lanham, Maryland 20706

PO Box 317
Oxford
OX2 9RU, UK

British Library Cataloguing in Publication Information Available

Library of Congress Cataloging-in-Publication Data

Bishai, Linda S., 1964-
  Forgetting ourselves : secession and the (im)possibility of
territorial identity / Linda S. Bishai.
      p. cm. — (Innovations in the study of world politics)
  Includes bibliographical references and index.
  ISBN 0-7391-0666-X (alk. paper)
  1. Secession. 2. Sovereignty. 3. Territory, National.
4. Self-determination, National. 5. National state. I. Title.
II. Series: Innovations in the study of world politics.
JZ1316.B57 2004
320.1—dc22   2003021931

Printed in the United States of America
⊖™ The paper used in this publication meets the minimum requirements of American
National Standard for Information Sciences—Permanence of Paper for Printed Library
Materials, ANSI/NISO Z39.48–1992.

for AB

Contents

Acknowledgments

It will be clear from the references in this text what some of my many intellectual debts are, but there are always, of course, many personal debts formed during the long and tortuous path to a book's end. I owe much to James Mayall, who refused to allow me a moment's complacency about any of my arguments. Much of this text was written in Stockholm, and while isolation makes scholarship difficult, the burden was often lightened by the comments and suggestions of Pål Wrange. My first chapter was improved by exposure to the research seminar at the Swedish Institute of International Affairs, and I am grateful to Walter Carlsnaes for his supportive and judicious suggestions. Thoughts on the narratives of secession were helpfully explored by a workshop on narrative at the European Consortium for Political Research in Mannheim, and in particular in discussions with Costas Constantinou. My understanding and appreciation of International Relations as a discipline were wonderfully enhanced through the process of introducing the field to students at the London School of Economics, Stockholm University, and Towson University. I am grateful for that opportunity. I have also benefited from the enthusiasm and encouragement of James Roberts, Marie Lall, and Janice Bially Mattern, who kept me thinking and reaching for the end of the book. Kind and helpful critiques from John Agnew, Charles Jones, and Chris Brown have made my own revisions a much less intimidating prospect, although obviously any failures of fact or analysis are mine alone. Jonathan Walker and Elizabeth Bishai stepped into the brink to save me from formatting and indexing torment. They have my admiring gratitude. Finally, my life has been immeasurably richer for the love, laughter, and intellect of my husband. For that I thank—not Andreas, who cannot help himself—but *Fortuna*, who, in one of her kinder moments, brought us together.

Introduction

Theorizing Theory

Now, a person who thinks should not try to persuade others of his belief; that is what puts him on the road to a system; on the lamentable road of the "man of conviction"; politicians like to call themselves that; but what is a conviction? It is a thought that has come to a stop, that has congealed, and the "man of conviction" is a man restricted; experimental thought seeks not to persuade but to inspire; to inspire another thought, to set thought moving.

Milan Kundera, Testaments Betrayed

What is the nature of the social and political organization of people? This might be considered the primary question of the social sciences. But how we ask this question, whether we put it as an open question or ponder it as impenetrable, determines to a great extent the path of scholarship that follows; that is, if we ask the question, "what is the nature of human social and political organization?" then scholarship must proceed with all empirical efforts required to muster a logically defensible answer. The asking of the question in itself contains the strong suggestion that the answer is determinable, is "out there," if only the scholar is brilliant or thorough enough to ascertain it. If, however, the issue is not put as a question but as a statement of a state of being, "humans are socially and politically organized," the emphasis shifts from the discovery of a determinable nature to the semantics of "social," "political," and "organization." Ironically, the statement contains more indeterminacy and interpretive space than the does the question. When we ask questions, we presume the existence of an answer, rather than the possibility that the answers are multiple and contextual. It is through the questioning of ontology, the nature of the real, and the implicit assumption that the answers are not singular or final but relational and inconstant, that scholars can adapt to change and theorize alternatives. Because theory both reflects and shapes our knowledge of reality, the ontological assumptions of the theorist have tangible implications for our collective experience. As Robert Cox puts it:

> Theory follows reality. It also precedes and shapes reality. That is to say, there is a real historical world in which things happen; and theory is made through reflection upon what has happened. The separation of theory from historical happenings is, however, only a way of thinking, because theory feeds back into the making of history by virtue of the way those who make history (and I am thinking about human collectivities, not just about prominent individuals) think about what they are doing. Their understanding of what the historical context allows them to do, prohibits them from doing, or requires them to do and the way they formulate their purposes in acting, is the product of theory.[1]

Theory, then, not only is intertwined with practice, but also is an inseparable part of the political culture and thus of the making of political decisions. For International Relations (IR) theory, concerned as it is with the nature of global political organization, the need to consider this indissoluble link between theory and practice is particularly decisive. The instability of formerly established patterns is becoming increasingly evident as the breadth and impact of globalization become clearer, and International Relations is uniquely positioned as a discipline to offer appropriately multifaceted perspectives on this flux in the spatial structures of the international.

Secession is one of the richest veins yet to be mined in International Relations, and it is especially responsive to an approach that questions ontological certainties. Persistent prodding at the assumptions of secessionists and many scholars who have theorized secession yields a wealth of mythical historical narrative, anti-political politics, illiberal liberalism, and problematic problem solving. An approach that is comfortable with ontological uncertainties readily exposes the contingency and ambiguity of conventional treatments of secession. The international disruptions caused by secessionist movements are constant evidence of the impact of theory upon practice as they strive to perform the required legal norms of self-determination and sovereign territorial integrity. As Cox suggests, secessionists' understanding of what the historical context allows them to do has been produced by theories of the nation and international order. Having been shaped by the expectations of the international legal and political structures of their era, secessionists respond with the preordained logic of the territorial state. All too often it is the habit of theorists to accept the practices of states and secessionists as prior to their theorizing, as a question to be answered, or as a problem to be solved through careful observation and analysis. But secession as a political phenomenon has not always been with us, nor did it abruptly appear as a nationalist fad. Secession implicates a host of historical accomplices related to the development of industrial modernity and considerable changes in the nature of sovereignty and the state. By historicizing secession, as I do in this book, it becomes possible not only to explain the historical transformations that have led to the current confluence of theory and practice, but also to better question the possibilities and impact of current transformative interactions.

Robert Cox's discussion of problem solving versus critical theoretical approaches provides a perfect illustration of the difference between the treatment of secession here and the treatment it has generally received in political science and theory (though not, strangely, in International Relations). Cox describes theory as belonging either to the problem-solving approach or to the critical approach, each serving different purposes. The problem-solving approach assumes the permanence of existing structure, while the critical approach explores the possibilities of structural transformation: "But whereas problem-solving theory assimilates particular situations to general rules, providing a kind of programmed method for dealing with them, critical theory seeks out the developmental potential within the particular."[2] Analyzing secession with the problem-solving approach assumes the timelessness of territorial states and national identities, thereby foreclosing any discussion about the historical validity of these structures and the possibility that they may be implicated in the phenomenon of secession itself. A critical theoretical approach "does not take institutions and social and power relations for granted but calls them into question by concerning itself with their origins and how and whether they might be in the process of changing."[3] Critically analyzing secession, therefore, requires a process of problematization, a *dis*-assumption of institutions and relations, which puts the issue in a wider (changing) context, revealing hidden connections and weaknesses in the structures. Thus, I seek here to historicize and question the concept of secession itself and the component assumptions of territoriality and identity upon which it rests.

This approach to secession is quite unexplored in International Relations literature, and I begin in chapter 1 with an explanation of the epistemological commitments that precluded IR theorists from analyzing phenomena "inside" the state. This chapter also contains a discussion of secession's historical meanings and examines two nineteenth-century cases commonly assumed to represent secession as we know it today. I argue that these cases do not reflect the politics of territory and identity that currently drive secessionist conflicts. Next, I examine the theories of secession developed in other disciplines and reveal the fixed assumptions under which they proceed to be firmly within a problem-solving theoretical framework that is therefore incapable of problematizing the constituent elements of secession. By treating secession as a structural feature of a stable system, conventional analysis has been unable to open new theoretical spaces that can view secession as a contingent rather than institutional phenomenon. Seeking to probe the historical conditions of secession's possibility, in chapter 3, *States Taking Place: History and the Territorialization of Politics*, I undertake a conceptual analysis of territoriality and the changing assumptions of political space that accompanied its development. Distinguishing between *territory* as space and *territoriality* as the political legitimation of space, I argue that it is not until the twentieth century that political space as territoriality came to be a source of such absolute regulation that it could lead to the secessionist imperative. The linkage between territorial affiliation and political identity is more institutionalized now than it has ever been. I illustrate this with a discussion of the concepts of foreignness, citizenship, and international, which converged with the modern state and nation to generate a regime of restrictions and control over identity.

It is the nature of identity, then, that I problematize next, in chapter 4, where I discuss the concepts of nation and minority and their dependence on boundaries both political and territorial. A discussion of identity in International Relations theory reveals that while many steps have been taken, there is some distance to go before the constructed nature of identity has been fully explored as relevant for IR. Using William Connolly's identity\difference discussion as inspiration, I reiterate the need for the acceptance of ambiguity in identity relations and show, through a telling of the secessionist stories of Québec, the dangers of assuming and requiring secured (fixed) identities. Chapter 5, *Secessionist Performances, Narrating Otherness*, carries this discussion further with a fuller analysis of the power of performative language in historical narrative. I examine several examples of secessionist literature, produced by the leadership of three movements (in Québec, Northern Italy, and Hawaii). While treating each as a separate historical example within a specific context, the one feature I find these secessionist narratives have in common is the need to establish a historical basis for the separateness of their identities and a validation thereby of the need for an independent state that will bound and protect those identities. This chapter concludes with a discussion of Nietzsche's typology of mankind's three relationships with history, and a plea for the encouragement of a critical engagement with history. Finally, in chapter 6, I discuss the implications of the previous discussion on (bounded) politics of democracy. Drawing on Derrida's concept of *ontopology* (the alignment of identity and territory in a social ontology of situated being), I introduce a variety of theorists who make it possible to question ontopological politics. I conclude, inconclusively, with a call for the practice of IR theory in the manner of Nietzsche's critical history—specifically, the practice of *forgetting* historical patterns in order to liberate theoretical space in our minds for future alternatives. Specifically, we must *forget ourselves* in terms of all the historical baggage that accompanies our identities. I was intrigued to find that the *Oxford English Dictionary* contains several definitions of the phrase "forgetting oneself."[4] One of these means "to lose sight of the requirements of dignity, propriety, or decorum; to behave unbecomingly"—referring perhaps to the kind of (unacceptable) behavior that happens when we depart from all of the social customs and norms that our selves accumulate from the past. But the primary meaning is "to omit care for oneself"—that is, to act selflessly or without protecting one's self—and this can happen in the positive sense only if we do literally forget who we are, even if only for a brief moment. Only by this kind of forgetting of the self can we engage fully in the ongoing process of negotiating identity with the other.

It is my belief that a critical historical engagement with secessionist movements reveals the constructed natures of both the identities and the territories they claim are justifications for sovereign independence. This book by no means asserts that identities are trivial, or that attachment to territory is insignificant, but rather, it intends to demonstrate that the drives that make secession appear as the only option for the enactment of international relations are neither founded in primordial history nor dictated by pragmatic considerations. The discipline of International Relations, by practicing theory differently, is remarkably well poised to make a significant contribution to a politics that will finally make secession a thing of the past.

Notes

1. Robert Cox, "Towards a Post-Hegemonic Conceptualization of World Order: Reflections on the Relevancy of Ibn Khaldun," in *Governance Without Government: Order and Change in World Politics*, ed. James N. Rosenau and Ernst-Otto Czempiel (Cambridge: Cambridge University Press, 1992), 133.

2. Robert Cox, "Social Forces, States and World Orders: Beyond International Relations Theory," in *Neorealism and Its Critics*, ed. Robert O. Keohane (New York: Columbia University Press, 1985), 244.

3. Cox, "Social Forces," 208.

4. *The Oxford English Dictionary*, 2d ed, s.v. "forgetting oneself."

Chapter 1

If at First You Don't Secede:
International Relations Theory
and Its Shortcomings

Secession is one of the few remaining options for the generation of new states in the international system; it would thus seem to be a subject of profound importance for the theory and study of International Relations. And yet it continues to be largely neglected by International Relations scholars both as a subject and as a concept. If the study of International Relations can be said to consist of the examination of relations between states, or the existence of a global system or society among states, or the relations between various state and nonstate actors in the international system, or a combination of all of the above, then secession—as an event that involves and affects all three of these types of relations—must be acknowledged as a highly relevant feature of the modern international system. Serious secessionist movements, as potential states themselves, affect relations among all by presenting the dilemma of whether to recognize them, and thus whether to bestow upon them the legal status of sovereignty and thereby establish international relations with them. Given the considerable privileges that accompany the status of sovereignty, as well as the likelihood of upsetting relations with the remaining parent state, the recognition decision is a weighty one. In fact, the untidy nature of the international system reflects this difficulty, with such important nonstate players as Taiwan and the Palestinian Authority.[1] The international system itself is also affected by secessionist movements since their success or failure indicates the relative balance of the tension between the principles of self-determination and territorial integrity. The prevalence of one of the principles over the other in the process of state generation has a great impact on the territorial nature of all states in the system. The more successful the principle of self-determination becomes in legitimating independence movements as states, the greater the threat to the stability and legitimacy of the system as presently constituted. Each successful introduction of a new state into the system, no matter how peaceful, swings the pendulum away from territorial integrity as a concept by drawing attention to the arbitrary nature of all territorial borders. However, the collective behavior of the society of states acts to safeguard its own perpetuation by continuing to emphasize territorial integrity as a binding principle, by limiting the definition of self-determination to decolonization and previously independent entities, and by condoning intervention only sparingly. Finally, secession involves nothing if not intense relations between state and nonstate actors, whether between the secessionist group itself and the resisting state, or between the group and international organizations that offer various forms of assistance or attention—including United Nations bodies.

Secession is thus implicated in all of the variations on the theme of International Relations studies. On any given day one might find upward of fifty secessionist movements worldwide of varying intensity and duration—but each with the potential to cause tremendous rifts in the geopolitical fabric, as well as violent conflict in social and cultural arenas.[2] Secession not only has great practical relevance in terms of stability and conflict, but it also raises important normative questions for International Relations scholars about the *rightness* of a system in which the players are so arbitrarily fixed and in which the fundamental rules are consistently challenged. In a theoretical analysis, secession sits at the juncture of the great abstract political concepts: sovereignty, legitimacy, territoriality, and identity. As a great breeder of violence and conflict, secession must be treated as a normative conundrum. As a concept on the borderline between the ideals of self-determination and territoriality, secession demands the most careful and rigorous theoretical analysis.

International Relations and Territorial Sovereignty: The Historical Context

Unlike the fields of history, law, and philosophy upon which it relies, International Relations is fundamentally a child of late modernity. The first inklings of the concept of "international" arose in the late eighteenth century when legal philosopher Jeremy Bentham coined the term in his *Introduction to the Principles of Morals and Legislation.*[3] What Bentham referred to, however, was not an international system or society, but the existence of international law. It was indeed through law and legal relations that politics came to be internationalized, for Bentham's term "international law" reflected the realization that the "law of nations" had come to mean law—and therefore relations—*between* nations rather than law applicable to all nations or peoples. So the secularization of politics was reflected in the secularization of law—from universal natural law principles toward more positivist practices. It was this shift from the universalist to the particularist in European law that enabled the concept of relations in the international, or "between," sense to flourish. Previously, the world had seemed to consist of politics and law internal to the world of Christendom. The non-Christian world, specifically the Ottoman Turk, was an external Other that did not make up part of a universal whole and to which European legal and political conduct did not apply.[4] Even Hugo Grotius, famous for his juridical writings on the laws of war and peace, acknowledged a dual layer in which all of humanity was subject to the norms of natural law and a select circle within Christian Europe followed the laws of Christ.[5] The concept of the international requires not only secularization, but also the possibility of relations between entities within a global environment that engage under apparently neutral rules. Thus, international law as "law between nations" provided the necessary stepping stone for International Relations.

One further development was also necessary to set the stage for the modern system of interacting sovereign states and thus for secession. This was the philosophical development of the concept of political legitimacy based on consent. The Enlightenment provided the momentum with its emphasis on rationality. Faith in the rationality of man fueled the growing sense of individual worth and allowed the doctrine of popular sovereignty to develop. At the same time, the sense of patriotism and national identity that was springing up in England and France complemented and motivated the political aims of the American and French Revolutions. These revolutions caused a seminal shift in the European political fabric—"[a]fter the American and French Revolutions the prevailing principle of international legitimacy ceased to be dynastic and became national or popular."[6] It was these late-eighteenth-century revolutions that colored the rise of nineteenth-century theories of nationalism as a political doctrine holding the nation-state out as its ultimate object. Change became possible, and people who had never been identified with the polity (or protected by it) became its fiercest defenders (and creators) in the name of nationalism.

> [T]he French Revolution introduced new possibilities in the use of political power, and transformed the ends for which rulers might legitimately work. The Revolution meant that if the citizens of a state no longer approved of the political arrangements of their society, they had the right and the power to replace them by others more satisfactory. . . . Here, then, is one prerequisite without which a doctrine such as nationalism is not conceivable. Such a doctrine would want to lay down how best a society should conduct its politics, and realize its aims, if need be by radical changes: the French Revolution showed, in a resounding manner, that such an enterprise was feasible.[7]

The French Revolution heralded the age of statehood and citizenship for *the people*. This anthem would survive a century of imperial conquest and sound from the mouths of twentieth-century statesmen attempting to construct a regime of world peace in the wake of World War I.

The conjunction of international law, popular sovereignty, and nationalism produced a cocktail of circumstances that nurtured the present-day international system of sovereign states. These circumstances, which made International Relations possible, were also the conditions of possibility for the concept of secession. Secession requires a modern theory of the state in order to make sense—that is, one that relies upon international law to guarantee its sovereign status as a nominal equal, popular sovereignty to guarantee its internal legitimacy and identity, and nationalism to provide the territorial definition of the state's "natural" boundaries and peoples. It is only when groups of people can self-identify as a nation and use the doctrine of popular sovereignty to claim their right to an independent territorial state that secession can even be imagined. Contemporary conceptions of identity and territoriality have such critical implications for secession that they will be explored separately in chapter 3: *States Taking Place* and chapter 4: *Begging to Differ*. The conclusion to be derived from all of this is that secession, like International Relations, is a twentieth-century phenomenon, and this is very nearly the case. There are two prominent events of the nineteenth century that must first be addressed to clarify this argument.

The Hungarian Revolution of 1848 and the American Civil War from 1861 to 1865 both involved fiercely contested movements for territorial independence. Both movements were defeated, and both events have been described as secessions. However, I argue that while it is possible to categorize these events as failed secession attempts, both are qualitatively different from the secessions of the twentieth century, and therefore should be regarded as distinct for the purposes of this analysis. In the case of Hungary, the nationalists wished to gain independence for their once-sovereign territories from the Habsburg Empire—which, I argue, involves a process different from that of a self-determination movement that tries to carve out a piece of a modern territorial state. In the case of the American Civil War, the Southern states were actually attempting to separate from what they believed was a loose federation on largely economic grounds and issues of social class—the question of Southern nationalism as separate from the American identity did not arise.

Early Separatism and the Habsburg Empire

In 1848, Hungary had been incorporated into the Habsburg Empire for nearly two hundred years, since the end of the seventeenth century, when it was freed from Ottoman Turk rule. Prior to that it had been a feudal kingdom, and in the early nineteenth century still retained certain feudal structures. The territory of Hungary contained many peoples not of Hungarian (Magyar) descent, including Germans, Serbs, Romanians, and Croats. Since the mid-eighteenth century, Hungary had been granted the status of a separate kingdom of which the Habsburgs were monarchs. But while nominally ruled through the national assembly, the final authority in Hungary came from Vienna. Despite the many non-Hungarian members of the society, a strong national movement of Hungarian-language speakers began in the late eighteenth century in response to a decree by Joseph II that German become the language of administration in Hungary. The uproar among the noble classes caused the decree to be withdrawn, and the official language reverted to Latin. As the Hungarian economy, population, and culture prospered, a desire to use the Hungarian language (the language of less than half of the people in the broader territory) in public life became more insistent. Although the ruling classes were largely conservative and the peasantry were ignorant of the ideals of the French Revolution, there were a number of lesser nobles and intelligentsia who had monitored the events in France and developed a close sympathy with the French (and Napoleonic) cause.[8] Two strains of pro-Hungarian sentiment developed. Hungarian revolutionaries wished to begin an inexorable process of Magyarization in the quickest manner possible, while moderates felt only that Hungarian should be the official language and other languages could continue in private and educational use. Although they included social reforms beneficial for the peasantry, the radical policies—promoted most powerfully by Lajos Kossuth, a landless noble and a lawyer—began to alarm the non-Hungarian segments of the population, who considered their allegiance to be to the emperor.

When the tempestuous events of the 1848 uprisings began in Paris and Vienna, the Hungarian Parliament took its cue and enacted a series of laws, the "April Laws," dealing with the taxation of noblemen, extension of the franchise (for Hungarian-speaking men), abolition of peasant obligations to landowners, and the development of voluntary troops, among other issues. The central government in Vienna, dealing with its own local uprisings, placated the Hungarian leadership (Kossuth) by accepting the April Laws while also encouraging Croat fears of Hungarian domination. Finally, in September, the Croat governor led a force, with the backing of the emperor, into Hungary. The new Hungarian volunteer militia successfully resisted the Austrian/Croat forces. In April 1849, Kossuth declared that the crown was now forfeit, appointed himself as regent—a royal rather than a republican term—and declared the independence of Hungary. But by this time, the new Habsburg emperor, Francis Joseph, had obtained a promise of help from Tsar Nicholas I of Russia, and in July the new Hungarian state was surrounded by Austro-Croatian and Russian troops. They were defeated on August 9; Kossuth fled and spent the remainder of his life in exile. The April Laws were revoked and Hungarian nationalists were imprisoned and executed. Although later the Compromise of 1867 led to a system of dual monarchy with Austria, Hungarian independence would remain a dream until the next century.

The point to make for a secession analysis is that the Hungarian Revolution took place within a political context (the Austrian Empire) that differed from the political context within which the discipline of International Relations grew up, that is, the post–Great War political society. So whether it is called a secessionist movement, a nationalist movement, a revolution—or all three—it is crucial to historicize the event, to try to gain insight into how it was understood at the time. Only by doing this can we understand the peculiarities of the relationship between secession and the development of International Relations theory. In taking this approach, I explicitly refrain from defining secession to include or exclude specific historical examples. As Nietzsche explained, "only something which has no history can be defined."[9] By this he means not that we are unable to insert definitions into our discourse for the sake of understanding and clarity, but that such definitions will always be the product of their historical contexts. Social and political concepts such as secession, nationalism, revolution, the nation-state, and so on—which certainly do have a history—must therefore be understood as signs or containers for social understandings which are in continuous flux. We must consider, in other words, "that anything in existence, having somehow come about, is continually interpreted anew, requisitioned anew, transformed and redirected to a new purpose . . . in the process of which their former 'meaning' and 'purpose' must necessarily be obscured or completely obliterated."[10] It is therefore crucial to understand that the same terms we use have been endowed with meaning over time by people whose lives and understandings were profoundly different from our own.

Given this introduction, what can be understood of these early separatist movements? In the case of the Habsburg Empire, it is crucial to remember that although the French Revolution had already unleashed the ideals of popular sovereignty into the continent, its major effects were still chiefly confined to France. The rest of Europe continued to operate under the assumptions of traditional monarchy, even if there were nominal parliamentary bodies working alongside the crown. This was even more so for Austria—which comprised a large unwieldy realm of multiple languages, races, and religions all connected by an inefficient bureaucracy and an allegiance to the person of the emperor. The majority of the population was peasantry living under a feudal system of dues, including both compulsory labor and a tithe of the crop paid to the lord. Nonetheless, there was widespread support and affection for the monarch among the peasants and common people as befitted the paternal image of the ruler for his "children." Even the severely handicapped Ferdinand I, who was epileptic and mentally retarded, was known by his loyal subjects as "Ferdy the Loony."[11]

The integrity and sovereignty of the Habsburg Empire was lodged in the person of the emperor, unlike that of post–World War II states that enforce their integrity by making their boundaries absolute. Rather than being defined by its outside boundaries, the Habsburg Empire was defined by the unity of control which could be exerted over disparate peoples.

> In the Habsburg Empire and Prussia the monarchy was essential above all as a unifying force. In each case a state which was the result of the haphazard accumulation over generations of territories with no common interest or common history was held together by the dynasty, and by the army and bureaucracy which that dynasty had built up around itself. . . . The emperor was not merely the symbol of unity but its active guardian and the only effective guarantee of its continuance.[12]

Not only did the monarch hold together disparate peoples, but his person was still considered to be sacred, as well. The awesome totality of the French Revolution caused many shudders amidst the cheers, and if many could sympathize with republican ideals, few could wholeheartedly endorse the execution of the monarch—heretofore the body of the state. Thus, Edmund Burke could write:

> They have seen the French rebel against a mild and lawful monarch, with more fury, outrage, and insult, than ever any people has been known to rise against the most illegal usurper, or the most sanguinary tyrant. Their resistance was made to concession; their revolt was from protection; their blow was aimed at an hand holding out graces, favours, and immunities. This was unnatural.[13]

In comparison with France, the Hungarian Revolution of 1848 was of a very different order. The radicals sought more control over their own affairs, but did not seek independence from the crown at first. Nor, given the demography of nineteenth-century Hungary, could the radicals have led an overtly nationalist revolution. Although the aims of the Hungarian leadership included greater political freedoms and benefits for the common man, the leaders themselves were of the nobility. The Hungarian leaders were hardly republicans, and they were not subversive of the Habsburg monarchy; they claimed that it was Metternich and the government ministers who were at fault. In a sense, the leaders of the revolution in Hungary were conservatives, since their chief goal was to restore the Hungarian Constitution, which had been subverted by Metternich.

Therefore, the claims made throughout the course of the revolution had a basis in the April Laws, which had been agreed upon by the king. They felt that their revolution was "lawful" since it was based on these laws which had received royal approval (and thus royal legitimacy). However, when the Hungarian leadership insisted on increasing its control over military and financial affairs, going so far as to raise its own military forces and print its own currency, the monarch withdrew his assent. In the eyes of the Hungarians it was this act by the king which destroyed the old order, not their wish for greater autonomy. Certainly, there can be no thought that the Hungarian Revolution was a secession in the late-twentieth-century sense. It was not about territorial sovereignty at all. Even if there were issues of nationalism at stake, the entire political menu differed. There was no question of carving out and establishing the legal boundaries of the new Hungarian state based on what could be militarily defended or who wanted to be included. Nor was there a question of legitimating the aristocratic Hungarian leadership, which already had a feudal entitlement. Although the French had introduced the idea of popular sovereignty, most Europeans (including Hungarians) had not removed the mantle of divinity from their monarchs, and continued to believe that hereditary princes offered a benevolent and even beneficially disinterested influence to counter the corruption of government officials. As the Archduke Albert explained:

> In a polyglot Empire inhabited by so many races and peoples the dynasty must not allow itself to be assigned exclusively to one of these. Just as a good mother, it

must show equal love for all its children and remain foreign to none. In this lies
the justification for its existence.[14]

In this sense, the Hungarian Revolution can be seen as more akin to a family quarrel
than the separation and formation of a completely new self-determined political
entity as are contemporary secessionist movements. It would be another seventy
years before Woodrow Wilson's "Fourteen Points" would explicitly mention the
right of "the peoples of Austria-Hungary" to a secured place among the autonomous
nations of the world, thus giving voice to the principle of self-determination which
would come to dominate the century.[15]

The Fight for the Definition of America

The American Civil War was an event in marked contrast to the troubles on the
continent. The United States was a wobbly new country trying to steady itself
against a common nationality based on individual freedom—as opposed to the
Habsburg's ancient amalgam of disparate peoples subject to feudal obligation under
a premodern sovereign. The tensions that finally boiled over in 1860 had been
brewing for some time. As the country's territorial waistline swelled with the
Louisiana Purchase, the annexation of Texas, and the settlement of the West, the
Southern states voiced ample concerns over the status of slavery in these areas. At
stake was not simply the socioeconomic culture of the new nation, but the legal
option of Southern plantation owners to move and settle westward with their slaves
in tow. As the western territories were increasingly being settled by those with
abolitionist or free state sympathies and the number of free states in the Union
began to rise correspondingly, feelings in the South began to crystallize into
hostility and paranoia against the North. In 1854, when Nebraska and Kansas were
applying for statehood, Congress could not agree on whether the Missouri
Compromise of 1820 (which permitted no slavery above the 36th latitude) should
continue to be applied. In enacting the Kansas-Nebraska Act, which left the choice
to the respective territories, Congress repealed the Missouri Compromise, which
had held the Union together for 30 years. Nebraska was clearly declared a free state
by its inhabitants, but Kansas was the subject of hot dispute. Northern abolitionists
raised money to finance free-voting settlers while thousands of pro-slavery men
from Missouri crossed into the state to vote illegally for a legislature which would
approve slavery. Open fighting broke out, and leaders on both sides were arrested
and killed in a melee which lasted until 1858 and cost 200 lives. Meanwhile, the
newly formed Republican Party was gaining strength with a platform which favored
banning slavery in the new territories, and by the time of the presidential elections
of 1860, the party was poised to put a man in the White House. South Carolina
declared that it would secede if a Republican candidate were elected.[16]

Although many historians have concluded that a majority of Southern voters
was actually pro-union (due to poor turnout in the state election polls), James

McPherson argues that this idea mistakes the nature of each side's concept of union. In an eery echo of the Hungarian revolutionaries' anti-Metternich, pro-monarch sentiments, the Southern Unionists felt betrayed by the election of an antislavery president:

> As a Mississippi "unionist" explained after Lincoln's election, he was no longer "a Union man in the sense in which the North is Union." His unionism was conditional; the North had violated the condition by electing Lincoln. Cooperationists in Alabama who voted against secession cautioned outsiders not to "misconstrue" their action. "We scorn the Black Republicans," they declared. "The State of Alabama cannot and will not submit to the administration of Lincoln."[17]

After the election results confirmed the election of Abraham Lincoln, six southern states seceded. The war began in April 1861 when troops organized by the Confederacy fired upon and captured a federal garrison at Fort Sumter in South Carolina. The war would last for four years, be led by veterans of the Mexican War who had fought side by side, pit brother against brother, cost 620,000 lives, and be one of the bloodiest wars in human history up to that point.[18]

One of the critical questions of the American Civil War was the nature of the bond between the states. The federal Union had never been fully challenged on the point of whether any one of the states had the right of separation. Until the Southern secession was successfully put down, the Union was regarded instrumentally as a useful means of protecting the revolutionary ideals of individual freedom and political equality. With its boundaries shape-shifting on a constant basis, and its internal composition continuously affected by immigration, the United States did not have a clear sense of its common identity in terms of a political union. The people called themselves American, but politically they hailed from different states. This was obvious to the visitor Alexis de Tocqueville, who wrote in the 1830s:

> The Union is a vast body, which presents no definite object to patriotic feeling. [The state] is identified with the soil; with the right of property and the domestic affections; with the recollections of the past, the labors of the present, and the hopes of the future. Patriotism, then, which is frequently a mere extension of individual selfishness, is still directed to the state and has not passed over to the Union. Thus the tendency of the interests, the habits, and the feelings of the people is to center political activity in the states in preference to the Union.[19]

Until the end of the Civil War it was normal to refer to the United States in plural rather than singular form. In fact, secession had already been threatened by the New England states over the War of 1812, but the issue faded when the war ended and the United States resumed good relations with Great Britain. Despite this tendency toward political regionalism, there was also a noticeable assimilation, toward a common society based on a general identification with the ideals of the Declaration of Independence.

So there was certainly a recognition of being a common people with shared political values and institutions. Nevertheless, the ease with which secession was raised as a policy option for the states suggests that at that time they took the Union to be a federation of convenience, not an entity to which they owed national allegiance. In fact, until 1865 "it was unclear what the relationship between the many and the one in *E Pluribus Unum* should be, and entirely possible that the United States would disintegrate into several American nations."[20] In other words, the issue of whether self-government was a right vested in the states or in the federal government had not been settled. This was precisely the issue that the Confederate states were testing when they argued that their right to self-government included the right to slavery as a way of life. Yet, unlike the separatist movements of the twentieth century, which would be based on the will and declared rights of national groups to be free of oppression by the central state, the Confederacy remains a political oddity: a movement which seceded in order to withhold freedom from much of its population, the slaves, whom the central government was attempting (in its commitment to a union based on principles of equality) to set free. Southerners argued that their freedom to have self-government was being denied by the Union, but Lincoln's response declared that the American protection of self-government was an individual not a collective one: "When the white man governs himself . . . that is self-government; but when he governs himself and also governs another man, that is more than self-government—that is despotism."[21]

The issue of individual political freedom was not at stake for residents of the Southern states. As Liah Greenfeld notes,

> It would be wrong to see the secession as in any way a result of Southern nationalism (namely the development of a specifically Southern identity, loyalty, and consciousness). Southern nationalism and secession were both responses to the unbearable inconsistency between American national ideals and slavery. In the framework of individualistic nationalism, secession was possible without the preceding development of a separate identity, as was so clearly demonstrated by the American Revolution itself.[22]

These American national ideals were what the North fought to apply to the whole Union, and neither slavery nor secession could be tolerated if the glorious American model of freedom and equality was to remain intact. In actuality, the North and the South were fighting to determine which image of American identity should survive—the one in which the ideal of equality was a unique model held out for the world to marvel, or the one in which there was thriving economic prosperity for the equals, but based on the exploitation of those who were not even politically visible, let alone equal. One of Lincoln's strongest arguments, and one which motivated even those who were ambivalent about abolition, was that America was a great political experiment which would be deemed a failure if slavery were allowed to continue. Philip Abbott points out that this was crucial for the Northern conception of American nationhood: "In essence, Lincoln was creating an argument that contended not only that slavery challenged American identity but that the fate of the nation had a world significance, that America's struggle with slavery constituted an even broader struggle, the outcome of which was of immense importance to mankind."[23] The fascinating aspect of this struggle over the defining characteristics of the national identity is that it was a struggle which did not rest on a conception of a sovereign territorial whole. Rather, it was a struggle over the final definition of the *American people*—including those living in territories which were not yet part of the Union. If the Southern states had succeeded in maintaining the Confederacy, they would have continued to be Americans—but their very existence as slave-owning Americans would have profoundly threatened the identity of the Northern states, who wished the world to see America as the exceptional country based on principles of freedom.

This clash of ideals within a people makes the American Civil War unique among separatist clashes. The closest contemporary analogy would be the kind of polarization which occurs over a political issue such as abortion—in which both sides are absolutely convinced that the other side must be made to see the issue in a specific way. In these cases compromise is failure. Indeed, the rhetoric which surrounded the slavery issue was as vitriolic as what now passes for dialogue in the abortion context. Like abortion, the issue of slavery could not be settled by negotiation because its very existence was moral anathema to many in the free states, and the very threat of its demise was social, economic, and political anathema to those in the South. Thus, even though for many Northerners abolishing slavery was not as important as keeping the Union, the issue was too important to the South for any kind of compromise. Technically, the central government had done nothing to curtail the rights of those in the South to own slaves. There were even strict fugitive slave laws in place to force the return of escaped slaves as "property." What the South could not countenance was the confinement of slavery to its geographical area and the loss of balance in national representation. In the end, the Civil War did more to clarify the American sense of unified identity formed at the national level than any event before. In this effect it is most clearly unlike any twentieth-century secessionist conflict.

Secession: Then and Now

The above discussion of nineteenth-century secessionist conflicts illustrates that whether or not the term "secession" is used to describe these events, they were understood very differently at the time from what we would recognize as secessionist conflict today—in the era of self-determination and the nation-state. This is relevant for understanding International Relations theory and the world it set out to describe. Two separate points are made in this section. First, secession has a changing meaning which rests on our conceptions of the state and the international system, both of which have been influenced tremendously by the ideals of nationalism, democracy and self-determination in the last century or so. Just as the nature of the state and the international system must be understood in historical context, so too secession cannot be taken as a timeless concept or possibility. The second point is that International Relations arose in response to an international system which had undergone profound change from the turn of the twentieth century onward, and thus the extent to which the discipline could account for secession depended upon its account of this radically altered political context. Furthermore, the concept of secession as a political act, unlike the concept of the state itself, actually has a reasonably fixed starting point of comparatively recent origin. The word "secession" can be dated from the seventeenth century according to *The Oxford English Dictionary*.[24] However, it was not used then in a political sense, but meant "the action or an act of going away from one's accustomed neighborhood, or of retiring from public view." The verb *to secede* was defined by Dr. Johnson in 1755 as "to withdraw from fellowship in any affair." Although the term was also used specifically to indicate withdrawal from a religious organization, as in the secession of the "Church, King and Kingdom of England from the Papacy" described by Coke in 1660, the first use of the noun *secession* in the political separatist context appears to have been in connection with the American Civil War. Ironically—for a political scientist—political usage of the verb *secede* is still described in the dictionary's etymology as "rare." The original root of the word is Latin—*secedere*: to withdraw.

The unfamiliar history of the usage of this word in the English language should not be surprising once one realizes the extent to which "political withdrawal" depends upon certain preconditions. For one thing, the origins of the root presuppose that the action is done unilaterally by the self—*se-ceder* or "self-cession." In seceding, one withdraws from a group; one does not cause the withdrawal of others. For this action to be translated into the political sphere, there must first exist the concept of a political collective from which a unit may withdraw, and there must also exist the concept of a political "self" within this collective which may effect the withdrawal. It is therefore understandable that the term does not enter political usage any earlier than the nineteenth century—it is practically dependent upon the concepts of the republic and popular sovereignty, and of course territoriality. In the age of princes and empires the state was indivisible because it was coextensive with the body of the sovereign and only vaguely associated with a delineated geography.[25] This is best illustrated by Louis XIV's famous phrase, "L'etat, c'est moi." The sovereign body was the source of the symbolic power of the execution of the king for the French revolutionaries. Only when the body of the sovereign had been (literally) destroyed could the people as a collective become (figuratively) sovereign. It is also, then, no accident that the term *secession* was first used extensively in the United States—a country in which the collective and the divisible notion of the people as sovereign had already been firmly established. One might say that before there can be a concept of secession, or withdrawal from the whole, there must first exist the concept of the whole—which is made up not only of state parts, but also from the union of all citizens. It was actually this latter definition of Union upon which the Northern states insisted in refusing the right of the South to withdraw.

Having established a historical starting point for secession as a concept does not mean that we have established any kind of fixed understanding of the term. If anything, the concept of secession has, until very recently, been inexplicable within International Relations theory due to the modernism of the discipline's dominant theoretical structures. This is reflected in the fact that the very conditions of possibility for the discipline of International Relations itself are the conditions of the twentieth century.[26] International Relations as a discipline requires both a concept of the international (in the global and not simply European sense) and of relations between units within an international sphere which is markedly separate from the domestic one. These concepts depend upon the historical mix of popular sovereignty with nationalism and territoriality to create the perception of an international system of sovereign nation-states, with clear boundaries between inside and outside concerns, upon which most International Relations work is based. This mix did not set until the end of World War I, when the balance of continental empire-states seemed to have reached the end of its viability as a system. This was due in no small part to the acceptance of the idea of popular sovereignty and its translation into the principle of national self-determination.

Popular sovereignty, as advanced by the American and French Revolutions, was offered as a universal principle of political legitimacy. This universality was the source of the idea's appeal. However, there was a difference between advancing the idea in theory and realizing it in practice. The ancien régime was so long established that the "abolition of the conceptual legitimacy of all privilege, first in theory and then in reality, was a momentous historical development, the final results of which are even now not fully determined."[27] Although popular sovereignty may be considered as a theory based on universal individual rights, it cannot be applied universally. James Mayall explains "that although the sovereignty of the people, and the conception of individual rights on which it is based, are essentially universal, i.e., they apply to all human beings or to none, the political claims to which they give rise are *always and necessarily* advanced by, or on behalf of, a particular group of people."[28] Thus, the application of popular sovereignty requires particularization of both the people and the state. Enter nationalism and the concept of the nation-state. The shift in the basis of legitimate sovereignty from the prince to the people required a fundamental reconsideration of the nature of the state. If sovereignty stemmed from the people, how were *they* to be delineated? National identity provided the seemingly obvious answer, and translated the eighteenth-century idea of popular sovereignty into the twentieth-century principle of self-determination. Or rather, as Mayall puts it, "an accommodation was reached between the prescriptive principle of sovereignty and the popular principle of national self-determination . . . the one expresses a timeless political principle, the other the only historically relevant basis on which it should be exercised."[29] This combination of principles provided the basis for the twentieth-century international order; but it was the logic of this order—taken to its extreme—that undermined itself in the form of repeated secessionist challenges to the established nation-states.

It should be noted that the triumph of nation-states over empires was by no means ensured until the outcome of the First World War and the fall of the continental empires left a vacuum and an opportunity. It was the American president, Woodrow Wilson, who did more than any other individual at the time to make the nation-state become the acceptable political model. Although Wilson failed in his vision for the League of Nations, the formulation of autonomy for national groups spelled out in his "Fourteen Points" speech to Congress in January 1918 was very important "in consolidating conceptions of national sovereignty as the 'natural' political condition of humankind, via a particular interpretation of the sovereignty-citizenship-nationalism relation. This was the most significant effect of the 'new system of law and justice' among states that Wilson wanted to achieve."[30] Another effect of Wilson's legitimation of the nation-state and the creation of the League of Nations was a newly globalized international system. It was no longer simply Europe which made up the system of sovereign states. The Unity of Christendom and the Peace of Westphalia had to give way to the League of Nations and the Permanent Court of International Justice, as well as many more international organizations to follow. The impact on Europe was compounded by the sudden emphasis on autonomy for colonial peoples, the fifth of Wilson's fourteen points. Although World War I and the Treaty of Versailles are often cited as the political turning point into the current modern system, it must be emphasized that such events only serve as convenient markers for historical trends. The world did not change overnight in 1918 anymore than the Soviet Union went from strength to pieces suddenly in 1992. And the nationalities which were to find their new international voices were crudely formed and ill suited to the political task of providing sensible boundaries for the state.

The Birth of the Discipline: "Ain't Gonna Study War No More"

It is necessary to tell the story of the birth of the discipline in order to understand how secession was not simply overlooked but made irrelevant through an epistemological framework that precluded it as a proper subject. The seeds of IR's early "Utopian" theories were planted decades earlier by classical liberalism. Although political liberalism had developed significantly in the nineteenth century by drawing on the writings of John Stuart Mill and the correlating economic theories of Adam Smith, theories of government and politics were still considered the prerogatives of philosophy and diplomacy. However, World War I—the Great War—caused both the public and statesmen in Europe and North America to believe that never again could diplomacy be left to the diplomats and war to the "professionals." There was then a perceived need to study relations between states in order to avoid another such catastrophe. The horror of the casualties and the ruin provoked a profound questioning within Europe of the great modern project of the rational man. Christopher Coker explains:

The Great War was the first historical event of significance to confront modern man with a question whose implications were particularly grave: was it any longer possible to see progress in terms of a long historical trajectory, and could progress itself any longer be considered necessarily redeeming? . . . For a few, the catastrophe of trench warfare destroyed all possibility of belief in the future.[31]

The feeling of hopelessness was compounded by its juxtaposition against the expectations of modernization and industrialization. Europe had seen many great wars before—but none had merited that explicit title. Men had died and lands had been ravaged, but this war left a different taste. What had gone wrong? One thing which was markedly different was the degree to which men were willing to die in the name of a cause. It was still an age of certainty and purpose, in which time moved forward and humankind was on a steady course of progress. Men believed in, and fought for, the notion of modern progress. Paul Fussell describes it as a world that was "compared with ours, a static world, where the values appeared stable and where the meanings and abstractions seemed permanent and reliable. Everyone knew what Glory was, and what Honor meant."[32]

In glaring contrast to the certainties of honor and glory at the time of the Great War, the 1991 Gulf War was the first armed conflict in which no U.S. Congressional Medal of Honor was awarded to any of the servicemen who participated.[33] As war becomes more mechanized, even virtual, the possibilities for heroic action have greatly decreased. Modernity was supposed to be the age of humanity's self-salvation—and instead, the Great War's aftermath reeked of an age of self-destruction. Yet, the salvationist element was still evident in President Wilson's last public speech.

> Why, my fellow citizens, should they [mothers who lost their sons in France] pray God to bless me?. . . I consented to their sons being put in the most difficult parts of the battle line, where death was certain. . . . They believe, and they rightly believe, that their sons saved the liberty of the world. They believe that wrapped up with the liberty of the world is the continuous protection of that liberty by the concerted powers of all civilized people.[34]

Ironically, the very fact that the war was fought under a moral banner was the source of the difficulty in finding a justification for its horror. How could the causes of such an immoral war have been moral? As Michael Walzer puts it, democratic idealism is objectionable because it declares goals which are impossible to reach, and this is a moral issue if soldiers are asked to die for these goals. "Their most heroic efforts, after all, can only bring a particular war to an end; they cannot end war. They can save democracy from a particular threat, but they cannot make the world safe for democracy."[35] But ending war was exactly the goal for which Western political thinkers began to aim. Surely, they concluded, the ultimate moral act would be to keep war from happening in the first place. And so the Great War became the "War to end all wars."

Despair over the failure of moral politics and diplomacy which led to the war ironically gave way to a modernist desire to approach war as a scientific problem which could be rationally analyzed and solved. The war had occurred, they theorized, because of an improper understanding of the facts which cause war. Political thinkers looked at peace as a goal obtainable through rational analysis, based on "the assumption that the world is thoroughly accessible to science and reason and that it contains in itself all the elements necessary for the harmonious co-operation of all mankind."[36] Thus, even while European society was feeling collective nausea at the horror and futility of the modern age as revealed by the Great War, theorists were responding from a perspective fully within the modernist framework, with further attempts to advance the cause of Enlightenment rationality. In keeping with this project was the League of Nations system championed so valiantly by Woodrow Wilson, in the belief that states would act rationally in their own interests in a voluntary self-policing system. Another famous "idealist" of the turn of the century was Sir Norman Angell, who became infamous in 1908 by arguing that war was both irrational and economically unsound. In the interwar period, Angell sided with those who wished to make—in the League of Nations—something that would supplant the anarchy of the international system and make war not only irrational, but also functionally illegal. In a sharply titled volume, *The Intelligent Man's Way to Prevent War*, edited by Leonard Woolf, the common approach of the idealists was spelled out. After stating that civilization cannot survive another "world war," Woolf valiantly asserted,

> War is not a "natural" catastrophe like a tidal wave or an earthquake. It is not inevitable; it is preventable in Europe like cannibalism, cholera, or witch-burning, all of which, though once common in this continent, have been abolished by civilization. . . . Any intelligent man can with a little trouble understand the problem of preventing war. Though it is not a simple problem, it is not nearly so complicated as that of making a six-cylinder engine for a motor-car, and it is child's play compared with the intricate mass of problems which have been solved to make modern broadcasting possible.[37]

While the bulk of idealist authors were not quite so simplistic, they were united in the belief that war was an effect whose cause could be studied and altered. It is also clear from Woolf's use of terms such as "civilization" and his idea of war being preventable "in Europe" that the early concept of International Relations was more Eurocentric than it is today. In some sense, these European writers still viewed the League of Nations as another multilateral great power security arrangement like the Concert of Europe. Peace was something that could come only to those states where democracy had taken hold. While the idealists clearly hoped that the spread of democracy could work its magic on the rest of the globe in time, the term "international" was still apt to refer only to the "civilized world." And the "world war" the idealists were trying to fend off was envisioned as another war with its center in the European continent.

The naïveté of the idealists, if not of their intentions, is encapsulated in the words of philanthropist Andrew Carnegie's bequest establishing the Carnegie

Endowment for International Peace. Carnegie instructed that "when the establishment of universal peace is attained, the donor provides that the revenue shall be devoted to the banishment of the next most degrading evil or evils, the suppression of which would most advance the progress, elevation and happiness of man."[38] Given the optimism of the discipline's formative years, it is no surprise that a discussion of secession as a problem was left off the laundry list of serious issues. In accordance with the methodology of rationalism, the question of secession might have been perceived as something contrary to national interest and which could, therefore, be avoided with studiousness and care. The days of the Peace Conference following the Great War were spent in serious consideration of the most effective national boundaries for the states arising out of the newly splintered empires of Europe. Once the frontiers were set in 1919, they were meant to be permanent. Article X of the League Covenant required that state members respect the territorial integrity of frontiers.

> [However] . . . if that peace was to mean anything else than licence to commit acts of tyranny with impunity—if it was to be a true peace and not a mere fastening of shackles upon the defeated States—it was absolutely necessary that the minorities should be ensured such treatment as would take away from them all valid excuse for disaffection and irredentism.[39]

So the problem of nationalist sentiment and state boundaries was recognized, but the remedy was the enactment of a system of minority protection treaties. In cases where the frontiers settled at the Peace Conference were simply unworkable, the appropriate procedure was deemed to be negotiation at the League Assembly—not that this procedure was observed in practice, but reworking the frontiers was considered an issue which could be raised. In short, the idealist approach was one which insisted on the maintenance of law and order in the international realm and which maintained that problems such as separatist movements would be dealt with by negotiation simply because this was the way which made the most rational sense.

From the Ideal to the Real: IR's Coming of Age

If Idealism was a perspective in which the harsh facts of real life were to be subjugated to reason, then the Realism which followed was a perspective in which reason was to be subjugated to the harsh facts of reality. In his discussion of the genesis of International Relations as a discipline, E. H. Carr quoted Engels as saying, "If society has a technical need . . . it serves as a greater spur to the progress of science than do ten universities." Carr then concluded that the "[d]esire to cure the sicknesses of the body politic has given its impulse and its inspiration to political science."[40] In responding to what he considered to be the misguided faith of Utopianism, Carr wrote what could be called a dialectical critique of the new discipline.[41] Carr differentiates the Utopian/Idealist approach to solving the problems of international politics (the inclination to ignore what was and what is in contemplation of what should be) from the Realist approach (the inclination to deduce what should be from what was and what is), and insists that they are both part of a continuing and necessary equilibrium. Carr is often cited as the chief destroyer of the Utopian school of theory during the interwar period, and as the father of Realism. But his work was more subtle than that, and he obviously did not intend to discredit the creativity and normative emphasis of the idealist.[42] Carr understood the need for the normative, and also the fact that normative issues and politics are inseparable since "[e]very political judgment helps to modify the facts on which it is passed. Political thought is itself a form of political action."[43] Carr actually located and defended the value of Utopian theory even while skillfully critiquing its primary faults. Although he advocated a healthy equilibrium of the two approaches, his feelings about the existence of international society were somewhat pessimistic since he focused on the structural inequalities that would always subvert any attempt at moral order.[44]

Another chronicler of the Realist genre, Hans Morgenthau, was far less patient with what he called "scientific utopianism":

> The "scientific" era of international relations resulted in the substitution of supposedly scientific standards for genuine political evaluations; in some cases this went so far as to impede, if not entirely destroy, the ability to make any intelligent political decisions at all. Power, however limited and qualified, is the value which international politics recognizes as supreme. . . . The quest for and the defense of power then become aberrations from the scientific attitude, which looks for causes and remedies.[45]

For Morgenthau, the neglect of power as a primary force in international politics was irresponsible and misguided. Although as a Realist, he shared the rationalist view of the Idealists that society is governed by natural laws that may be ascertained through reason, Morgenthau's fundamental principle for the international system—and the one that became the cornerstone of International Relations theory—was that it was based on "interest defined in terms of power." According to Stanley Hoffmann, it was the missionary impulse of Morgenthau, his air of conviction and certainty, that helped to establish the discipline of International Relations in the United States. "Steeped in a scholarly tradition that stressed the difference between social sciences and natural sciences, he was determined both to erect an empirical science opposed to the utopias of the international lawyer and the political ideologues, and to affirm the unity of empirical research and of philosophical inquiry into the right kind of social order."[46] In his attempt to describe the "real" and to make the social science of International Relations policy practical as well as policy relevant, Morgenthau mapped a field that took states and power as the actors and the interests, and considered the balance of power to be a fundamental natural law of the system. Almost as Carr predicted in his simplified model of realism, the Realist school of IR became focused on the deduction of what should be from the nature of what was and is. Thus, Realists tended to take the international system as they found it and to theorize about states and power as if the system had always existed and would continue to do so in an unproblematic manner. Needless to say, this theoretical gaze found secession to be an issue beneath its notice.

Although it began in the 1930s as a response to the Utopian nature of Idealism, the Realist school became well established after World War II, in the era of confirmed cynicism and the beginning of the American-Soviet nuclear standoff. The structuralist assumptions of the basic Realist stance have resulted in scarcely a glance cast at matters involving substate entities. Even Hedley Bull, a scholar with great knowledge of political and legal history, felt that the task of International Relations was restricted to the analysis of relations between states. He emphatically declared: "The starting point of international relations is the existence of *states*."[47] With the field so strictly circumscribed, it is hardly surprising that Realist theory (in response to the positivist methodological challenge) became rarefied and formalized, focusing strictly on state power and interests. This theoretical perspective reached its apex with Kenneth Waltz's *Theory of International Politics*. The formalized Neorealist world is carefully defined by the sovereignty divide of inside/outside, domestic/international. Given this definition of the space of international politics, social movements such as national separatist groups are problems for public administration or sociology, but should not concern the scholars of International Relations until such movements become responsible for state actions beyond internal borders. The Neoliberal challenge to this form of Realism, articulated by Robert Keohane, did not serve to increase the scope for International Relations theory. The main differences between the two perspectives can be distilled to a general shift in focus by the Neoliberals to forms of state cooperation, regimes, and political economy. The Neoliberal view encompasses intentions and perceptions and the role of institutions in mitigating anarchy, in contrast to a more hard-line Neorealist insistence on relative gains, security, and anarchy as driving forces behind state behavior.[48] In ontological terms, however, the two perspectives are merely variations on a Realist theme, neither of which questions the existence and formation of states.

Realist ontology, with its assumption of the reality of states, cannot account for the making and breaking of states, and for the complexity that arises when the status of a state is called into question, as it is by secession. Because states simply *exist* as part of the "real world" for Realist theorists, they do not theorize how states come into being and what the nature of that being is. In Realism's defense, it can be argued that all academic disciplines must theorize from some starting point, thus taking certain things for granted, and that International Relations has clearly from its inception been about the relations between established states. However, when the ontological boundaries of the discipline blind it to political events that take place just beyond its theoretical gateways, there is a pressing need for reassessment. Realist International Relations theory describes a world so narrowly circumscribed that it cannot correspond to observable events. International Relations has been so concerned with inter-*state* relations that it cannot comprehend inter-*national* relations and all of their implications for politics at every level. Critical theorists, those for whom the reality of the world "out there" is one constituted and continually changed by human knowledge, do not assume the reality of states. Rather, critical International Relations theory must question the formation of states and the very nature of their existence. Secession, then, is a phenomenon that is an integral part of a critical theoretical approach to International Relations.

Realism continues to be the dominant ontological perspective within International Relations, although it has gone through several permutations, and power politics has continued to serve as the dominant theoretical justification for state policy. Certainly, there have been significant challenges, and it can be argued that International Relations in its "interparadigm" stage is now "the site of a hundred (theoretical) flowers blooming," but there is also much reason to believe that this is an overly optimistic view.[49] There has been a traditional unwillingness within International Relations theory to grapple with certain philosophical questions as other social sciences have. This unwillingness has resulted in an extensive disciplinary practice of dichotomizing the relationship between facts and theory. This dichotomized approach has remained prominent even though in recent years International Relations has seen a fanning out of the field into areas well beyond the tradition of state-centered approaches. Texts designed to introduce students to the discipline must now include perspectives and topics as widespread as feminism, environmental issues, security studies, foreign policy, postcolonialism, poststructuralist, and critical social theory, and culture and identity, to name a few.

Naturally, the discipline has become a much more interesting intellectual space as a result, with various texts questioning the nature of sovereignty, the state, and transnational interaction. But while the Realist ontological view (of a world beyond our reach) persists, there are serious epistemological consequences. A perspective in which states and regimes are "real" leads to a system of knowledge that assumes there is no human influence over them. This is the most profound implication of the theory/fact dichotomy discussed by Jim George. Although International Relations theorists are beginning to look beyond the state, as it becomes clear that the sphere of the global is much more complex than simple interstate relations, there is still a pervasive tendency to practice social science as a deductive exercise. Theory that maintains its distance from practice also maintains silence on the foundational questions of modernist understanding. Questions of culture and identity cannot be adequately treated. The contingency of history and human existence must remain irrelevant.

These silences are nowhere more obvious than in a recent attempt to take up secession as an International Relations subject, in response to its increased visibility in post–Cold War international dynamics.[50] The author of this work, Viva Ona Bartkus, compares a great many examples of secession and separatism and applies a framework of cost/benefit analysis to quantify the factors that go into the decision to secede. This treatment, while welcome for its focus on secession, remains limited by its traditional theoretical perspective, which envisions secession as an event susceptible to causal analysis and secessionist groups as fixed and unitary actors. The attempt to describe the causes of secession is comprehensive but silent on the crucial question of the formation and maintenance of social group identity. By accepting group identities and perceptions as "facts" that may be interpreted by the "theory" of an objective observer, this text cannot engage with the concepts of identity, difference, territoriality, and sovereignty that—as mutually constitutive and contested concepts—must inform our understanding of secession. As long as these crucial issues remain unexplored, our understanding of secession will remain truncated and out of context. Thus, the features of international politics that make secession a possibility, and one that affects all of us, cannot be analyzed from Bartkus's perspective, and remain entirely outside of its theoretical reach.

The fact/theory dichotomy reflects one of the most important developments in the evolution of International Relations as a discipline, that is, there is now an irreconcilable division between two metatheoretical perspectives. Steve Smith calls them "constitutive" and "explanatory" theories. The divide is "between those theories that seek to offer explanatory accounts of international relations, and those that see theory as constitutive of that reality. At base this boils down to a difference over what the social world is like; is it to be seen as scientists think of the 'natural' world, that is to say as something outside of our theories, or is the social world what we make it?"[51] The constitutive theoretical perspective, imported from philosophy and social theory, has only recently taken hold in International Relations and has yet to achieve anything like parity with traditional explanatory theoretical approaches in the discipline. Even within each metatheoretical approach there are widespread conflicts over various theoretical commitments. But the goal the constitutive theory schools have in common is to adopt an approach that "reformulates basic *questions* of modernist understanding in emphasizing not the sovereign subject (e.g., author/independent state) or the object (e.g., independent world/text) but instead the historical, cultural, and linguistic practices in which subjects and objects (and theory and practice, facts and values) are constructed."[52] This recent development has freed the theoretical space for a look at secession that does not assume the objective presence of states and ethnonational identities. The point of all this theoretical space, as George points out, is not to establish a newly dominant "paradigm," but to disrupt discursive certainties; it is not to dismiss dominant readings in the discipline, but to show that they are actually contextual readings of reality rather than reality itself.[53]

This complex ancestral chart, only briefly described here, goes a long way toward explaining why International Relations theorists have traditionally failed to address the problem of secession in any meaningful way.[54] The hold that Realism has maintained over the many theoretical perspectives that have emerged in the last few decades has limited the ways in which the world can be viewed. Indeed, the very term *international* has been limited by the perception that this is a realm made up of states and organizations of states. So not only do Realist (explanatory) perspectives fail to adequately address the impact of substate separatist movements on the international system, but they also cannot account for the diverse qualities of present-day states. Secession, as a concept that challenges the very underpinnings of sovereignty, statehood, and territoriality, can be treated only as an effect with determinable causes rather than as an integral part of the current (historically contingent) system. Thus, any avenues for creatively thinking beyond the territorial state and secessionist self-determination are blocked. It is only through a constitutive theoretical approach, which does not accept international structures as given or unproblematic, that secession and all of the political difficulties it encompasses can be seen in a meaningful way.

While International Relations theorists have only rarely looked past the nature of the system as unquestionably based on states, there have been writers in other disciplines for whom the substate nature of secession has not posed a problem. These fields include political philosophy, political science/government, sociology, and law. When secession is handled by these theorists, it is examined either in terms of moral justification for certain cases, or in terms of causal analysis. Such treatments have provided interesting if narrow discussions, but they have not problematized the nature of the state or the formation of political identities, that is, they have remained explanatory (or justificatory) rather than constitutive. Thus, there continues to be a pressing need for a "theory as fact" analysis of secession as a concept.

Notes

1. Even if the Palestinian Authority eventually becomes a state, the existence of any nonstate entity with international presence, even a short-lived one, is an exception to the system rules.

2. On a recent visit to the *Homelands* website, which lists "autonomy, secession, independence and nationalist movements," I counted more than seventy sites dedicated to some form of change in the interstate structure. See http://www.visi.com/~homelands/. Accessed 25 March 2003.

3. Discussed in Hedley Bull, *The Anarchical Society: A Study of Order in World Politics* (New York: Columbia University Press, 1977), 36.

4. See Iver B. Neumann and Jennifer M. Welsh, "The Other in European Self-Definition: An Addendum to the Literature on International Society," *Review of International Studies* 17 (1991): 327-348.

5. Neumann and Welsh, "The Other in European Self-Definition," 339.

6. Bull, *The Anarchical Society*, 35.

7. Elie Kedourie, *Nationalism*, 4th ed. (Oxford: Blackwell, 1993), 4-5.

8. Zoltán Halász, *A Short History of Hungary*, trans. Csaba Szabó (Budapest: Corvina Press, 1975), 133.

9. Friedrich Nietzsche, *On the Genealogy of Morality*, trans. Carol Diethe (Cambridge: Cambridge University Press, 1994), 57.

10. Nietzsche, *Genealogy of Morality*, 55.

11. Alan Sked, *The Decline and Fall of the Habsburg Empire 1815-1918* (London: Longman Group UK Limited, 1989), 81.

12. M. S. Anderson, *The Ascendancy of Europe 1815-1914*, 2d ed. (London: Longman Group Limited, 1985), 65.

13. Edmund Burke, *Reflections on the Revolution in France* (New York: Anchor Books, 1973), 51.

14. Sked, *Decline & Fall of the Habsburg Empire*, 265.

15. Woodrow Wilson, "Address to a Joint Session of Congress, January 1918," in *The Nationalism Reader*, ed. Omar Dahbour and Micheline R. Ishay (Atlantic Highlands, N. J.: Humanities Press, 1995), 309.

16. While the Hungarians in 1848 thought of themselves as "revolutionaries," the Southern separatists called themselves "secessionists," thereby initiating a political meaning for the term that had not been in common use previously.

17. James McPherson, *Battle Cry of Freedom: The American Civil War* (London: Penguin Books Ltd., 1990), 239.

18. Both of the famed Civil War generals, Robert E. Lee and Ulysses S. Grant, fought as officers in the Mexican War. Captain Lee commended Lieutenant Grant for his services in the attack on Mexico City. These thanks were delivered to Grant by Lieutenant Pemberton, who surrendered to Grant sixteen years later at Vicksburg. McPherson, *Battle Cry of Freedom*, 5.

19. Alexis de Tocqueville, *Democracy in America*, vol. 1., Everyman's Library (London: David Campbell Publishers Ltd., 1994), 386.

20. Liah Greenfeld, *Nationalism: Five Roads to Modernity* (Cambridge, Mass.: Harvard University Press, 1992), 432.

21. Greenfeld, *Nationalism*, 480.

22. Greenfeld, *Nationalism*, 476.

23. Philip Abbott, "The Lincoln Propositions and the Spirit of Secession," in *Theories of Secession*, ed. Percy B. Lehning (London: Routledge, 1998), 185.

24. *The Oxford English Dictionary*, 2d ed. s.v. "secession."

25. For a complete treatment of this topic, see Ernst Kantorowicz, *The King's Two Bodies: A Study in Mediaeval Political Theology* (Princeton: Princeton University Press, 1957).

26. That is, contrary to Neorealist assumptions of the continuity of state forms since the ancients, the discipline of International Relations as it exists today could not have existed before the twentieth century (in contrast to, say, the disciplines of history and philosophy).

27. James Mayall, *Nationalism and International Society* (Cambridge: Cambridge University Press, 1990), 38.

28. Mayall, *Nationalism and International Society*, 40 (emphasis in original).

29. Mayall, *Nationalism and International Society*, 35-41.

30. Anthony Giddens, *The Nation-State and Violence* (Berkeley: University of California Press, 1987), 259.

31. Christopher Coker, *War and the 20th Century: The Impact of War on the Modern Consciousness* (London: Brassey's, 1994), 126.

32. Paul Fussell, *The Great War and Modern Memory* (London: Oxford University Press, 1975), 21.

33. Medal of Honor information is available from http://www.army.mil/cmh-pg/moh1.htm. Accessed 25 March 2003.

34. Quoted in Daniel Patrick Moynihan, *On the Law of Nations* (Cambridge, Mass.: Harvard University Press, 1990), 52-53.

35. Michael Walzer, *Just and Unjust Wars: A Moral Argument with Historical Illustrations* (New York: HarperCollins Publishers, 1977), 111.

36. Hans Morgenthau, *Politics among Nations: The Struggle for Power and Peace*, brief edition, rev. Kenneth W. Thompson (New York: McGraw-Hill, 1993), 41.

37. Leonard Woolf, introduction to *The Intelligent Man's Way to Prevent War*, ed. Leonard Woolf (London: Victor Gollancz Ltd., 1933), 9.

38. Quoted in Moynihan, *On the Law of Nations*, 131.

39. Gilbert Murray, "Revision of the Peace Treaties," in *The Intelligent Man's Way to Prevent War*, ed. Leonard Woolf (London: Victor Gollancz Ltd., 1933), 122.

40. E. H. Carr, *The Twenty Years' Crisis 1919-1939: An Introduction to the Study of International Relations* (London: Macmillan, 1993 [1939]), 2-3.

41. Tim Dunne, *Inventing International Society: A History of the English School* (London: Macmillan, 1998), 37.

42. Carr can even be read in support of the normative claims of critical theory. See Andrew Linklater, "The Transformation of Political Community: E. H. Carr, Critical Theory and International Relations," *Review of International Studies* 23 (1997): 321-338.

43. Carr, *The Twenty Years' Crisis*, 5.

44. Dunne, *Inventing International Society*, 35.

45. Morgenthau, *Politics among Nations*, 48.

46. Stanley Hoffmann, "An American Social Science: International Relations," in *International Theory: Critical Investigations*, ed. James Der Derian (London: Macmillan, 1995), 217. First published in *Dædalus* 106, no. 3 (1977).

47. Bull, *The Anarchical Society*, 8 (emphasis in original).

48. Steve Smith, "The Self-Images of a Discipline: A Genealogy of International Relations Theory," in *International Relations Theory Today*, ed. Ken Booth and Steve Smith (Cambridge: Polity Press, 1995), 23.

49. Jim George, *Discourses of Global Politics: A Critical (Re)Introduction to International Relations* (Boulder: Lynne Rienner, 1994), 14.

50. Viva Ona Bartkus, *The Dynamic of Secession* (Cambridge: Cambridge University Press, 1999).

51. Smith, "The Self-Images of a Discipline," 26-27.

52. George, *Discourses*, 192 (emphasis in original).

53. George, *Discourses*, 192.

54. The notable exception is James Mayall. See *Nationalism and International Society*, 61-69; James Mayall and Mark Simpson, "Ethnicity Is Not Enough: Reflections on Protracted Secessionism in the Third World," *International Journal of Comparative Sociology* 33 no. 1-2 (1992): 5-25; "Self-determination Reconsidered: Should There Be a Right to Secede?" *The Oxford International Review* 4, no. 1 (Winter 1993): 4-6; Rick Fawn and James Mayall, "Recognition, Self-Determination and Secession in Post-Cold War International Society," in *International Society after the Cold War: Anarchy and Order Reconsidered*, ed. Rick Fawn and Jeremy Larkins (London: Macmillan, 1996), 193-219.

Chapter 2

Why the Patient Cannot Be Cured

While International Relations literature has given only the barest nod in the direction of secession (it is an inconvenient failure of statehood best left to human rights lawyers and conflict researchers), there has been no lack of interesting discussion and analysis of the subject. Two distinct categories of the conceptual treatment of secession have developed. Political philosophers in the liberal tradition have provided ample argumentation for the nature of secession as a political right that might be justified in certain circumstances. They tend to deal in abstract models and are concerned with legitimate consent and representative democracy. Secession in this framework is seen as a possible political right—a necessary tool for meting justice, so analysis is required for when it is justified. Causal analysts, on the other hand, consider secession in terms of dispute resolution. Secession in this framework is seen as causing conflict and disorder, but also as a possible resolution to conflict, and so its causes must be understood in order to yield useful policy results. While many researchers in the latter category are political scientists, they rarely supply a theoretical framework based on International Relations theory.[1] Their work tends to fall into subdisciplinary categories such as conflict resolution or peace research.

But the approaches taken by non-IR scholars are also unsatisfactory. Both categories of analysis—rights-oriented and causal—deal with secession only in part, and both analytic categories remain firmly within the explanatory theoretical framework. Thus, many of the constructed elements of secession as a phenomenon are taken for granted. This theoretical perspective imposes strong limitations on how secession may be perceived and dealt with. Political theory (moral analysis) tends to sanitize secession by making all of its arguments based on assumptions about the rights of individuals. Causal analysis tends to simplify secession by making all of its arguments based on assumptions about group behavior and the conditions of conflict. Neither approach considers secession to be the by-product of problematic assumptions about International Relations and the nature of statehood and national identity. Rather, secession is seen as a problem which can be solved, a patient who can be cured, if only the appropriate model can be developed. This chapter grapples with the existing literature on secession and demonstrates that the problems with it are twofold.[2]

First, the stated aims of these two tendencies in the literature are unattainable: the rights of all individuals to be protected within a territorialist self-determination framework can never be guaranteed, nor can a scheme or model be devised in which the decisions of national groups will be consistently predictable. Second, because this literature regards secession as a "problem" susceptible to a solution, it can never go beyond the creation of models and policy suggestions which continue to operate within the same parameters of an antiquated international system. Firmly grounded in Realist-style explanatory theory, and modernist epistemology, these models reproduce old assumptions about the nature of the international system which are limited both in terms of descriptive accuracy and in terms of ability to respond to international normative concerns. Ironically, although International Relations has long neglected this issue, the secession nut can best be cracked by an approach which critically (and constitutively) examines the meanings of both *international* and *relations*, that is, secession is most productively theorized in terms of an approach which sees theory as constitutive of reality and which assumes that the social world is not only socially constructed but also socially (and thus diversely) perceived, and so it cannot be objectively theorized through scientific deduction of the "laws" of International Relations. A constitutive approach requires a problematization, a questioning, of the primary assumptions upon which secession rests. These assumptions go to the heart of statehood itself: the territoriality and sovereignty assumption, and the construction of identity on both the individual and collective levels. The theoretical approaches hitherto applied to secession have not dealt with the implications of these questions.

The Political Philosophy of Secession

Few states can unabashedly claim to be composed of a single ethnic group. Yet, the evolution of the modern political state has produced a system in which legitimacy derives from sovereign control over bounded territory even though the citizens who reside within may feel multiple forms of allegiance, which not only transcend cartography but also change in response to internal and external events. These multiple identities create enormous problems for modern political philosophy. The "people" who confer legitimacy upon the state may be defined as those who live within the fixed territorial boundaries of the state. But reading those "people" as members of a "nation," assuming that they feel both civic and cultural loyalty to each other, is a doubtful conclusion that endlessly calls into question the very concept of "nation-state." Self-determination has taken a strong grip on the political imagination as a means of solving this legitimacy dilemma. However, problems of interpretation have divided theorists into those who would limit self-determination to decolonization—i.e., a "one shot" framework—and those who believe that self-determination must logically include a continuing right of secession for people who define themselves as oppressed or alienated by their current governments. Since the international system bulges with such oppressive regimes, and since national separatist movements are so often fought with bloody ferocity, allowing for a right to secede seems the only way to solve the problem. After all—theorists argue—the best way to stop a fight is to split up the antagonists. When couples fight irreconcilably, they are allowed a divorce. But the solution promised by secession is illusory. Political separation cannot be as clean and effective as a marital one. In fact, it is worth noting that perhaps the marital metaphor is apt in a way its proponents never intended since marital breakups are notorious for causing exploitation and pain to the involved parties, even when the laws are as liberal as possible. The problem is that these concepts of separation as a right or as a means of conflict resolution do not account for the fact that human beings become attached to each other in many different ways, and these bonds (not all of them necessarily ones of affection) cannot be broken by the "simple" process of separation. These social ties transcend time and space and efforts to essentialize them; they cannot be locked in or out by borders and walls. Secession merely continues to draw new boundaries around timeless patterns of shifting populations and evolving identities.

It is necessary at the start to define secession for the scope of this discussion. I use the term here to denote "self-cession"—the unilateral withdrawal of territory and people from a state for the creation of a new and separate state. The assumption therefore will be that secession is always disputed by the parent state as illegitimate. Undisputed separations, such as that of Sweden and Norway, or the Czech Republic and Slovakia, are not secessions for the purposes of this discussion; rather, they are peaceful political agreements for constitutional separation—deemed legitimate by both sides. I suggest this limitation in meaning, because to do otherwise is to obscure the very serious theoretical difficulty which secession presents for political theory of any sort—that is, the impasse between self-determination, territorial sovereignty, and political rights. One further qualification will help sharpen the analysis: I do not consider colonial independence movements to be true cases of secession within this discussion. Colonies contain populations which lack the benefits of full membership in the parent state to begin with; they are territories without a history of statehood in the modern international sense, and therefore a colonial independence movement is closer to the creation of a state de novo than it is to the unilateral "withdrawal" of territory and population from a bounded state proper.[3] While these qualifications may appear restrictive, they are meant to clarify the debate. And a definition which regards secession as inherently conflictual more truly mirrors the nature of the debate surrounding the concept.

Secession is an idea antithetical to the modern state. It is opposed by political leaders almost without exception because it involves a loss of territory—the lifeblood and defining characteristic of the state. While the precise nature of the boundaries, population, government, and capacity of a state may all be called into question, there is no exception to the rule that a state must have control of some territory (however small) to be recognized as a state.[4] Territorial withdrawal by a disaffected group not only risks weakening a state economically and politically, but also redefines the very identity of the state in question. The state which remains after secessionists have withdrawn must redefine itself as a state with a population which no longer contains that group or territory. Although the name of the state may remain identical, it is no longer identical with its presecession population, borders, and sovereignty. Thus, its national identity must change in response to these differences. In addition to the basic foundation of the right to self-determination, theorists often rationalize a right to secession in terms of the rights of groups to protect their cultural identities or economic welfare. But theories which justify certain types of secession often fail to adequately account both for the rights of trapped minorities (on both sides of the new borders) and for the futility of matching territorial boundaries to the many variations on human political affiliation. Secession can be only a temporary and incomplete solution to problems of political consent. Its fatal flaw is that it perpetuates a framework in which territorial sovereignty is the only means of protection for disaffected groups. Separatists feel that fully fledged statehood is the only satisfactory option. While statehood may appear to be the best option for members of the primary secessionist group, it creates new types of minority groups, within the seceding territory, or within the territory of the parent state, thus re-creating the original problems inherent in state structure.

Not only does secession create difficulties as a long-term stable solution, but it also poses strong normative problems because it ultimately sanctions segregation rather than cooperation and participation. Secession allows and encourages an increased number of boundaries between different groups of human beings—reinforcing the idea that exclusion is essential to the nature of territorial control and the maintenance of social identity. Even if separation is the best means of stopping two individuals from fighting, it is no guarantee that they will not fight again when next they meet. The immediate violence may be halted, but the conflictual nature of the relationship has not been resolved. Separation is simply a sweep of identity conflict dirt under the territorial rug. A state border between two groups is no guarantee of cooperation and peace, nor is it a guarantee that the majority identities will be secured and settled. John McGarry notes:

> Discontent in new states created by secession is not limited to ethnic minorities who want their own state, to be part of another state, or substantial political accommodation with the new state. In addition, there are those members of the majority group who have dual identities and who, while accepting the new state, regret the passing of the old.[5]

Calling it a "right" for secessionists to build the barriers of modern statehood between themselves and those in the remaining state represents an approach to political problems which condones the deepest intolerance. It is in fact a sanctioned form of ethnic cleansing because it is always based on the assumption of difference between two groups and therefore the assumption that separation is a right. Territorial boundaries do not guarantee freedom; and freedom does not require boundaries to be regarded and protected as a political right.

Justification Theories: When Is There a Right to Secede?

Among liberal democratic theorists who analyze secession in terms of moral rights, the marriage and divorce metaphor appears most compelling. This is rooted in a theoretical framework which places maximum emphasis on freedom of individual choice in the political sphere. This emphasis on the voluntary nature of political relationships underpins the analysis of Allen Buchanan, a prolific theoretician of secession, who states in his seminal book on the subject that political association is like marriage in the sense that it is an artificial institution designed to meet the needs of those subject to it.[6] Buchanan's marriage analogy, with its emphasis on the voluntary nature of political relationships, frees him to find a rationale for secession much broader than the commonplace one of oppressive government. Although in his book he exhaustively covers no fewer than twelve possible reasons for political "divorce," Buchanan later refines the argument by dividing normative theories of secession into two types: primary rights and remedial rights.[7] Primary right theories are based on the principle that any group which decides through a plebiscite should be entitled to secede. There are variations on whether the group may be based on national identity, but primary right theories are basically supportive of a general right to secession based on choice. Remedial right theories are based on the idea that secession is a qualified right, one which must be restricted to special cases. Again, there are variations on what the qualifications actually are, but, as Buchanan puts it, "What all Remedial Right Only theories have in common is the thesis that there is no (general) right to secede from a just state."[8] Buchanan, himself a firm advocate of remedial right theories, argues that secession should be permissible in two particular cases: (1) actual physical safety of a group is threatened, or other grave violations of human rights, or (2) a group's territory was unjustly taken. In considering secession as a remedial right rather than a general one, Buchanan confirms the present international legal order, which continues to hold state territorial integrity sacrosanct. Since territorial integrity actually benefits citizens by maintaining a stable international legal order and creates incentives for cooperation and investment in legitimate political processes, Buchanan argues, "States, so far as their authority rests on their ability to serve the basic interests of individuals, have an *obligatory* interest in maintaining territorial integrity."[9] He is not alone in this approach. Anthony Birch also finds that any justification for breaking up an existing state must be serious and persistent.[10]

Birch's framework, not unlike Buchanan's, starts from the assumption that secession should not be encouraged, but should be available as a last option in certain troubling cases. The justifications Birch finds most persuasive are: (1) continuous refusal on the part of a people to give consent to membership in a union; (2) failure of the government to protect the basic rights of certain citizens; (3) failure to safeguard political and economic interests of a region; and (4) failure to keep a bargain made to preserve the interests of a region which would be outvoted nationally.[11] Though differently worded, the justifications presented by these two theorists are very similar. Birch's first justification, refusal to consent, can be viewed as the primary element of Buchanan's unjust taking of territory argument—since a territorial taking would be considered unjust only if the resident population continuously and vociferously protested. Protection of basic human rights is a straightforward justification for both writers and is certainly intended to address the persecution of minorities in various forms. Birch's third and fourth justifications, failure to protect interests and failure to keep a political bargain, are variations on the possible qualifications of the remedial right theory category. The similarities evident between two liberal writers on secession indicate the limitations of liberalism as a framework for analyzing the problems of secession. With its emphasis on the rights of the individual, liberal theory can address secession only as a necessary evil; one which should be controlled but cannot be banished. Any approach which provides "guidelines" for justifiable secession will be subject to broad disagreement about the applicability and practicality of those criteria, especially when the rights of nonsecessionists are added to the equation.

Even the most morally appealing justification, that of protection of general human rights, still yields contradictions when placed within the remedial right theoretical framework. For example, in the case of Kosovo, compelling human rights violations suffered by the Kosovar Albanians are countered by the Serb claim that Kosovo is a land which was unjustly "taken" from them and settled by Albanians when Serbia did not have control over it. Which argument is more compelling? Obviously, threats to the physical safety of civilian people can never be justified, but which group has the right to the land? One might continue to apply the marriage analogy and liken a repressive state to an abusive spouse. A battered spouse certainly has a right to a divorce, and in comparison, the specter of brutal massacres in ethnically divided states compels a drastic solution. But the analogy cannot really be applied so neatly. The rights and obligations which regulate relations between two individuals do not translate into political relations among large groups of people. Separating even the lives of a single divorced couple is difficult; how can it be possible to cleanly separate groups of people who have been living amongst each other on the same territory for generations? While there is certainly a general human right to personal physical integrity, it is not clear that secession would be an outcome of that right. Buchanan compares the situation to the right of self-defense against lethal threat. But secession is not like self-defense in that it is not a defense open to everyone. It can be claimed only by groups privileged enough to be concentrated within a definable territory, and even then they must be powerful enough to withstand a military campaign by the state against secession. What about the self-defense of groups which are spread throughout the territory of a state? They are left exposed and defenseless by this "right." It is also interesting to note that neither Buchanan nor Birch seriously discusses the obligation of other states to intervene in cases of genocide or severe human rights abuses.[12] Further, neither writer addresses the question of why the creation of a new state would serve as protection of general human rights. Territory cannot itself serve as protection—it must be defended. Even states with control over large land masses have no "security" without peace treaties, cooperative agreements, and military strength. A political regime (or private group) bent on a campaign of ethnic eradication would not cease because its victims declared their independence. Such activities are not stopped by the declaration of a state border; they are stopped by force—or rather, by the *enforcement* of law and order. The sad example of Bosnia, where "ethnic cleansing" began in response to secession rather than being forestalled by it, serves to illustrate that secession can help to create a climate of fear and difference rather than a protective barrier between threatened and threatening groups.[13]

Also attractive as a justification for secession is the rectification of unjust takings of territory argument. Buchanan defines this as the previous incorporation of the seceding area directly by annexation into the existing state and gives the example of the Baltic republics and the Soviet Union. Birch considers the Catholic counties of Ireland and also the difficult cases of indigenous peoples in lands conquered by settlers. The power of the argument stems from its analogous link to stolen property. But again the analogy is not secure because it does not make sense in the collective form. Finding a right of secession for annexed groups is substantially more problematic than finding that these people have the right to remain in the land where their ancestors lived. A right of secession in this case depends not only on a firm commitment to the concept of collective ownership of territory, but also on the means to legally organize and ratify such ownership. This position is fraught with practical pitfalls, and is difficult to support legally. For example, decisions about when such ownership becomes vested, when it lapses, and which persons are to be considered members of the "ownership group" would require the difficult foundation of an international recorder of deeds. Even Buchanan admits that "the history of existing states is so replete with immoral, coercive, and fraudulent takings that it may be hard for most states to establish the legitimacy of their current or past borders."[14] Allowing a right to secession in this case ignores the evolving and locomotive nature of group identities. It would allow groups to claim that a right to territory legally attached and remained fixed at some indefinable point in time despite subsequent processes of immigration and nation-building which may have gone on since. This analysis is not meant to condone conquest and land-grabbing, as, for example, the invasion of Kuwait by Iraq. The point is that by the time a territory has become fully integrated so that its inhabitants are citizens with the full complement of civil rights, then secession becomes extremely problematic. Groups from the parent state who have moved into the territory and consider it home also have rights which should be protected. This is the case in Northern Ireland, and also in the Baltic republics, where the rights of ethnic Russians are proving a difficult issue. When this occurs, the "rights" of two or more groups come into direct conflict and the creation (or "reinstatement") of a new state is no longer a pristine solution. As Birch admits in his discussion of the Indians of North America, "[t]here is undoubtedly a sense in which these indigenous peoples have suffered cruelly from the white man's invasion, but it would be romantic to suggest that secession is now an appropriate answer to their problems."[15] A right of secession in these cases only encourages groups to remain isolated and separate and works against beneficial cooperation and political integration. The question then should not be whether a group has "title" to territory, but whether the rights of the group as citizens and human beings are being protected by the existing political machinery.

Finally, there is the justification of discriminatory redistribution. This occurs, according to both Birch and Buchanan, when a political system sanctions deprivation, or ignores the crucial interests of a region. The interesting aspect of this type of unfair situation is that it can occur even in states which observe liberal democratic principles if they implement schemes which arbitrarily advantage some groups and disadvantage others. Both writers illustrate their concerns with examples from the U.S. Civil War. Buchanan mentions the fact that discriminatory tariffs were enacted against the Southern states through proper congressional procedures, causing Southern leaders to feel that their interests could never be protected in the Union. Birch discusses the fact that Congress broke the negotiated agreement that new states admitted to the Union would alternate between slave state and free state. Southern leaders felt that this move threatened their economic interests. Birch concludes that "[i]n terms of the liberal principles here proposed, this attempted secession was probably justifiable."[16] Amazingly, Birch does not discuss the moral imperative of slavery in this case. Nor does it seem to matter to his calculation that the inhabitants of the western territories which were being admitted to the Union as new states largely did not depend on slave labor and did not wish to enter as designated slave states. How were their rights as free citizens being protected in this framework? What this viewpoint fails to address is exactly why discriminatory redistribution translates into a good argument for secession. If a democratic state commits a serious injustice against the interests of a group or region within its jurisdiction, why should a newly seceded democratic state not turn around and reproduce similar unfair schemes on its own populace? There is no certainty that repartitioning territory will result in an equitable distribution of assets, either for those seceding or for those remaining behind.[17] In fact, liberal democracy has never been about the right to equal distribution—it is only about the right to an equal opportunity to participate in the political process. The voice—not the result—is all that democracy guarantees.[18] Why should secession be the answer to that political problem?

The discriminatory redistribution argument requires the assumption that governmental legitimacy depends upon nonexploitation of its citizens, that is, although "the state's distributive policies are to be allowed to affect different groups differently, there must be some sound moral justification for the differences."[19] What moral justifications would be considered acceptable for such differences? To whom must the arguments be presented? The argument implies that failure on the part of the state to justify its distributive policies effectively voids its claim to the territory in which those who are discriminated against reside. This seems a harsh solution for a problem which must be perceived and argued subjectively. Patterns of economic distribution are notoriously difficult to interpret normatively in the absence of the kind of discrimination or mismanagement which results in widespread physical suffering.[20] In addition, there is the factor of time—discriminatory redistribution will cease to be profitable to the exploiting parties if, for example, the resources become hopelessly depleted or political fortunes change. As Buchanan acknowledges, it is part of the nature of political association and the construction of the state that the wealth of certain areas will be redistributed for the benefit of certain other areas.[21] Accurate determination of the point at which this activity ceases to be cooperation and becomes exploitation or neglect would prove prohibitively difficult. Since economists can scarcely agree on how best to stimulate and manage wealth, it seems exaggerated to find that a state has lost its legitimate claim to territory because wealth has been unfairly redistributed. This justification for secession begins to sound increasingly like a right to wise and good governance—a desirable but elusive thing in this world. Of course, some governments include discriminatory redistribution in a laundry list of oppressive and autocratic acts of state. These are serious issues. But secession is not a plaster which can patch broken or harmful states. It only allows concentrated groups of people to redraw their political boundaries. To see secession as a solution is to be blind to the problems of discrimination and the designations of "otherness" which occur every time a piece of territory is delineated.

While Birch and Buchanan approach secession as a remedial right, one which should kick in only when wrongs have been manifested, Harry Beran approaches it from the opposite side of the fence as a primary moral right from which there should be a presumption that secession is just.[22] Beran also compares his theory of secession to marriage and divorce, illustrating his point with three types of legal divorce: (1) cases in which it is allowed only on specific moral grounds such as adultery or cruelty; (2) cases in which the parties are so incompatible that they both wish to be apart; and (3) cases in which the marriage ends even at the wish of only one of the parties. Beran prefers the last case as a model for his theory of secession because it provides the greatest scope for satisfying parties in unhappy marriages. Ultimately, Beran argues, "liberal political philosophy requires that secession be permitted if it is effectively desired by a territorially concentrated group within a state and is morally and practically possible."[23]

From the starting point of democratic consent theory, Beran argues that the closer adult decisions are, in a contemporary democracy, to being voluntary, the closer such a society comes to matching the ideal liberal model. Citizens in a liberal state may work and live and marry as they choose, and governments are voted in and out of office by their choice. Under this scheme, according to Beran, no state can be indissoluble since that would limit the freedom of choice to the generation which formed the state in question. In other words, a group's right of self-determination is "the right to freely determine its political status."[24] There are two flaws in this argument. First, it is not so easy to determine which individuals belong to the group with this right; and second, it is based on the assumption that "political status" must mean the determination of a state with borders. Beran's reply to the problem of calculation of group members is quite simple: the reiterated application of the majority principle. In other words, Beran's theory holds that the determination of groups by continued referenda on the issue of secession is the only solution that is consistent with democratic principles. The elegance of this solution is chimerical. People will not be so cleanly divided into groups on the issues of identity and territory. They have plural identities, not majority/minority ones. In addition, the language of any proposed referendum will itself largely dictate the outcome. Depending on how the secession issue is stated, different groups will find their interests represented, and the result will not necessarily protect the political choice of all the parties. Forcing nonsecessionists to choose a political identity under these circumstances may actually offer them none of their preferences. For example, what protects the freedom of individuals within a seceding group who do not wish to leave? Their only means of remaining within the parent state is to move—hardly a protection for these involuntary victims whose actual choice is to remain within the original (whole) state.[25] Also, reiterated referenda do not affect the problem of dispersed or integrated minorities; they are people whose interests can never be addressed territorially.

The second flaw is the assumption that the right to determine "political status" must mean the right to create new state borders. Political organization has existed in many forms throughout history, and it is a narrow interpretation indeed that restricts its manifestation to the modern state. Territorial states as they are now, with strict border delineation and control, are a modern outgrowth of the nineteenth century.[26] There is no preordained requirement that our conception of political organization be fixed to a territorial entity. Our understanding of what is meant by "the state" has already undergone alteration and continues to do so, especially in the face of increasingly private control of economics and finance. Within this context, liberal theory provides a restricted vision of political freedom. For many ethnic or national groups, the "freedom" of a territorial state is more responsibility than they have the resources to handle. For these groups, the notion of the state as the only manifestation of political freedom is actually a burden that limits them by presenting them with an all-or-nothing choice. Freedom can be truly protected only by flexible conceptualizations of political organization, conceptualizations that recognize that political free choice can be directed at group membership rather than state citizenship.[27]

Beran further elaborates that his democratic theory of self-determination is meant to produce rightful borders, not necessarily good ones.[28] This statement assumes both that the right of secession is a moral right and that stable and peaceful borders are not necessarily morally justified ones. In fact, Beran criticizes Birch and Buchanan for failing to account for "the compatibility of such a highly qualified right of secession with the fundamental principles of democracy."[29] But Beran then confuses the issue by allowing for limitations to the right of secession on practical grounds, and even for the suppression of secession by force where there is a "moral justification." Making a distinction between "ideal world" and "real world" theory, Beran concedes that in the "real world," secessionists may be resisted if they refuse to allow joint control of militarily essential territories, or if they refuse to share the benefits of scarce natural resources with the rump state, or if they will oppress minorities in their midst. He even hypothesizes the case of the disintegration of the former Yugoslavia, saying that "if the Slovenes thought that the disintegration of Yugoslavia would in turn lead to a catastrophic war in Europe and the loss of millions of lives, they ought not to have exercised their right of secession at the time."[30] By conceding that the right of secession can be limited by certain expediencies such as territorial viability, monopoly of resources, oppression of minorities, and the potential for catastrophic war, Beran conflates a moral/normative analysis of secession with a Utilitarian analysis, based on practicality and maximized interests. If the right of self-determination is tied to the individual right of free political association, how can the use of force to suppress secession ever be justified? A true *moral* right cannot be limited by the potential unhappiness it may cause. It is the concept of balancing benefits which ultimately weakens Beran's thesis. Once he allows for practical limitations on the "permissive" right, it becomes difficult to differentiate his outcomes from those of Birch and Buchanan. Beran's starting point of secession as a moral right which should be freely allowed ends in an intricate pattern of situations in which secession should be discouraged and even actively fought. The argument ends on a much less radical note than the one on which it opened.

The final writer to be examined under this approach is legal philosopher Lea Brilmayer, whose "territorial interpretation" also seeks to overturn the standard account of secession and the right of self-determination.[31] Brilmayer seeks to reconcile the contradiction between the principles of self-determination and territorial integrity which arise in the secessionist context by making the argument that secessionist claims are actually much more about territory than they are about a distinct people. The current emphasis on self-determination, according to Brilmayer, obscures the debate rather than clarifies it, since the real normative force of a bid for secession comes from a claim to territorial legitimacy and not from the argument that the group constitutes a distinct people. By making this argument, one can clarify the confusion which reigns over contemporary international law about how the right of self-determination can be meaningful without necessarily supporting indefinite subdivisions of states. Brilmayer supports this limitation of the right of self-determination by attacking the understanding of consent as the key to legitimacy in liberal democratic theory. Although interestingly Brilmayer does not mention Beran, she tackles his arguments head on. Liberal theorists, she argues, have never intended for consent to be actual in the sense that refusal exempts the individual from state authority. Liberal democratic consent is, in fact, tacit and encompassed in the right to participate.

> Government by the consent of the governed does not necessarily encompass a right to opt out. It only requires that within the existing political unit a right to participate through electoral processes be available. Moreover, participatory rights do not entail a right to secede. On the contrary, they suggest that the appropriate solution for dissatisfied groups rests in their full inclusion in the polity, with full participation in its decision-making processes.[32]

As Brilmayer rightly points out, then, self-determination need not be considered as the necessary basis of secessionist claims since it does not encompass the right to "opt out" of state processes. She also raises the classical critique—where is the "self" in self-determination? Since the identification of peoples is notoriously arbitrary, Brilmayer argues that basing secession on territorial claims instead self-determination ones provides a more liberal and more consensual means of determining the right. After all, "[o]ne's geographical location is more nearly voluntary than one's ethnic identity."[33] What Brilmayer neglects, however, is the possibility that ethnic identity and territorial association go hand in hand. Her point that every secessionist claim must include a justification of territorial taking is correct. Obviously there are many national groups which may not make a claim to a discrete piece of territory given their level of assimilation within the area of the entire state. Thus, Brilmayer's shifted emphasis forces us to realize the problematic nature of current understandings of nations and peoples as territorially defined. Shifting the basis of the right of secession to territory, she seems to think, will make the assessment of the legitimacy of claims much fairer and simpler. But such a result is far from clear. Why should it be easier to assess the legitimacy of claims to territory than of claims to independent nationhood?

Brilmayer does provide two categories of argument which might indicate the superior legitimacy of one party against another over territory. First is the case of conquest or annexation in which the wrongdoer is the current state. The second argument involves the action of a third party (imperial power) which improperly fixed the borders but is no longer involved in the current conflict. Brilmayer illustrates the annexation argument with the example of the Baltic republics and the Soviet Union, and the colonial case with the example of East and West Pakistan and Great Britain. She asserts that a territorial framework allows for a proper focus on the history of such disputes rather than the simplistic "rights of nations" analysis. It is the history of these claims that gives them the normative strength to attain legitimacy. Otherwise, all claims are dealt with equally on the basis of whether the seceding group constitutes a valid people. If United Nations principles of self-determination are taken literally, Brilmayer asserts, "then Turkish guest workers in Germany have claims on par with black Africans fighting colonial powers. So static a view of the division of a society into peoples cannot fully capture an important normative feature of separatists' demands, namely that the asserted historical grievance confers on it the right to a particular territory."[34] What Brilmayer does not provide is any kind of consistent guideline for prioritizing normative rights. For example, why should black Africans fighting colonial powers have greater normative priority than Turkish "guest workers" who have been in Germany for several generations and yet continue to be refused basic citizenship rights? Presumably Brilmayer's reply would be that the historical association of the black Africans to their native soil creates a much stronger claim to territory than that of the Turks in Germany. This suggests that normative claims to territory can be quantifiable; for example, a claim might be "created" if a certain number of years were spent by a group on a territory. But if we wished to establish such quantifiable standards for territorial benefits, how would we establish a fair international standard? Brilmayer seems to advocate an international legal principle of adverse possession for territorial claims. She recognizes this problem and explicitly provides several factors which should help determine whether the status quo or the historical claim has more validity, including (1) length of time since the historical grievance occurred, (2) the extent to which the separatist group could keep the controversy alive, (3) the extent to which the population in the territory consists of members of the dominant group, and (4) the "degree of wrongfulness" of the original grievance itself. These factors are as susceptible to difficulties as those of the political philosophers described above. None of them would clarify the difficult territorial conflicts in Northern Ireland or Palestine, for example. Furthermore, there are two issues Brilmayer does not discuss which are crucial to an understanding of territorial claims. The first is that claims to territory are much more about power than they are about rights. It is only because control of territory is the prerequisite for the powers of sovereign statehood that groups fight so viciously for control of it. And it is only groups which are affiliated with statehood that gain recognition in the international sphere. Otherwise, why would groups which live in democratic states where the rights of citizenship give them protection and the tools of cultural maintenance nevertheless maintain such tenacious separatist struggles? The second issue, glaring by its absence, is the question of the extent to which a people is created and identified by its affiliation with some territory, whether it is sovereign or not. Brilmayer writes as if a group's claims to be a people and its claims over a territory can be conceived of separately. In fact, the only groups for which this is true are nomadic ones, and they are rarely implicated in the problems surrounding separatist conflicts.[35] It is a serious oversight to neglect the extent to which national identities are territorially based. The relationship between territory and ethnic identity is not simply, as Brilmayer supposes, the purpose of keeping the historical grievance alive year after year, but it is also a constitutive one. It is precisely because territory provides a basis for identity that such fierce battles are fought over it—the same piece of territory may give meaning and identity to more than one group. Thus, the "conquerors" come to feel like the "natives," and the aggrieved group may seem aggressive in turn, when it attempts to regain control of its homeland. These sentiments are not adequately captured by Brilmayer's use of the technical term "adverse possession," which implies that one might occupy the territory of a state as a business venture.

Brilmayer admits that her territorial interpretation does not provide easy answers, but she claims that it does force us to examine the crucial questions: "When a group seeks to secede, it is claiming a right to a particular piece of land, and one must necessarily inquire into why it is entitled to that particular piece of land, as opposed to some other piece of land—or to no land at all."[36] These are indeed crucial questions, however, a "territorial interpretation" goes very little way in answering them.

Causal Analysis: How Do We Fix the Secession Problem?

The political theorists discussed above share similar approaches to secession in that they are concerned with rights under liberal democratic theory and all ultimately find that secession must be permitted under certain circumstances to protect these rights. Writers in the causal analysis category have a slightly different focus. Their concern is with decreasing the level of separatist conflict, and they therefore tend to see secession both pragmatically, as a necessary evil, and as a problem which may be solved through careful study. Causal analysts may also discuss the rights of separatist groups, but their chief concern is with international policy not political theory. While liberal theorists look past the nature of national group identity to analyze individual rights, causal analysts are more likely to perceive national identities as an intransigent stumbling block to conflict resolution. Rather than speaking in terms of marriage and divorce (a metaphor premised on liberal individualist assumptions), causal analysts speak in terms of power relations and violence:

> Bloodshed, chaos and suffering tend to accompany the birth of the secessionist child. It is likely to be illegitimate, spawned in conspiracy and the result of rape. The mother country must be dismembered. Maimed fractions must now become healthy wholes. Territory is lost, and with it, tenacious memories, people and vitality. Prolonged struggle demoralises all sections in the conflict equally, polarises and demoralises nearly all members, creates a garrison mentality, cripples democratic institutions, breeds fanaticism and helplessly accepts a distorted existence as normal and inevitable. . . . The right to secede is as valid as the capability of forcibly wresting territory and people from another state.[37]

These analysts are drawn to study secession as a phenomenon not because of a concern with moral rights but because secession poses a significant problem for politics and policy in both the international and the national spheres. The first instinct for these scholars, then, is to identify recurring variables in secessionist cases (the usual suspects are national identity, territory, and sometimes economic benefit) and deduce processes which will ensure the smoothest possible resolution and transition to peace. These theorized processes involve judgments of some kind by the international community or a specially designated United Nations body. Other writers have concluded that secession only begets further conflict and that the best chance for a stable international order is one in which there is interethnic cooperation and nonstate forms of political representation.[38]

One of the first writers to discuss secession as a relevant concept on its own was Lee Buchheit.[39] Coming from a legal background, Buchheit sees secession as an integral part of the concept of self-determination. Refusing either to state that self-determination is limited to arbitrary categories such as decolonization, or to leave the validation of secession to the future while focusing on nonintervention and use of force norms, Buchheit offers a third approach—a balancing test for determining which claims of secession are legitimate and should be allowed to proceed. Starting from the premise that secessionist movements are unlikely to decrease in number, Buchheit believes that setting international standards for the types of secessionist claims which can be considered legitimate will moderate both the reactions of external states and the tenor of the claims made by separatist groups.[40] His starting assumption is based on a sort of state-centered utilitarianism, which requires that "the institution of the existing State will be respected, unless to do so would contribute to more international disharmony than would result from legitimating the separation of a component group."[41] Buchheit finds that the factors of viability and "self"-ness for the separatists, and the increased balance of harmony for the world community, are not capable of being measured by absolute standards. Since each separatist case will contain a different blend of these elements, Buchheit suggests a balancing analysis between the interests of international peace and the strength of the separatists' claim. Although he discusses the nature of legitimacy and the possibilities for greater harmony in further detail, Buchheit never fully identifies what he means by the concept of world community. This is a fatal theoretical weakness for his argument. The attempt to ascertain whether an act will increase world harmony will surely fail if the "world community" remains undefined. Hence, the expectation that this world community should perform the balancing analysis must also fail.

Buchheit's scheme depends on two factors which are both incapable of determination. Neither the subject nor the method is specified in his case by case approach. While Buchheit wishes to avoid the problems of theoretical rigidity, his suggestion for determining legitimacy is so vague as to distill into a single obvious maxim—that the international community should act toward secessionist groups in ways that resolve the situation peacefully and most beneficially for all concerned. The normative strength of this argument seems to be based on the premise that only those groups which are attempting to secede under conditions which are favorable for the rest of the international community will actually have a right to do so. Not only is this unhelpful as a solution to secessionist conflict, but it also is of dubious moral value. Furthermore, Buchheit's "balancing test" approach seems wildly out of context in the international community. It is a term borrowed from American constitutional legal analysis, which requires both a body of law and a body of judges to make adequate use of its principles. Unless there is a designated body of individuals whose capabilities are recognized and trusted to carry out this balancing test, it remains a paper solution.

While Buchheit stopped short of proposing a more specific term than "international community," another legal scholar, Lawrence Frankel, takes his analysis further.[42] Agreeing with Buchheit that cases of secession must be decided by a neutral body on an individual basis, Frankel proposes a U.N. Commission that will be triggered as an automatic mechanism by the petition of organized secessionist groups. The commission would apply a set of generally applicable standards that should be determined by international consensus:

> What is critical . . . is for there to be clearly enunciated, established standards for
> when secession should or should not be encouraged. Fortunately, there is reason
> to believe that principled, legitimate, workable guidelines for evaluating
> secessionist claims can be formulated.[43]

Frankel thus remedies the vagueness of Buchheit's balancing test, but falls prey to
problems of his own. Asserting that both moral legitimacy and practical politics
should be considered in the determinations of the commission, Frankel suggests six
standards that might find international consensus. They are a combination of human
rights concerns with the practicalities of territorial control and economic feasibility.
However, what Frankel does not provide is a realistic assessment of why the reports
from his commission will carry any more weight than those of the current Human
Rights Commission, which is influential but hardly capable of resolving major
conflicts. Frankel asserts that the recommendations will carry great moral force
through the effects of "world opinion" since "[t]he hypocrisy of states voting against
an impartial, carefully justified recommendation would be uncomfortably apparent,"[44]
although he concedes that further U.N. action might be necessary if individual states
refuse to take action. While Frankel goes some way toward specifying the kind of
system to which Buchheit alludes, his framework remains little more than a variation
on the international diplomatic means currently existing. Frankel relies upon the
moral coercion of an established regime put in place by an international consensus.
But in the absence of any serious treatment of the establishment of international
norms, he fails to provide evidence that such a consensus on secession might ever
be reached (especially given the tendency of states to see it as a vital threat to their
interests) or that states might heed the recommendations of such a commission.

The writer who perhaps best exemplifies the approach to secession as "a
necessary evil" is Alexis Heraclides. While writing from within the Western liberal
perspective, he is far less concerned with whether secession is a right than with
confronting the realities of separatist movements in the international system.[45]
Heraclides examines three possibilities for a normative approach to secession and
discards two of them. First, he considers the "Pandora's Box" option—which permits
unilateral secession for those capable of achieving it and allows outside states to
become involved as they see fit. The logic of this approach is something akin to a
political version of the survival of the fittest, but with the additional corollary that
"the unfit won't try." Not surprisingly, Heraclides finds this prospect destabilizing
and blind to the merits of each prospective case, "rewarding military prowess and
diplomatic adroitness as if 'might' could be 'right.'"[46] Next, Heraclides examines
the "Window of Opportunity" approach, which basically describes the postwar
limited-permission regime in which separation was possible only through partition
or by mutual agreement. Heraclides believes this framework actually lasted until 1990
and the break up of the Eastern Bloc. The Window of Opportunity tradition,
Heraclides suggests, could be updated by adding an emphasis on minority protections
and various forms of federation. Heraclides maintains that this scheme is unjust on
the basis of unequal treatment of certain groups, since the idea cannot be maintained
"that an arbitrarily carved colony or a unit of a federation which does not suffer

inequality should have more of a right to independence than an ethnic or regional group which suffers systematic and flagrant discrimination . . . with no realistic prospect of change."[47] Ironically, Heraclides' distaste for this type of discrimination cannot be cured by any framework regarding the disposition of state territory, since the historical legitimacy of claims to territory can be disputed indefinitely.

Heraclides' final plan is the one he advocates—that of allowing secession in specified cases. He retains the emphasis on the protection of distinct cultures and suggests, in addition, a method for ascertaining the legitimacy of unilateral independence. Heraclides also recognizes a variety of interesting possibilities for minority self-rule without the need for secession, calling them "ethnosocial contracts." Such possibilities include an agreement on the part of a minority group to remain loyal to the state, or a nonsecessionist oath, in exchange for mutual acceptance and accommodation. An ethnosocial contract, according to Heraclides, might also provide for nonsecessionist autonomy or for some type of communal federation for the minority group. Ultimately, Heraclides sees the need for a specific framework which would identify justifiable cases of secession. His criteria sound familiar. Justifiable cases must be those where there is alien domination. Specific circumstances which would justify a unilateral secession must include (1) the existence of a sizeable compact community strongly in favor of statehood; (2) a pattern of exploitation on the part of the state against this group; (3) cultural rejection or attempts to forcibly assimilate this group on the part of the state; and (4) the refusal of the state to consider any form of internal autonomy for the group.[48] Although Heraclides' step-by-step analysis for legitimating secession attempts to consider the needs of all parties, it still fails to account for the poverty of secession itself as a solution to political problems, and it leaves some confusion about its application.

If a state neglects the needs of a minority group within its borders, does that group have the right to secede? What exactly would constitute "neglect" in such a case? Since secession is widely considered to be disruptive, is it really a desirable approach in such a case—especially recalling Brilmayer's discussion of the tacit nature of political consent and the right of exit? Most glaringly, is it fair to grant the right of secession to aggrieved minority groups within a state simply because they have the good fortune to reside in concentrated numbers on delineated areas of territory? What a right of secession actually amounts to in this case is a right to a group identity and a state frozen at the moment of the vesting of that right. But cultural groups and their interaction with territory cannot be fixed in this way. Populations have been moving and mixing over the surface of the globe since time began. Now that travel has become faster, safer, easier, and cheaper, it seems hopeless to assume that the only means of political organization available is one in which territorially bounded sovereign states must mirror the location of cultural and national groups as they adapt and change. Political freedom can be manifested and protected in other ways.

The writer who best epitomizes the causal analysis approach is political scientist Donald Horowitz.[49] Horowitz's concern, with the causes of ethnic conflict in general, covers a much broader category of political and social relations, yet he does provide a fairly focused analysis of secessionist conflict. From the preface of his substantial volume, Horowitz espouses a positivist empirical methodology—that is, he works on the assumption that there are objective patterns of ethnic conflict which are discoverable. Once having discovered these patterns, he aims to provide an analysis of methods of reducing conflict and their effectiveness. To that end, Horowitz asks the classic causal questions: "What accounts for the emergence of secession? What kinds of groups attempt to secede and under what circumstances? What accounts for the success of such movements, and what effects does success have, both in the secessionist state and in the rump state?"[50] Given his aspiration to ascertain the natural patterns of ethnic conflict, Horowitz's procedure seems somewhat arbitrary. While obviously well versed in many different histories and cultures, and able to provide numerous examples of separatist movements and secession attempts, Horowitz does not provide relevant data to back up his stated categories. Quoting from Immanuel Wallerstein's comments on the likelihood of relative wealth strengthening a secessionist attempt, as it did in Katanga, Horowitz borrows the link between ethnic claims and the economic characteristics of the regions involved to create a matrix indicative of potential secessionist groups.

Noticing that many wealthy regions made no effort to secede, while many poorer regions did, Horowitz tries to expand Wallerstein's remark into a more explanatory framework. His matrix therefore counterposes "backward" and "advanced" regions against "backward" and "advanced" groups. Within Horowitz's analysis, "backward" groups are those with lower average education and per capita income, and "advanced" groups are ones with generally higher education and higher levels of "non-agricultural employment." Regions can be characterized, in this analysis, by the relative economies measured by per capita regional income. These data are in fact, according to Horowitz himself, difficult to come by, especially for regions in Africa and Asia. Nonetheless, Horowitz insists that "identification of backward and advanced regions is not difficult."[51] Even if one willingly accepts that the determination of backward (as opposed to advanced) groups and regions is straightforward without precise assessment data, it would still be difficult to understand how Horowitz selects his "groups." His matrix includes twenty-one potential secessionist groups in four different categories, depending upon whether the groups are backward or advanced, and whether their regional economies are backward or advanced. Interestingly, Horowitz does not explain how he selected these groups from the myriad of cases he discusses throughout the book. He also includes six examples that are problematic both in terms of being distinct groups, and because they have never had a strong secessionist movement. If they have not had a strong secessionist movement, why should these groups be categorized within a matrix of potential secessionist groups? If the lack of a secessionist movement is no barrier to the analysis, then Horowitz might as well have included every territorially discrete group he could legitimately label as "ethnic" for the sake of comprehensive analysis. Notwithstanding the richness of the empirical observations throughout the book, there are notable lapses in his categorization of secessionist groups, specifically in examples from Western Europe and the Americas. The

Québécois, for example, are missing from the matrix, as are the Catalans—although Basques are mentioned, as an advanced group within an advanced region. In addition, many groups are included that have severe internal differences and/or divergent goals that make them problematic for consideration as single distinct separatist groups. These include the Southern Sudanese and the Kurds in Iraq.

Horowitz readily admits that his framework overlooks certain difficulties for the sake of simplification. He states, for example, that deciding upon regional categories on the basis of per capita income excludes relevant information on varying levels of development between rural areas and urban centers. He also acknowledges that he does not account for the various differences within ethnic groups concerning choices about secession, but will rather deal "with central tendencies or merely with the outcomes of such debates."[52] What remains unclear is how this simplified categorization can lead to the proposed goal of determining the causes of secession and the indicators of its probable success. Horowitz states that "[t]he interplay of relative group position and relative regional position determines the emergence of separatism," but he also wishes to "reject direct causal relationships between regional economic disparity and ethnic secession."[53] This confusing formulation obscures the question of whether Horowitz can make any predictive or prescriptive claims on the basis of his matrix. He seems to want a foothold in both camps, claiming that regional position is a causal element in secessionism, but that it does not predict secessionism directly; rather it "conditions the claims ethnic groups make and their response to the rejection of those claims."[54] What, then, can one conclude from the juxtaposition of these ethnic group variables?

Horowitz summarizes his claims in a second matrix, showing that the backward and advanced group and regional categories reveal tendencies in terms of types of political claims they make, the events (precipitants) that will most likely indicate rejection of group claims, the calculations each group tends to make, and the timing and relative frequency of actual secessionist claims. Thus, the most likely secessionist groups are "backward groups in backward regions," while the least likely to secede are groups (both backward and advanced) in "advanced regions." There are no calculations provided of how many groups were considered in total, and which ones were placed in which categories. Horowitz simply presents his summary, conceding that every category has negative cases. Given the methods by which the matrices have been constructed, one concludes that their main purpose is descriptive rather than predictive. Despite a detailed discussion of the nature of ethnicity elsewhere in the book, Horowitz is forced to organize his analysis of secession in ways which take ethnic groups for granted as stable, unproblematic, and self-evident. Because of his chosen causal aims and methodology, Horowitz must ignore the very features of ethnic groups and secessionism which make them difficult to understand and predict in the first place. Classifications based on empirical methods always involve a cost in detail and abstraction, and these limitations are acknowledged. But Horowitz attempts to derive a causal explanation from a categorization, and this is where he fails. These methods yield a framework which is not effective in explaining a number of secessionist cases very well, if at all. It also fails to account for the rarity of successful secessionist attempts in general. Horowitz argues that it is not the international principle of territorial integrity and the legitimacy of boundaries which has stood in the way of successful secession attempts. Rather, he concludes, it is the fact that intervening states provide inadequate support for secessionist groups, central governments exert great efforts to defeat them, and the groups themselves suffer from internal problems. But it is precisely the strength of the territorial principle which moderates the aid of intervening parties and increases the efforts of central governments to put down secessionist attempts. Also, it is international recognition of the legitimacy of a secessionist movement which will result in the creation of a legitimate state—or not. Thus, the international community and the principle of territorial integrity play crucial—actually constitutive—roles in the success and failure of secessionist movements. A framework which does not consider them (and which ignores the contingency of group identity and group decision making) has limited explanatory value.

Conclusion: Re-Placing Politics

The political philosophy approach which focuses on the rights of secession is essentially an outgrowth of the philosophical search for a good life and the liberal assumption that individuals must be free to determine (and consent to) the good life for themselves. Secession, however, assumes that a sizeable group of individuals agrees that a certain precise type of state (territory, population, structure, etc.) is necessary to preserve their ability to live the good life. Given the fact that such decisions are extremely difficult to reach precise agreement on, and that the result of imprecision is the denial of similar rights to those who disagree with separatism, it is far from obvious that secession really provides an assurance of the liberal right of free political association. The main source of inconsistency of the frameworks put forward by secession's apologists is the lack of protection for the rights of the groups which either become trapped within the seceding territory or remain behind in the parent state. Such groups are the "children" of the metaphorical political divorce espoused by these theorists, and their best interests are as difficult to protect as those of the children of real broken marriages. Rights analysis which gives no consideration to the contingent and constructed nature of identities will never be able to fully account for the plurality of individual needs and preferences. Such "rights," then, require that those who claim them essentialize and privilege parts of their identities to the exclusion of others. This injustice is not accounted for in moral rights analysis. The arguments of political philosophers regarding the rights of secession are therefore internally inconsistent. Moreover, they do not take into account the practical weakness of secession in that it does not provide a long-term solution to conflict. Secession does not "solve" problems of group conflict; it merely redraws the boundaries around them.

The causal analysis approach to secession also yields confusion. Regarding secession as an objective problem which must be studied and thereby minimized or "solved" results in methods which can at best yield a case-by-case approach. Because causal analysis cannot account for the contingency of ethnic or group identities, and because it must necessarily reduce the difficulties of identity and group decision making into the simplistic model of unitary actor behavior, it provides only shallow descriptive accounts. The identities of actors in secessionist conflicts are too intertextual and constructed to be captured completely within the presumption of state boundaries and political freedom upon which secession is premised. Presenting independent statehood as the sole legitimate political form for separatist groups only perpetuates the conditions which allow nationalism to flourish in its most virulent forms. Once this is recognized, secession becomes illusory, both as a solution to intrastate conflict and as a means of protecting political freedom.

The problem which both of the theoretical approaches examined here share is what Bonnie Honig calls "the displacement of politics." Honig argues that political theorists of all persuasions have long attempted to remove conflict and contingency—the political—from political theory. Political theorists

> converge in their assumption that success lies in the elimination from a regime of dissonance, resistance, conflict, or struggle. They confine politics (conceptually and territorially) to the juridical, administrative, or regulative tasks of stabilizing moral and political subjects, building consensus, maintaining agreements, or consolidating communities and identities. They assume that the task of political theory is to resolve institutional questions, to get politics right, over, and done with, to free modern subjects and their sets of arrangements of political conflict and instability.[55]

By assuming the need for stable subjects and institutions, by depoliticizing their theories of secession, many of the political theorists discussed above must take for granted the very contestations and constructions which make secession what it is. That is, they assume the stability of the minority and majority identity relationships in question, they assume the value and need of historical justification of claims, and they assume that territorial boundaries necessarily protect and secure the identities of national groups. By making these assumptions, political theorists shut out the very contingencies which are most at stake in secession. The failure to recognize or account for the ongoing unstable nature of identity formations results in theories which effectively lock identities in place, perpetuating a different kind of violence to the multiplicity of the self and failing to provide for the remainders caused by "the self's perpetual ill-fittedness" to established identities.[56] Engaging with Nietzsche, Honig suggests that the contestations of politics are necessary to continuously call into question the sedimentation of moral concepts. In Nietzsche's terms, resistance to such sedimentation is the equivalent of the battle between life and death.

> To attribute particular features, qualities, or moods to the world is to attempt to fix and order a world characterized above all by an impulse to change, although moving in no particular direction, an impulse Nietzsche identifies with life itself, sometimes calling it will to power.

God, virtue, the ego, and the subject are not given; they are interpretive
creations, fictions. To insist on their givenness (or rightness or expressiveness) is
necessarily to conceal their varied, violent, haphazard, and tenuously constructed
origins.[57]

Secession, as the embodiment of conflict, must not be ordered into stable categories,
nor should it be seen as the product of given forces such as identity, history, and
territoriality. All of these forces are the contingent and unstable outcomes of the
impulse to change. The most productive way to analyze secession, then, is to call
its assumptions into question, to loosen its sedimentation to free the creative powers
brought forth by an awareness of politics and the will to power. The rest of this book
attempts to do just that, by unsettling the settled and resisting the will to order.

This chapter examines and demonstrates the difficulties of current secession
literature both in justifying secession as a right and in attempting to solve it as a
problem of ethnic conflict. These approaches cannot achieve their aims because they
continue to view secession as an established feature of international politics. It may
be good or bad or neither, but it exists and must be examined almost as a structure.
Such treatment, by institutionalizing secession, creates a theoretically closed space
within which to analyze it. By questioning the roots of territoriality as a concept, and
by analyzing the conditions for secession's possibility, one can view secession more
constructively—not as a self-evident feature of international politics, but as an
outcome of contemporary international impulses. It is not a disease, then, that we
should try to cure, but rather a symptom of underlying and too often unquestioned
structures of the system. Attempting to analyze secession without taking this step
is a Sisyphean endeavor, not only fruitless but also blind to the conditions of
generation and thus of possible change. Secession, then, should be regarded as a
troubling symptom of the international system that should induce us to make a wider
analysis of the process of its construction. In the next chapter, I penetrate the roots
of the concept of secession through a conceptual history of territoriality and the rise
of the modern(ist) state.

Notes

An earlier version of this chapter originally appeared as "Altered States: Secession
and the Problems of Liberal Theory" in *Theories of Secession,* edited by Percy B.
Lehning (London: Routledge, 1998); reprinted here with kind permission of Routledge.

1. Indeed, as I assert in chapter 1, this is because International Relations theory, as
dominated by Realist assumptions of statehood and sovereignty, makes a sustained analysis
of secession extremely problematic.

2. Although there has been a proliferation of literature dealing with secession in recent
years, the epistemological assumptions I discuss here have not changed. The texts used in
this chapter represent secession literature that is well established in the subject area and to
which many recent texts have responded. Most noticeable among recent publications on

secession are: *Theories of Secession*, edited by Percy B. Lehning (London: Routledge, 1998); and *National Self-Determination and Secession*, edited by Margaret Moore (Oxford: Oxford University Press, 1998).

3. Thus, the American War of Independence in 1776 was just that—a war to gain independence, to create the possibility of the status of citizenship for the revolutionaries—not a war of secession. In fact, there is some evidence that had British colonial policy been more conciliatory, the American colonists would not have had the collective will to fight for independence from the "mother country." See Philip McFarland, *The Brave Bostonians: Hutchinson, Quincy, Franklin, and the Coming of the American Revolution* (Oxford: Westview Press, 1998).

4. For an amusing and thought-provoking (as well as legally accurate) text on the subject, see Erwin S. Strauss, *How to Start Your Own Country* (Port Townsend, Wash.: Loompanics Unlimited, 1984).

5. John McGarry, "'Orphans of Secession': National Pluralism in Secessionist Regions and Post-Secession States," in *National Self-Determination and Secession*, ed. Margaret Moore (Oxford: Oxford University Press, 1998), 222.

6. Allen Buchanan, *Secession: The Morality of Political Divorce from Fort Sumter to Lithuania and Quebec* (Boulder, Colo.: Westview Press, 1991), 7.

7. See Allen Buchanan, "The International Institutional Dimension of Secession," in *Theories of Secession*, ed. Percy B. Lehning, (London: Routledge, 1998), 227-256.

8. Buchanan, "Institutional Dimension of Secession," 232.

9. Buchanan, "Institutional Dimension of Secession," 242 (emphasis in original).

10. Anthony H. Birch, *Nationalism and National Integration* (London: Unwin Hyman, 1989), 64.

11. Birch, *Nationalism and National Integration*, 64-66.

12. Buchanan does discuss the strengthening of international institutions but not in a manner that recognizes the implications of a norm of intervention for the concept of secession as a right.

13. Although analyses of the conflict in the former Yugoslavia usually refer to its history of violent ethnic clashes, there is also no doubt that many peaceful mixed communities were forcibly polarized after Bosnia's secession by calculated political campaigns of terror.

14. Buchanan, *Secession*, 68.

15. Birch, *Nationalism and National Integration*, 64.

16. Birch, *Nationalism and National Integration*, 66.

17. Charles R. Beitz, *Political Theory and International Relations* (Princeton, N.J.: Princeton University Press, 1979), 109.

18. Buchanan does in fact further tease out the relationship between democracy and secession in terms of both involving a form of self-determination. See Allen Buchanan, "Democracy and Secession," in *National Self-Determination and Secession*, ed. Margaret Moore (Oxford: Oxford University Press, 1998), 14-33.

19. Buchanan, *Secession*, 44.

20. I am thinking here of the widespread starvation that occurred under Stalin and Mao Zedong. These famines clearly overstep the category of simple distribution and become issues of the general human right to life. The fact that Buchanan and Birch did not use these examples to illustrate the justification of discriminatory redistribution indicates that their conceptions of the right fall within the highly capricious parameters of western contemporary political economy.

21. Buchanan, *Secession*, 42.

22. Harry Beran, "A Liberal Theory of Secession," *Political Studies* 32 (1984): 21-31; Harry Beran, *The Consent Theory of Political Obligation* (London: Croom Helm, 1987).

23. Beran, "A Liberal Theory of Secession," 23.

24. Harry Beran, "A Democratic Theory of Political Self-Determination for a New World Order," in *Theories of Secession*, ed. Percy B. Lehning (London: Routledge, 1998), 34.

25. Beitz, *Political Theory*, 110.

26. See E. J. Hobsbawm, *Nations and Nationalism since 1780: Programme, Myth, Reality* (Cambridge: Cambridge University Press, 1990). This point is further discussed in chapter 3.

27. One liberal theorist, Will Kymlicka, notably stands out in addressing the importance of group membership for the protection of free choice. See Will Kymlicka, *Liberalism, Community, and Culture* (Oxford: Clarendon Press, 1989); and Will Kymlicka, *Multicultural Citizenship: A Liberal Theory of Minority Rights* (Oxford: Clarendon Press, 1995).

28. Beran, "A Democratic Theory," 39.

29. Beran, "A Democratic Theory," 41.

30. Beran, "A Democratic Theory," 54.

31. Lea Brilmayer, "Secession and Self-Determination: A Territorial Interpretation," *Yale Journal of International Law* 16 (1991): 177-202.

32. Brilmayer, "A Territorial Interpretation," 185.

33. Brilmayer, "A Territorial Interpretation," 186.

34. Brilmayer, "A Territorial Interpretation," 191.

35. Somalia, with roughly 85 percent of its population remaining nomadic, is an interesting partial exception to this.

36. Brilmayer, "A Territorial Interpretation," 201.

37. Ralph R. Premdas, "Secessionist Movements in Comparative Perspective," in *Secessionist Movements in Comparative Perspective*, ed. Ralph Premdas, S.W.R. de A. Samarasinghe, and Alan Anderson (London: Pinter, 1990), 12-13.

38. Judgment-oriented writers include Buchheit, Heraclides, and Frankel, discussed below. Horowitz and McGarry strongly favor nonsecessionist forms of settlement such as devolution and EU-style suprastate unification. Premdas limits himself to providing an analytic framework for comparing secessionist movements with the goal implied (but unstated) of developing policy solutions for secessionist conflicts.

39. Lee C. Buchheit, *Secession: The Legitimacy of Self-Determination* (New Haven: Yale University Press, 1978).

40. Interestingly, though, Buchheit is willing to suggest several nonstate forms of political association for dealing with compelling claims from entities that are not viable as states.

41. Buchheit, *The Legitimacy of Self-Determination*, 227.

42. Lawrence M. Frankel, "International Law of Secession: New Rules for a New Era," *Houston Journal of International Law* 14 (1992): 521-564.

43. Frankel, "International Law of Secession," 548.

44. Frankel, "International Law of Secession," 560 n. 116.

45. Alexis Heraclides, "Secessionist Conflagration: What Is to Be Done?" *Security Dialogue* 25, no. 3 (1994): 283-293.

46. Heraclides, "Secessionist Conflagration," 285.

47. Heraclides, "Secessionist Conflagration," 286.

48. Heraclides, "Secessionist Conflagration," 289.

49. Donald L. Horowitz, *Ethnic Groups in Conflict* (Berkeley: University of California Press, 1985).

50. Horowitz, *Ethnic Groups*, 229.

51. Horowitz, *Ethnic Groups*, 234.

52. Horowitz, *Ethnic Groups*, 235 note 9.

53. Horowitz, *Ethnic Groups*, 235.

54. Horowitz, *Ethnic Groups*, 235.

55. Bonnie Honig, *Political Theory and the Displacement of Politics* (Ithaca, N.Y.: Cornell University Press, 1993), 2.

56. Honig, *Displacement of Politics*, 9.

57. Honig, *Displacement of Politics*, 44.

Chapter 3

States Taking Place:
History and the Territorialization of Politics

Political scientists have long recognized that the term "nation-state" is only marginally accurate as a description of contemporary political structures. While closely entwined in modernity, the concepts of the state and the nation were not born together. However, both can be represented as subjective contexts for political identity—as constructions of the modern world. Modern individuals are embedded in interrelated spaces and identity possibilities endlessly engaged in the process of becoming different; and regardless of which definition of nation is operative, individuals may identify with or feel sympathy for a number of various identities either simultaneously or consecutively. R. B. J. Walker describes modern political identities as "fractured and dispersed among a multiplicity of sites, a condition sometimes attributed to a specifically post-modern experience but one that has been a familiar, though selectively forgotten, characteristic of modern political life for several centuries."[1] It is ironic, then, that the international political system is based upon a presumption which privileges identities that are fixed arbitrarily and externally by territory and residence, thus limiting national identities to a concept of the state which apparently defines the outer limits of political possibility. National identities are too contingent and too infinite to be confined by the arbitrary and finite boundaries of the state. Onora O'Neill concludes that "[t]he concepts by which people define who they are—in which they articulate their sense of identity—are all of them concepts without sharp borders, and hence cannot provide a basis for sharp demarcations such as political boundaries between states."[2] Thus, while boundaries may make sense for practical administrative purposes, there is a strong disjunction between the strictly controlled territorial border and the boundless receptivity of human identities to the impulses of change.

Political theorists forge the link between national identity and territory with the concept of sovereignty. As the defining characteristic of statehood, sovereignty has become the focal point of the nation/state/identity nexus. This definition is problematic because identities cannot be constrained to finite categories without dangerously overlooking, and thus delegitimating, certain diverse categories. These overlooked categories are the "remainders," which become focal points for contestation (often violent) of the categories themselves. Furthermore, the tenuous identity/territory link relies upon the concept of sovereignty as territorial control. It is critical, then, to recall that neither states, nor nations nor sovereignty are fixed historical entities. According to Walker:

> The patterns of inclusion and exclusion we now take for granted are historical innovations. The principle of state sovereignty is the classic expression of those patterns, an expression that encourages us to believe that either those patterns are permanent or that they must be erased in favour of some kind of global cosmopolis. . . . Its fixing of unity and diversity . . . or inside and outside, or space and time is not natural. Nor is it inevitable. It is a crucial part of the practices of all modern states, but they are not natural or inevitable either.[3]

Just as many state boundaries were determined incidentally by military battle lines rather than by agreement, so the concepts of "state," "territory," and "sovereignty" themselves are historically contingent. These basic political concepts, which we so freely use, have developed and changed in response to human patterns of domination and organization. From feudal princes, to the Enlightenment principle of popular sovereignty as manifested in the French and American Revolutions, to the twentieth-century incarnation of nationally self-determined states, each age has understood the meanings of these terms in its own contextual way.

Successive manifestations of sovereignty and statehood have produced and have been produced by changing political identities in a dynamic interrelationship. For example, an early twentieth-century shift from popular sovereignty to national sovereignty as the basis of state legitimacy mirrors an emphasis on the concept of the collective as opposed to the individual self as the basis for political identity. As James Mayall points out, there are no naturally given national boundaries for the collective self and thus: "the nation is ultimately a group whose identity is forged by a particular interpretation of its own history."[4] The boundaries of such a nation, then, are limited only by the collective imaginations of its members. The boundless vitality of the collectively imagined nation puts it on a collision course with the intrinsically limited nature of the modern conception of the territorial state. Contemporary notions of statehood and nationhood are incapable of producing a perfect fit. This is not to suggest that states cannot be formed with nations in mind and vice versa, or that there are no possibilities for the growth of a "civic" national identity within the boundaries of the state. The problem arises with the introduction of the conception of sovereignty itself as territorial. Sovereignty over territory has come to symbolize privilege and superiority in the politics of the international such that "it is almost impossible for a people to feel equal to others if it does not enjoy the privileges of sovereign statehood. . . . [A]s long as state sovereignty allows for the subjugation of peoples, it will continue to be sought by those who fear its use against them."[5] Because territorial sovereignty has become a badge of international legitimacy and a symbol of power, it aggravates the disjunction between nations and states. Secessionist movements are the inevitable result. Territory has not always been, and does not have to be, the source of sovereign legitimacy. Likewise, territory has not always been, and does not have to be, the foundation and security of national identities.

The failure to account for the dynamic of the interaction among territorial sovereignty, national identities, and secessionist movements within the liberal framework is a theoretically fatal flaw. How can liberal theory claim to justify secession when its analysis is founded on the rights of the individual? Furthermore, how can liberal theory form a coherent framework when the identities of individuals are taken as fixed? Not only does this approach fail to address the plurality of group identities available to individuals, but it also assumes that individuals will remain within groups and thus that group characteristics will not alter. Otherwise, why would secession be worth justifying for any group, given the violent tendencies involved? In fact, since identities continue to change, territorial solutions—such as secession—cannot provide long-term peace or guarantee rights. The focus must shift to strategies of social accommodation that allow forms of political control to be socially rather than territorially determined. Before this can happen, we must problematize the concept of territory and the many meanings with which it has been endowed to free ourselves from the discursive restraints of late-twentieth-century understandings. It is only with this intellectual liberation, or temporary forgetting, that we can be open to creative thinking about the problems of secession.

Understanding Territory

The very term "territory" comes loaded with a myriad of contextual under-standings and historical associations. What do we really mean when we refer to the territorial state? Or to territorial sovereignty? Understanding this concept is much more complex than it would first appear. As Nietzsche wisely counseled, nothing that has a history can be defined. All definitions are products of their time and space. Just as sovereignty and statehood have undergone numerous metamorphoses, it is obvious that territory has played different roles throughout the course of human history—its meaning is highly contextual. Territory, then, may be examined in a similar fashion as sovereignty—through conceptual history. Concepts reveal historical experience, and thus close analysis of conceptual terminology leads to an understanding of contextual meaning.[6] Jens Bartelson compares sovereignty, as a concept, to fire—a substance that has never been scientifically defined but whose effects are both devastating and life-giving. Bartelson proposes an analysis of how sovereignty is spoken of rather than a questioning of what it is.[7] Implicit in this approach is a problematization of any foundational assumptions about the concept. If we are to understand territory through analyzing the manner in which it has been discussed, we are maintaining an epistemological commitment to ambiguity. Ironically, then, we can gain clearer understanding of modern concepts only through a procedure which is antithetical to modernity.

The examination of texts which reveal historical concepts appears to be a logical and simple procedure; it is not. Unlike sovereignty and fire, territory may be touched, walked on, measured, quantified, and captured in numerous physical ways. Like all physical objects, it is both an abstract and a concrete noun—a signifier and a signified. Unlike sovereignty and fire, territory is intricately bound up—as space—with the very existence of each human being. No one can fail to occupy some of it. But this does not make territory either ahistorical or primordial. Some have argued that since human history has been written in terms of civilizations which occupy and defend specific territories, this must indicate the enduring, presocial, nature of territoriality.[8] This perspective assumes that because certain groups of people have always occupied a certain place their concept of that space (their concept of territory) has remained constant. Such an assertion confuses the idea that all people must occupy a space (and thus have a high likelihood of forming attachments to that space) with the notion that the relationship people maintain with a designated space can be some kind of objective constant. To assert that territoriality as a source of political legitimacy is primordial is to assert that all the things which are implicated by territoriality—human social and political relationships—are also somehow primordial or timeless. Certainly, they are not. I deliberately reject the term *primordial* since its connotation of "from the beginning" would seem ontologically presumptuous in human social historical terms. The *beginning* is something we cannot know.

How then are territory and space related? What is the question of territoriality? The "secret" of territoriality, in Bartelson's phrase, is the transformation of space from something that must be occupied to something that must be controlled. In other words, the question of territory depends upon the question of how space became politicized, transformed into the prerequisite for political legitimacy (in the form of the state). There is no history of this transformation, and we are left with a chicken and egg conundrum trying to determine which came first: society or territorial polity. In other words, did structured political entities arise before they came to be associated with specific territorial parcels or did territorially specific societies evolve into structured polities? How did space become politicized? As Bartelson points out, "what comes first in this rather elliptical chain of development seems theoretically undecidable, unless we quite uncritically assume some exogenous shock in the dawn of statehood, lifting European man up from some primitive form of life to a more developed stage of spatial politics."[9] Thus, any attempt for complete mapping of the concept of territory must be thwarted for lack of a discernible origin for the very concept itself. It is perhaps the better part of intellectual valor to focus instead on the discernible effects of this conceptual transformation of space. Even if we accept that the physical nature of territory as an object gives it certain lasting characteristics, the fact that territory has been perceived differently (politically, religiously, materially, etc.) by various societies at various times gives it a social (constructed) meaning which is as abstract as any philosophical concept.

The etymology of *territory*, unsurprisingly, turns out to be both unsettled and fascinating.[10] It has possible origins both in the Latin *terratorium*, meaning earth (*terra*), and *terrere*, meaning to frighten (suggesting *territorium* as a place from which people are warned off).[11] Early references to territory as an administrative unit occurred in the fifteenth century, when it was used both to refer to the land surrounding a town which is under its jurisdiction, and to the lands of a ruler. In the seventeenth century, the term's usage also included references to regions with undefined boundaries. And by the eighteenth century, the term was occurring in legal documents regarding jurisdiction and the state. The United States Constitution, ratified in 1789, gave Congress the power to make all necessary rules "respecting the Territory or other Property belonging to the United States."[12] Ironically, contemporary usage of the term includes both the land which makes up a sovereign state's *territory* and a nonsovereign entity, non-self-governing *territory,* which is administratively subject to another state. The meaning which partially emerges from these various examples of *territory* is one of ancient and widespread use. Territory has generally referred to a specific type of space—a particular area of earth/land (*terra*) which has been categorized or mapped in some fashion so that it can no longer be considered unknown (*terra incognita*). The act of mapping and categorizing is, of course, a means of exerting control over such space. Hence, territory is a place where one is "warned off"; it is a place surrounding a town which has local jurisdiction; it is a piece of land which has been mapped and settled but which is not a state; and it is also the extent of the land which is controlled by a state's "internal" jurisdiction and which thus defines the borders of its sovereignty and of its citizens. Territory means all of these things. All of these things mean some form of control over land.

These understandings do not seem to contradict the thesis that territoriality is a primordial social form. But there is a crucial distinction to make. A simple shift to the derivative word form yields profound semantic consequences. Territory is a word with a basic meaning which probably predates written human history. It refers to the very condition of physical existence—that is, to the habitation of a particular space. Because every human being must occupy space, and because humans are social beings who tend to occupy space in groups, the concept of mapping space may be considered to be of very cognitive and linguistic ancient origin. It is important to note here that nothing in the meaning of territory itself requires the existence of either concrete physical borders or ownership. Territory as mapped or controlled land is not even inconsistent with nomadic social patterns, since nomads do not continually roam in unknown places but instead form distinctive and repetitive cycles. The profound difference in meaning occurs with the simple addition of an ending meaning "of or pertaining to." The simple grammatical process of going from noun to adjective creates a very different meaning. While *territory* can be as simple as mapping and categorizing a piece of land, activity which is *territorial* presumes some kind of behavior which is already based on territory. Territorial behavior—*territoriality*—is one step removed from territory and already contains assumptions about territory. It describes not the simple designation of space, but the behavior patterns which emerge from the political use (the occupation) of territory. Territoriality thus requires territory to be definitively bounded rather than loosely so, and thereby creates the conditions for the physical exclusivity of people. Politics may take place within a territory and yet be nonterritorial politics. Such politics may be based on personality, class, kinship, or other form, and while territory is necessary as the ground on which such politics occur, it is not the fundamental basis of the system. Territorial politics, on the other hand, require the control of territory as the very basis of legitimacy. In this case, territory is not simply a location—it is a prize and a prerequisite. It is *territoriality*, which cannot be considered to be of ancient origin. Territoriality assumes that politics depends upon the control of a delineated space. It is no accident then that the term does not enter common usage until the nineteenth century.

The clearest illustration of the modern manifestation of politicized space as territoriality is through the legal definition of statehood. According to customary international law, a state must include a territory, population, and government. This territory must be well-defined since "[t]he legal competence of states and the rules for their protection depend on and assume the existence of a stable, physically delimited, homeland."[13] Indeed, state leaders themselves codified the criteria in the 1933 Montevideo Convention on Rights and Duties of States, which declared that a state should possess a permanent population, a defined territory, a government, and the capacity to enter relations with other states. These criteria are accepted as generally indicating the customary international standard for the requirements of statehood. Since recognition of statehood is a domestic matter and tends to be highly political, the application of these criteria has been tried in several respects. The matter of a defined territory has already been called into question. However, even in finding that a state may be recognized with its borders under dispute, the international community accepted the deeply rooted assumption that the entire state system rests upon the foundation of territorial legitimacy. In the debate over whether to admit Israel to the United Nations in 1948, the following argument was made:

> The reason for the rule that one of the necessary attributes of a State is that it shall possess territory is that one cannot contemplate a State as a kind of disembodied spirit. . . . [T]here must be some portion of the earth's surface which its people inhabit and over which its Government exercises authority.[14]

The assumption of the necessity of territory for the existence of a state, as revealed in this argument, indicates the operation of an extremely strong conception of territoriality—or the complete territorialization of politics. The statement above asserts, with an interesting and recurring metaphor, that the idea of a "disembodied" state cannot even enter the imagination. And yet it was not always the case. The "body" of the state was not always seen in such concrete and territorial terms. While social entities such as tribes, kingdoms, empires, and states have always, of necessity, occupied territory, the derivation of political legitimacy from territorial control is a relatively recent matter. In the next section I analyze the concepts of territory and territoriality in historical context, with an eye to the clearer understanding of the former and the modern development of the latter.

Historicizing the State

One of the difficulties of conceptual historical method is the struggle against "presentism" in the interpretation of terms which have remained static while the meanings attached to them have changed. Thus, words such as *state, people*, and *territory* occur in the Renaissance texts of writers such as Machiavelli, More, and Hobbes, whose existence and circumstances bore little resemblance to contemporary conditions. What did they mean when they used these terms? More important, what impact did these meanings have on political patterns? While the concept of the *state* could certainly be interpreted to refer to delineated entities occupying and controlling territory during the Renaissance, the states of that period were not precisely those of today. For example, the political system was not *territorial* in the sense discussed above. The main argument of this chapter is that territoriality in the twentieth century arises from a specific conception of territory that links it to the identity of the citizens, and it thus depends upon the rise of nationalist sentiment and popular sovereignty. The concepts of state and territory found in these early texts are ones in which territory is a source (and a symbol) of power, but not of identity or legitimacy. Thus, there is an open-endedness to the classical concept of statehood. Territorial borders were approximate and negotiable. Princes could fight, marry, and bargain for more territory and greater political power. While these states or duchies or principalities were certainly territorial in the sense of being delineated territories under rule, they were not territorial states in the sense of being necessary for the creation and maintenance of national identity.

The archetype of such a fully territorial state is a creature of the twentieth century: the noninterventionist, anti-imperialist member of the international society of equals. The greatest impact of this concept of territoriality is a fully developed sense of the border as the beginning and end of national identity. Thus, the territorial state seeks to stop both itself and others at its border. It wishes not only to defend against intrusion, but also to avoid invasion and thereby incorporation of anything outside or other than itself. This conception of the territorial state relies heavily upon (and in turn contributes to) the concept of national identity. Given this understanding of the changes wrought by territoriality, it is clear why secession was not possible before the nineteenth century, and why it fully blossomed as an international concern in the twentieth. The acquisition of territory prior to this time was not an act which created or destroyed national identities. International relations were a kind of statecraft played as a game by aristocrats who were born or fought into its ranks rather than legitimated through political consent. Legitimacy was inherited or patronized. The *people* were largely irrelevant. Territoriality began to occur when the people started to have an identity, when they started to share an abstract sense of belonging—the "imagined community."[15] The territorial state arises from the identification of a people with a territory as a basis for political legitimacy. Thus, the story of territoriality is indeed intertwined with the concepts of class struggle, the industrial revolution, literacy, and the philosophy of individual rights. Within the scope of this book, however, the emphasis will be on the historical and political understandings of territoriality as revealed in the assumptions occurring in representative texts.

Dante's *Monarchy*

Like all writers, the authors of the texts examined here were responding to the currents of their age. The eminent thinkers discussed here are not chosen because they accurately represent the politics of their age, but rather because they represent the reflections of what it was possible to think in their time. They are presented, then, as the problem solvers of their ages, attempting to solve questions of political identity as they were present in their day, just as—today—we consider secession as a response to problems of political identity. The impossibility of secession as a plausible response for these writers only emphasizes the distinctiveness of our contemporary conceptions of sovereignty as deeply territorial.

Dante wrote *Monarchy* as a strong argument in favor of the power of the Holy Roman Emperor, "the Monarch," over that of the pope. Dante equated the papal bid for political power with the disintegration of the empire and thus of peace. He makes a universalist argument which would seem modernist if it were not for Dante's assumption of Christendom as the obvious basis for human commonality. Universalism under one monarch is the only system which ensures justice, liberty, and peace for all, Dante asserts. The image Dante creates is one of harmony and wholeness: "mankind is most one when the whole human race is drawn together into complete unity, which can only happen when it is subordinate to one Prince."[16] Notably, Dante speaks not only of Christendom, but also of the entire human race—equating humanity with Christianity in a particularly late medieval way. Local identities, languages, and customs are irrelevant to his conception of the appropriate ruling structure. Dante argues that the emperor's political legitimacy stems from approval by God, "as should be obvious." But Dante also presents numerous practical arguments for universal rule. Throughout the course of the work, it becomes increasingly clear that he abhors disunity. The modern international system with its anarchical relationship among states would have signified the utter collapse of human goodness for Dante. He sees in the person of the emperor a natural judge over the disputes of princes, believing that "Justice is at its strongest only under a Monarch; therefore Monarchy or Empire is essential if the world is to attain perfect order."[17] The secret to order and justice, for Dante, is the power of the monarch to "render each his due." Thus, Dante's universalist conception of order is not only nonterritorial, but also antithetical to a territorialist order because of its emphasis on political hierarchy. The monarch, by having no territorial limits—"unlike other princes, such as the Kings of Castile and Aragon, whose jurisdictions are limited by one another's frontiers"[18]—would have no wish to acquire new territories and would be unclouded by unjust thoughts and warlike desires. Dante firmly believed that the breakup of the empire would spell political disaster. But even this dichotomy was not between territorialist states and the empire—for the states of the fourteenth century were not such exclusivist entities. Although Dante was arguing against a nearly foregone conclusion, the result of a weakened emperor was not the creation of modern territorial states, but the consolidation of local princely powers. Although their territories and jurisdictions were defined, these states had no meaning independent of the various princes who used them to extend their power. It was the chaos of all the overlapping monarchs that led Dante to argue so passionately for the benefits of a single overlord in the person of the emperor. But these princes and their so-called states were still a far cry from twentieth-century states recognized under modern international law. As Benedict Anderson aptly describes it:

> [I]n fundamental ways "serious" monarchy lies transverse to all modern conceptions of political life. Kingship organizes everything around a high centre. Its legitimacy derives from divinity, not from populations, who, after all, are subjects, not citizens. In the modern conception, state sovereignty is fully, flatly, and evenly operative over each square centimetre of a legally demarcated territory. But in the older imagining, where states were defined by centres, borders were porous and indistinct, and sovereignties faded imperceptibly into one another. Hence, paradoxically enough, the ease with which pre-modern empires and kingdoms were able to sustain their rule over immensely heterogeneous, and often not even contiguous, populations for long periods of time.[19]

Not only were the monarch's subjects irrelevant for his legitimacy (a divine right), but monarchs were frequently "foreign," having gained rule through marriage or invasion from another kingdom.

The sense of universalism to which Dante tried to appeal in *Monarchy* was strengthened by the widespread use of Latin among the literate classes. Since Latin was the only language in which one could be educated, there was in effect a single community of literacy throughout European centers of learning. Although vernaculars continued to flourish, amongst the intelligentsia there was a cross-cultural, cross-temporal dialogue. This "sacral language" allowed Dante of early fourteenth-century Florence to write in what was essentially the same language as Grotius, of the seventeenth-century Netherlands. Before the spread of printed works in the vernacular and of literacy, there was no medium for the development of regional identities. Before identities were recognized in the abstract as based upon language and culture, they could not have been territorial. They were at this point, if anything, identities of subjection—deriving from common status as "subjects" of the prince. This form of political identity emerges quite clearly from Machiavelli's sixteenth-century study *The Prince*.

Machiavelli's *The Prince*

This work has been written about and interpreted in many ways since it was published in 1513.[20] It has variously put its author on a pedestal as the "father of political science" and also condemned him as an unprincipled "immoralist." These labels are unhelpful for a contextual understanding of Machiavelli's concepts. His handbook for the political success of sixteenth-century princes carries an irony in its very title. Machiavelli's perception of a need for such a work—a book containing advice for the acquisition and maintenance of *states* by *princes*—and the structure and characteristics of the work itself indicate the vast changes in the meanings and understandings of these terms between the ages of the Renaissance and the United Nations. These different meanings are, in fact, the constant source of translator's complaints, most notably with Machiavelli's use of the term *virtù*—a characteristic word with a highly contextual meaning and virtually untranslatable into any single word in English.[21] For the purposes of this chapter, the most important shift in meaning occurs in the word *Principe*—Machiavelli's chosen title. Our contemporary understanding of the term "prince" is a far cry from the subject of this Renaissance work. In the late twentieth century, princes are quaint reminders of by-gone times, and they retain a faint mythical quality that evokes the agelessness of children's fairy tales. They do not do the one thing that Machiavelli's *principe* did—they do not rule.

> Machiavelli's prince is not our prince by a long shot—he may, for example, be what we would call a king or he may be a mercenary soldier; he may be elected, like a doge, or be a churchman like a pope. . . . A "principality" [in English] is what a "prince" governs, and he is defined chiefly as not a king, not a duke, not a president, not a pope, not a condottiere—not even a prince, really, because in English usage a prince (like the Prince of Wales) doesn't govern, and that's one thing that Machiavelli's *principe* emphatically does. "Prince" and "principality" are chiefly defined in English by negatives, whereas for Machiavelli they are nothing if not positive and inclusive.[22]

Although explained by this translator as a difficulty between English and Italian, it is quite clearly more than that. The difficulty of translating Machiavelli is a temporal as well as a linguistic one. Not only has the meaning of the word *prince* changed, but there are no twentieth-century equivalents of *il principe* or *principato*. These terms, which described Machiavelli's world, are no longer relevant—even for contemporary Italian politicians.

Machiavelli addresses a world where the concepts of state and republic exist, but where the system as a whole had a profoundly different reality from what we understand by these terms today. Territorially delineated polities abounded, to be sure, but they were open targets for enterprising schemers. It is perhaps in contrast with twentieth-century notions of state sovereignty, nonintervention, and the sanctity of borders that Machiavelli's advice to his prince acquires its most sinister aspect. But Machiavelli was not suggesting that modern states with national identities, symbols, and sovereign recognition be invaded for personal gain. He had no concept of such uniform and territorialized units—and his concept of relations with other states was not one of a system of "international relations," but rather one of diplomacy amongst a variety of different political entities. Florence in 1513 was one of five major units of political power in the area of Italy, comprising Milan, Venice, Naples, and the papal states (under the dominion of Rome). These five city-states had maintained an uneasy balance of power because none was strong enough to rule the other four. They each had revolving internal struggles for rule and various systems of leadership. Naples was a kingdom (the crown of which was claimed by France, Spain, and the pope); the Venetian doge and the Roman pope were nominally elected; Milan had been ruled by a family dictatorship which in 1450 was ousted by a professional soldier who had been born a peasant. Florence had an ancient history as a republic, but had recently been subject to sporadic rule by the Medici. In short, Italian Renaissance politics consisted of a motley bunch of wealthy successful cities which had control over the surrounding countryside and which were the objects of power struggles by various and sundry important people. Residents of the five city-states were, however, all considered to be Italian, and spoke dialects of the same language. They were all Catholic and had similar customs. This did not stop them from plotting each others' demise. Machiavelli's Florence was a city with a long history as a republic—yet it was not a "republic" in the contemporary sense of a "state with representative government" for it was not a state in the modern sense. Moreover, although Florence had the luxury of a history as a republic, that did not stop it from exercising rule over other cities in surrounding Tuscany. With a population of roughly 100,000, sixteenth-century Florence (along with its four sister states) belongs in a category by itself.

Machiavelli begins his advice to the prince with a discussion of the types of states. There are two kinds, he says, republics and princely states. He designates the latter as his main concern, and specifically princely states which are newly acquired by the prince. Machiavelli advises the ruler of newly acquired lands to extinguish the line of the previous prince and to keep the laws in place, "because in other matters, as long as you keep their old way of life and do not change their customs, men will live quietly enough."[23] Also, if the new acquisitions are in an area with different language and customs from the prince's own, "[o]ne of the best and most effective policies is for the new possessor of territories to go there and live."[24] Regardless of his own preference for republicanism in Florence, Machiavelli's assumption about the "people" here is that they are subjects. They may cause trouble if their customs are forcibly altered, but there is no expectation that the prince's rule is illegitimate because they did not consent to it. The "state" or "territory" is a possession, and Machiavelli uses that term quite literally in terms of its being acquired, kept, and lost.

These states were not equal and sovereign. They were given political attention according to their military might and economic wealth. Machiavelli learned this lesson to his chagrin during his mission to the French court.

> Machiavelli discovered that his native city's sense of its own importance seemed to the French to be ludicrously out of line with the realities of its military position and its wealth. . . . Although he tried making a speech "about the security your greatness could bring to the possessions held by his majesty in Italy," he found that "the whole thing was superfluous," for the French merely laughed at him.[25]

There were various territories, but the governing principle was anything but territoriality. There was no concept of permanency or of strict borders. Machiavelli does not even discuss sovereignty. It is not relevant as a principle of legitimacy for his historical context. Machiavelli would have found extremely odd the suggestion that a state's power was proportionate to the strict control of its boundaries regardless of the competence of its prince. The legitimacy of Machiavelli's prince derived from his *virtù*. If a man could rule well, then he was a prince—even if he were born a peasant (as Francesco Sforza) or the illegitimate son of a pope (as Cesare Borgia). Thus, "a new prince taking charge of a completely new kingdom will have more or less trouble in holding onto it, as he himself is more or less capable [*virtuoso*]."[26] For Machiavelli, then, *virtù* acts as a new principle of legitimacy, operating independently of divine right. So although the pope continued to be acknowledged as God's representative on earth, he also played a political role and as such was included as one of the group of princes who would find Machiavelli's work useful. Two hundred years later, Dante's nightmare about the loss of universal allegiance and the disintegration of order amongst states seems to have come true. But it was not as simple as that. The Holy Roman Emperor was still a presence in the sixteenth century, but one with a decreased sphere of influence. Thus, Machiavelli's world incorporated Dante's and also involved substantially different perspectives. Ironically, the men were both, two centuries apart, writing from Tuscany—thus illustrating the devastating effects wrought by temporal distance over the same geographical space.

More's *Utopia*

Sir Thomas More's *Utopia* was published in 1515—not even three years after *The Prince*. Thomas More and Niccolò Machiavelli were living at opposite ends of the European continent as well as under very different local political circumstances. The English More was largely exempted from the turmoil of the constant exchange of rulers which plagued the Italian city-states. The two scholars were joined, however, by a common humanist upbringing with its emphasis on mastering the classical languages, history, philosophy, and rhetoric. In fact, More wrote a number of works, including *Utopia*, in Latin. While More and Machiavelli had distinctly different intellectual commitments (one was willing to lose his life standing up for the unity of Christendom while the other maintained a frankly pragmatic approach to the papacy as another example of a power-seeking prince), they each spent years in the service of their princes, including diplomatic missions abroad. They both drew on years of political expertise in writing their works. But while Machiavelli's book contains many historical examples and aspires to be a genuine handbook, More's work resembles a parable which teaches through illustration. More's target is not the prince but the entire fabric of English society. Nonetheless, it is clear from their texts that Machiavelli and More inhabited the same Renaissance time frame. The two writers share the same concept of the "prince" as ruler. More begins his book by referring to King Henry VIII as "most accomplished in all the virtues of an outstanding prince."[27] During that period, rulers as diverse as kings, popes, nobles, and even accomplished military leaders were unified in one category. Although the Medicis (who sometimes ruled Florence and to whom *The Prince* was addressed) were not rulers in the same dynastic sense that the kings of England and France were, they were nonetheless entitled to recognition as legitimate rulers—"princes." This discrepancy between power and title indicates that the principle of political legitimacy had far more to do with personal power than any concept of territoriality. Borders were not assumed to be permanent indicators of the beginning and end of the state, much less of the nation. Even dynastic kings had to exhibit competent leadership skills or suffer the humiliation of losing parts of their realm to enterprising neighbors. It was this world that Machiavelli and More shared—and criticized.

More's *Utopia* operates on dual levels of understanding, crossing easily back and forth between fact and fiction. While the story of the mythical island country, where money is unnecessary and all needs are provided for, offers sharp social criticism through a description of an imaginary life without certain evils, it also reveals the life and times of its author through contemporary details and More himself as first-person narrator. Like *The Prince*, *Utopia* is about *virtù*, but in this case the meaning is confined to *virtue*. More is concerned with men's souls rather than political success. He describes in his mythical "non-place" of Utopia a society in which "what is cherished as examples of virtue in More's present is turned into utmost vice."[28] The foremost of the vices targeted for criticism by More is the concept of private property. Every facet of Utopian life is meant to mitigate against the greed and unfair distribution of private ownership. While More's arguments must have seemed at the time like a glorification of the simple peasant communities of the Middle Ages, today they also have a distinctly proto-Marxist flavor. In fact, both nostalgic and futuristic hints can be discerned in the text.[29] Using classical rhetorical skills, More could not conceal his humanist education, nor could he hide the social assumptions of the world in which he lived. He imagines a new and unfamiliar world, but he cannot completely remove himself from his own perspective.

Territory in Utopia plays a much more definitive role than it did in More's Renaissance Europe. The Utopians are blessed with a naturally perfect geological basis for their state. By artificially creating an island out of a peninsula, they have provided themselves with boundaries against both invasion and their own greed, for Utopians have abolished pride and greed as the greatest vices, and obtaining territory for the sake of power would amount to an evil on the largest of scales. Indeed, More's narrative device, in the character of Raphael Hythloday, who recounts to More (as first-person narrator) the wonders of Utopia, provides an ample platform for More's own commentary on the nature of European politics. If he were to give counsel to princes in the midst of their most secret negotiations, Hythloday says, he would advise "that Italy should be left alone and the French stay at home; that the kingdom of France is practically too big to be conveniently administered by one man, so that the King should not think of adding others."[30] In this startling contrast to the typical princely concerns of the time, Hythloday verbalizes More's own frustration at the effects of willful princely rule. A virtuous society can arise only when the prince keeps his focus on the territory he already has. Hythloday would advise such a prince to "look after the kingdom he inherited, and embellish it as much as he could, and make it as flourishing as possible; to love his people and be loved by them; to live together with them and make his rule gentle; to say good-bye to other kingdoms, since the one that had fallen to his lot was enough and more than enough."[31] In fact, Machiavelli gives similar advice, asserting that the people who feel no connection to their prince will be troublesome and difficult to rule. More and Machiavelli are both responding to a world in which such civic attention was not the norm. Rule over territory was a matter of acquisition, and the prince who cultivated the love of his people—his subjects—was a rarity.

The loyalties of the inhabitants of Utopia are to the collective project—which acts in More's scenario as a unified whole. Instead of owing allegiance to a prince, Utopians submit themselves to the good of the system. This applies even to such personal matters as family planning. Each household in Utopia is kept between ten and sixteen adults. If the number increases for one family, the surplus will be transferred to smaller households. If an entire city exceeds its limits, the surplus is transferred to other cities or colonized. Thus, the inhabitants of Utopia are moveable goods—filling in the gaps in the cultivable territory. This conception of More's assumes a far greater civic awareness than was common in his time, but it also leaves out any notion whatsoever of national attachment to place. The development of nationalism was yet embryonic, and More could not have conceived of it in his vision of "no-place." So nonexistent is the link between people and territory for the Utopians that when their island population grows beyond its limits, citizens are chosen to colonize the nearby mainland, absorbing or conquering the native inhabitants.

They take in any of the inhabitants of the country who wish to live with them. . .
But those who refuse to live by their laws they drive out of the boundaries they

mark out for themselves. If they resist, they go to war against them. For they think it the justest reason for war when any nation refuses to others the use and possession of that land which it does not use itself, but owns in idle emptiness, when the others by the law of nature ought to be nourished from it.[32]

There could be no more convincing evidence for the lack of territorial attachments at the time than the suggestion by a scholarly man attempting to provide meaningful social commentary that justice would be served by violently expelling those who are unwilling to share their territory with a fair and industrious people. What a far cry from the *jus cogens* of the twentieth century and the near universal response in favor of territorial sanctity during the events of the 1991 Gulf War.[33] Given the impact that statement would have had if territorial sentiments were strong and widespread, More could not have made it without further explanation. He makes the suggestion as one who knows that it differs from the norm, but that it has some merit.

It would not be long in fact before the concept of nationalism would begin to take hold and the first inklings of nonintervention would provide a peaceful solution to the Thirty Years' War. More's own perspective was certainly still based on universal Christendom, and when Henry VIII decided to create his own version of the church, More's steadfastness cost him his life. Greenfeld argues that More's beliefs were already out of date, and he was a prenationalist in a nationalist world (at least in England).

> Sir Thomas More was a Christian; this was his identity, and all his roles, functions, and commitments that did not derive from it (but were implied, for example, in being a subject of the king of England) were incidental to it. The view that "one realm" could be a source of truth and claim absolute sovereignty was, to him, absurd. "Realms" were but artificial, secondary divisions in the ultimately indivisible body of Christendom. . . . He found the position of his judges incomprehensible. He failed to realize that they were already transformed, that being Englishmen, for them, was no longer incidental to their allegiances, as it was for him, but had become the very core of their beings.[34]

Whether this level of nationalism had already taken hold in England in 1532 does not matter for the present argument. Even if Henry could command his subjects to abandon Christendom as they knew it because he was the symbolic head of their nation, this only indicates that personality, not territoriality, was still a primary factor in political legitimacy. National allegiance, such as there was, was fixed upon the person of the king. Territoriality itself was still a thing of the distant future. The important point to take from More is the complete lack of the concept of the *outside* in his *Utopia*. This is the clearest indication that his notion of sovereignty was nonterritorial. The body of Utopia is an inside which has no outside because all of the territory beyond its borders is a potential part of itself. Utopia's borders have nothing to do with sovereignty, history, or the identity of its people. They are adjustable borders in accordance with the needs of the population for land resources. Any people living on this land which the Utopians simply absorb may become Utopians themselves. Thus, all lands and peoples are potential Utopias in the making. This total elasticity in the conception of borders surely reflects More's commitments to the unity of Christendom. But it also indicates the extent to which the inside/outside dynamics of the territorially sovereign border were unthinkable for him.[35]

The Treaty of Westphalia

The seventeenth century was one in which the processes of both war and peace transformed the structures of European leadership. On the continent, the Thirty Years' War devastated the resources and terrain of Germany and finally broke Habsburg claims to Christian hegemony, while in Great Britain the question of religion plunged the country into a brutal civil war. The medieval theoretical model of the unity of all of Christendom was shattered by the spread of Protestantism and the increasing willingness of Catholic princes to proclaim political independence from the pope. As the hierarchy of the empire gave way, and the coalition of French and Protestant powers succeeded in destroying the strength of the Habsburg forces, a new kind of relationship grew among the political units which had not existed previously. Without the nominal universal authority of the emperor, the variety of kingdoms, duchies, and principalities suddenly stood in roughly equal relation at the negotiating tables. This is in stark contrast to the experience of Machiavelli as a forlorn Florentine diplomat in the court of the French king.

Two of the most memorable minds of this memorable century were Hugo Grotius and Thomas Hobbes. Grotius was an eminent diplomat who served both the Netherlands and Sweden during the course of the war. He died before the Treaty of Westphalia was negotiated, but not before he had noted and written about the need for some kind of ordering principle governing the relations between the newly autonomous segments of the empire. In writing his major work, *De Jure Belli ac Pacis* (On the Law of War and Peace), published in 1625, Grotius explored the basis for laws in and among nations. Although writing as a devout Christian with an assumption of divine providence, Grotius attempted to create a secular basis for law among nations based on "unbroken custom." Thus blending natural law concepts with customary ones, Grotius intended to describe a body of laws acceptable to both divine and princely wills.[36] The concept of laws governing war had already been developed in the sixteenth century, but the aftermath of the Thirty Years' War had created an atmosphere which gave new potency to the concept of law among nations. Nonetheless, it would still be two hundred years before the word "international" would be coined. It is significant, however, that while the elements of the empire were becoming more and more independent, even to the point of being recognized as equals, the concept of territory was still relegated to a background role. Grotius himself defines the state as simply "a complete association of free men, joined together for the enjoyment of rights and for their common interest"[37]—thus emphasizing the voluntary contractual aspect of the state as a political unit rather than its control over a specific territory. Grotius goes on to discuss the nature of the state as an association where an individual or a group has a relation of supremacy to the others, but again without explicit reference to territory. While Grotius's discussion of personal property rights implies that the state may indeed exist to protect territory, "these implications fall short of the conception of an area of exclusive jurisdiction, and they require assumptions other than those constitutive of Grotius's conception of the state."[38] Again, while territory continued to be vital to the existence and maintenance of political units, it was yet to become the sole legitimating basis for a national state in the manner of the contemporary territoriality of the twentieth-century state.

The other great seventeenth-century theorist of the state was Thomas Hobbes. A well-traveled and well-known intellectual both in France and in England, Hobbes took refuge from the ravages of the English civil war (and from possible retribution for his political views) at the Court of Louis XIV of France. The Thirty Years' War must have affected him personally, but instead of discussing peace between states, his famous *Leviathan* was concerned almost exclusively with maintaining stability within the state and avoiding civil war. *Leviathan*, subtitled *The Matter, Forme and Power of A Commonwealth Ecclesiasticall and Civil*, was published in 1651, just three years after the signing of the Treaty of Westphalia. Hobbes is often credited with having provided the model for the modern state because of his proposition that all men have equal status. Hobbes's citizens, using their naturally given freedom, voluntarily join a commonwealth for the sake of protection against the violence of the state of nature. The sovereign described in *Leviathan* may be a single person as in a monarch, or may be a group of people in the form of an assembly, but Hobbes insists on the necessity of its being absolute. Naturally, given that the basis of legitimacy for his sovereign was secular, and that his model for the equality of the citizenry precluded both aristocracy and bourgeoisie, Hobbes was politically unpopular with both sides in the English civil war. Whatever his social standing, Hobbes was nonetheless recognized as one of the great thinkers of his time. It was during this period, as Grotius's concept of law among nations implies, that the concept of sovereignty began to take hold. Something beyond mere power of rule, sovereignty includes the idea of both internal absolutism and external equality. While Hobbes does not explicitly treat of relations among leviathan-type commonwealths, his sovereign provides order through absolute power to regulate the commonwealth within. The corollary of this notion of sovereignty is that it creates an inside and an outside—a peaceful orderly commonwealth inside, and a brutal state of nature outside.

Thus, Hobbes hit upon the very element of sovereignty which makes up the modern territorial state—its ability to delineate the borders between members and nonmembers, inside and outside. There is one crucial distinction, however. Unlike the sovereignty of the twentieth-century state, Hobbes's delineation between commonwealth and state of nature was metaphysical and explicitly nonexclusive. Hobbes was not interested in allowing only certain national types into his commonwealth. His model was for all men. It offered the way out of the state of nature for any man who exercised his will and submitted to the laws of the sovereign. It is not accidental, then, that Hobbes's definition of the commonwealth does not include any mention of territorial boundaries or control. Hobbes's "Essence of the Common-wealth" is

> One Person, of whose Acts a great Multitude, by mutual Covenants one with another, have made themselves every one the Author, to the end he may use the strength and means of them all, as he shall think expedient, for their Peace and Common Defence.[39]

Hobbes's only mention of borders for the commonwealth occurs in connection with sovereigns defending their realms with "Forts, Garrisons, and Guns upon the Frontiers of their Kingdomes."[40] But this is meant to contrast the state of war among sovereigns, which upholds "the Industry of their Subjects," with the natural condition of individual men in anarchy, which is "misery," and not as a statement of the necessity of the territoriality of sovereigns. Seventeenth-century political thought, then, was beginning to develop away from the universalism of medieval Christianity and from the princely board game of the Italian city-states. The concept of the state as a container of peoples, and thus of relations among states as relations among units entitled to equal recognition and treatment, was making its first appearance. But it would still be over two centuries before states completely shed their erstwhile role as a measurement of princely power.

It was this concept of territory as princely property that was perpetuated in the Treaty of Westphalia, even though the treaty is often cited as the foundational document for the European state system. Westphalia's contribution was to eliminate the top, unifying, layer of European politics, the authority of the emperor. Fought partially on religious, partially on power-balancing grounds, the Thirty Years' War resulted in the end of any concept of the unity of Christendom. The Catholic kingdom of France fought with the Protestant powers of Sweden and the German principalities to put an end to the ability of the Austrian-Spanish coalition of the empire to exert control in their realms. The Treaty of Westphalia, signed at Munster, October 24, 1648, confirmed and redistributed territories among the victors. The treaty also confirmed the terms of the ninety-three-year-old Peace of Augsburg, which granted religious tolerance within the empire according to the religion of each prince in his realm (*cujus regio ejus religio*). The negotiations forced the emperor onto a level field with the rest of the "Electors, Princes, and States" of the empire. As Adam Watson describes it, Westphalia was a profoundly anti hegemonic act; it was the "charter of a Europe permanently organized on an anti-hegemonial principle."[41] So, although Westphalia can be said to have begun a new ordering principle within Europe (making it for the first time an order *among* the states of Europe), it still fell short of creating a system resembling that of the contemporary United Nations system.

Territory was an important part of the Westphalian settlement, but it was still clearly regarded as the property of the prince, the stuff of the realm. Territory was not considered essential to the legitimacy of the prince, and also was not yet equated with the identification of the nation. The words of the treaty itself indicate that it codifies the redistribution of goods among the princes—not only land, but all that goes with it. The victorious French king acquired Alsace and a frontier west of the Rhine.

> All the Vassals, Subjects, People, Towns, Boroughs, Castles, Houses, Fortresses, Woods, Coppices, Gold or Silver Mines, Minerals, Rivers, Brooks, Pastures; and in a word, all the Rights, Regales and Appurtenances, without any reserve, shall belong to the most Christian King, and shall be for ever incorporated with the Kingdom of France, with all manner of Jurisdiction and Sovereignty, without any contradiction from the Emperor, the Empire, House of Austria, or any other: so that no Emperor, or any Prince of the House of Austria, shall, or ever ought to usurp, nor so much as pretend any Right and Power over the said Countrys, as well on this, as the other side the Rhine [sic].[42]

These items listed *shall belong* to the king of France. They are not the property of an abstract state or even of the French nation, for such entities did not exist. The Thirty Years' War was fought and won on behalf of individual princes. Its concluding treaty instituted the novelty of a promise to refrain from involvement in each other's affairs, but it did not create a system of national territorial states. The prevailing order was still one in which politics was based upon personality. The state was not an abstract unity of peoples, but was still a "realm" ruled patriarchally by the prince. Westphalia can be noted for changing the principle of legitimacy from one of divine right to secular mutual recognition and agreement.

The Eighteenth Century

Once political legitimacy came to be seen as an earthly (though not secular) matter instead of a divine one, the way was paved for notions of individual rights and equality to become widespread, as indeed they did throughout the eighteenth century. The most famous formulation (if not the first) of these ideals was perhaps the Jeffersonian one found in the American Declaration of Independence: "We hold these truths to be self-evident, that all men are created equal, that they are endowed by their Creator with certain unalienable Rights, that among these are Life, Liberty and the pursuit of Happiness." The colonists of North America were antagonized into a revolutionary fervor by precisely the fact that their sense of what was due to them as *Englishmen* had been gravely violated. The American Revolution is sometimes mistakenly characterized as a secession. This is inaccurate since the Americans sought to create a state de novo where one did not exist. Their status as colonies of Britain was precisely what was so irksome to their political expectations. Furthermore, the independence of the colonies and the creation of the "united States of America"[43] left the government of Britain in form, structure, and identity essentially untouched. Not only is this because the colonies were never fully integrated into Britain proper, but it is also because the concept of territoriality, so necessary to secession, had yet to make an appearance.[44]

The world of colonial America still largely operated on European assumptions and models. As famous as Jefferson's opening sentences are, few are familiar with the paragraphs that follow. These contain a long and irritated litany of the faults of King George III, whose entire purpose in life, if the declaration is to be credited, was none other than "the establishment of an absolute tyranny over these States." The king is charged with several exaggerated sins, including calling meetings at distant locations "for the sole purpose of fatiguing them into compliance with his measures," and creating so many new offices that "swarms of Officers" appear "to harass our people, and eat out their substance." While the inconvenience of distant meetings and a multitude of public officials may seem an unlikely justification for revolution, there are several serious charges that were more calculated to boil an Englishman's blood. The monarch had imposed taxes without any form of representation or consent, he had cut off colonial trade, and he had deprived the colonies of trial by jury, thus removing the legal protections that all Englishmen had come to expect. The colonies, then, were both *of* and *other than* Britain. They expected the full rights of Englishmen, but were not fully integrated into a union with Britain. They had reached a point where it was either union or revolution. Americans found themselves increasingly treated with condescension by the British administration and continued to point out that they were entitled to the full complement of English liberties. John Adams stressed, "Is there not something exceedingly fallacious in the commonplace images of mother country and children colonies?. . . Are we not brethren and fellow subjects with those in Britain, only under a somewhat different method of legislation and a totally different method of taxation?"[45] The answer to this query came to be more and more clearly in the negative, and the union with Britain grew less and less desirable or likely.

As modern as the rights asserted in the Declaration of Independence seem to the contemporary ear, the structure of the document still bears traces of the hierarchy of feudal Europe. Rather than directing their ire to the British parliament, the colonial delegates focused their address upon the person of the king. *He* refused, and *He* imposed, and *He* abolished. The hated entity was not the abstract state with which we now deal in the international system, nor was it the English nation with whom the revolutionaries claimed brotherhood. It was the Machiavellian prince. In short, the king was deemed in the declaration to be "A Prince, whose character is thus marked by every act which may define a Tyrant, [he] is unfit to be the ruler of a free people." It was not the office of monarchy itself that the colonists rejected; it was the perceived injustice of the monarch's rule. While even Machiavelli had mentioned the need for judiciousness on the part of the wise prince in order that his people would love him and not rise up, the theoretical ease with which the declaration claims the right to freedom from tyranny indicates that the newly secularized principles of legitimacy were already at work.

The concept of territory in the colonies was still a European one. Spheres of jurisdiction and control were certainly delineated between the states, but there was no concept that the current borders were the final ones and must not be tampered with. In fact, the newly independent united states were in the uniquely privileged position of having vast amounts of frontier territories into which they could expand (the native inhabitants being only a temporary impediment). So far were the Americans from seeing their original thirteen colonies as constitutive of their boundaries and identity that one of their most grievous complaints against the king in the declaration involved his attempts to control the growth of the colonies. He "endeavoured to prevent the population of these States; for that purpose obstructing the Laws of Naturalization of Foreigners; refusing to pass others to encourage their migrations hither, and raising the conditions of new Appropriations of Lands."[46] Americans were aware that the physical resources of their vast land was one of the sources of their greatness. Far from being defined and contained by the boundaries of the established colonies, American identity was geographical in the continental sense. A federal union, and therefore the possibility of a national identity, was not ensured until the Constitution was ratified in 1789.

The International System in the Twentieth Century: Citizens and Foreigners

The twentieth-century international system differs from any order that has gone before in being the first truly global order based on the nominal equality of all its members. Also for the first time, the acquisition of territory by conquest has been universally acknowledged to be illegal. The quintessential text of twentieth-century territoriality is the United Nations Charter, which asserts in Article 2.4:

> All Members shall refrain in their international relations from the threat or use of force against the territorial integrity or political independence of any state, or in any other manner inconsistent with the Purposes of the United Nations.

States, by becoming members of the United Nations, agree to refrain from interfering in the internal affairs of other states; thus, the territorial boundaries of states that have exercised the right of self-determination are held to be inviolable. The combination of these aspects has produced a type of territoriality that is more absolute than anything that existed previously. Geographical space has been claimed politically in all but the polar and deep seabed regions. As every inch of space has been labeled and deemed to be under a specific sovereign, so also has every individual been labeled as a *national* of a specific state. Those identities not aligned with any sovereign polity have become both precarious and defensive, as the term "stateless persons" so aptly illustrates. State identities have become institutionalized, as can be represented by the importance of passports for international travel. While no one would think of traveling abroad without one today (with the exception of intra-European Union travel and across certain neighboring borders deemed friendly by treaty), passports as national identity documents are a feature of the twentieth century.[47] The international passport regime first became established after World War I with the attempt to regulate (and also to help guarantee) travel rights. But travel was not impossible without such documents for most people until after World War II. For example, it was not illegal for American citizens to travel abroad without passports until legislation to that effect was passed in 1941. While passports are meant to extend to their bearers protection and the right to leave and reenter the issuing state, the fact that they are an almost universal requirement for entry into states can have the opposite effect. Rather than merely aiding travel, passports serve to simplify the means by which states patrol their borders and maintain control of the people over whom they exert sovereignty. It is this form of control which is a recently developed feature of our conception of the world.

According to David Campbell, this conception of citizen inside and alien (or foreigner) outside is dependent on the conception of the international itself—thus linking the study of International Relations very closely with the study of foreignness, and lending a new meaning to the making (of) foreign policy.

> The passage from difference to identity as marked by the rite of citizenship is concerned with the elimination of that which is alien, foreign, and perceived as a threat to a secure state. . . . [I]t was not until Bentham coined the phrase *international* in the late eighteenth century that *foreign* came to be firmly associated with the different character of other nations. *Foreign* always signified something that was on the outside and therefore distinguished from the inside, but the parameters that constituted the demarcated space differed greatly from our contemporary understanding. In the first recorded use of *foreign* in the English language, the thirteenth-century term *chamber foreign* represented a private room in a house. From then until the seventeenth and eighteenth centuries, *foreign* served to indicate the distance, unfamiliarity, and alien character of those people and matters outside of one's immediate household, family, or region, but still inside the political community that would later comprise a state.[48]

There are several interesting correlations to the development of the word *foreign* and the coining of the word *international* in the late eighteenth century. It was at this time that the first appearance of the term *immigrant* occurred in the English language; it began specifically in reference to the population of the United States. It was also at this time that the concept of *citizenship*, which had lain dormant since the demise of the Roman Empire, had a revival in the wake of the American and French Revolutions. While the Romans used citizenship as a means of distinguishing residents of Rome from those of the conquered territories, it eventually came to cover all the incorporated residents of the empire. At that time, it had more to do with one's personal status as free versus slave than with any concept of national identity. Now, however, citizenship and nationality have become closely bound. With a universal presumption of free status (notwithstanding immense differences in relative statuses among individuals), citizenship is no longer a social classification. One's citizenship creates legal ties to the associated state which preclude obligations to other states regardless of prior or ancestral national affiliations.

The concepts of *citizenship, foreignness*, and *international* which began in the late eighteenth century are by now closely intertwined with state and national identity. Taken together, they reflect the late modern tendencies of the state to assert sovereignty through territorial control. States achieve this through strict control over their borders and through control of the categories of citizens and foreigners or—even more bluntly—aliens. Nowhere is this more evident than in the interrogations involved in the process of *naturalization* or making the unnatural natural. In its process of admitting foreigners to the privileges of citizenship, the United States Immigration and Naturalization Service (INS) must make several determinations of eligibility based on certain factors. Aside from the various residency requirements, the INS informs applicants in its pamphlet *A Guide to Naturalization* that "to be eligible for naturalization you must be a person of good moral character. INS will make a determination on your moral character based upon the laws Congress has passed."[49] Thus, the INS suggests to prospective citizens (outsiders) that not only are those in the privileged (inside) class of superior moral standing, but the nature of that superiority may be determined by the subjective decisions of the inside class itself and may be subject to change. Should the determination of moral character and other procedural requirements be made in the affirmative, an "alien" must then take *The Oath of Allegiance*:

> I hereby declare, on oath, that I absolutely and entirely renounce and abjure all allegiance and fidelity to any foreign prince, potentate, state, or sovereignty, of whom or which I have heretofore been a subject or citizen; that I will support and defend the Constitution and the laws of the United States of America against all enemies, foreign and domestic; that I will bear true faith and allegiance to the same; that I will bear arms on behalf of the United States when required by the law; that I will perform noncombatant service in the Armed Forces of the United States when required by the law; that I will perform work of national importance under civilian direction when required by the law; and that I take this obligation freely, without any mental reservation or purpose of evasion; so help me God.[50]

The first half of this oath in particular evokes a much older era of sworn allegiance amongst crusading knights. It is the language of a sovereign commanding his (its) subjects, and the required renunciation of "all allegiance and fidelity" goes beyond the old citizenship concept of voting rights, tax obligations, and military service. This is an oath of identity. It binds the declarant to the inside of the sovereign state and requires her or him to defend this inside against all *enemies, foreign and domestic*. Ironically, once one has become a citizen of the United States, one cannot be made to pledge allegiance, as freedom of political speech and conscience is a constitutional right. The naturalization process, however, remains a policing one, in which the character and allegiance of the *un*-naturalized must be proved, and the collective identity of the inside must be protected.

Territoriality Lived—Characteristics of the Contemporary State

Nothing illustrates the odious novelty of contemporary systems of citizenship and identity as well as a social anthropologist's perspective on the changes that occurred in a European border town after World War II.[51] The village of Leidingen is a tiny place of 200 inhabitants that has existed on the German-French border of the Saar-Lorraine region since 1815. Before World War II, the villagers had managed to ignore the border and maintain a village life with both French and German populations using the single church and school, which were located on the German side of the border. Starting with the aftermath of World War I, however, the German government maintained tight controls over the border, and by the end of World War II, a separate church and school had been built on the French side. At this point, the earlier local German dialect was replaced by compulsory French on the French side. Not surprisingly, many village families were split by the war, with different members fighting on opposite sides. An ethnographic study of the perceptions of themselves by the children of the village revealed some surprising things about modern political identities. The close connections of the two national identities in the village had all but been wiped out for the children born after the war. The ethnographer's project involved having the young students of both the French and German schools visit the cemeteries on the opposite side of the border. Already there was a lack of familiarity with and connection to this part of their tiny village.

> The mood of these German students changed noticeably when we crossed the border, unmarked by customs posts or other indications and all but invisible for those who do not know about it. Arriving at the French cemetery, the girls had a laugh when they discovered plastic flowers on the graves, which were mostly covered with marble tombstones, and which displayed other features not common in German cemeteries. It was clear that only two of the girls had previously visited the French cemetery, although all four had lived in the village since birth. Their friends immediately demanded an explanation of the two who knew the cemetery, and suggestions were made about their apparent ancestral connections to the French. But the girls who were the butt of these jokes were to have the last laugh when it emerged the following day that in fact all four girls had relatives buried in the French cemetery.[52]

When asked to note the similarities and differences between the two churchyards, the students failed to notice the most obvious feature—both churches are Roman Catholic. A close look at the older German cemetery also revealed several graves from the eighteenth century, one of which, dated 1772, was that of Jost Hillt. Hillt's family had a long history in Lorraine, and had come to Leidingen in the sixteenth century. "That he, as a Lothringian [i.e., from Lorraine], was buried in Leidingen is an indication of the minor importance of linguistic and regional boundaries to the population at that time, and is a clear example of how kinship and economic relationships extended across a number of social boundaries."[53] Not only had the recent generation been shielded from their connections across the (invisible) national border, but they also had learned to apply national stereotypes and suspicion of motives to their French and German counterparts. When the two school groups were brought together there was much apprehension, and in a short time a fight broke out.

> Apparently some of the German boys, aged 10-11 years, had initiated the conflict by imitating the French attempts to speak German. The French had immediately formed a bloc to defend themselves. The Germans who had begun the conflict now felt threatened and had called for their class mates. They began to push the French girls and earned some slaps on their faces in return. Stones were thrown, fists were brandished, and insulting gestures were made. Abuse was hurled at the other side, such as, "this will be the reason for the next World War, you bloody spiked helmet!", and "baguette head!". . . . When a German boy pointed out a French one, asking in German for his name, the French boy replied by hitting him before I could do anything about it. I told him that the German boy had only wanted to know his name, nothing else, and he answered: "How could I know that? I don't understand him, so I decided to beat him as a defensive measure. What he said might have been an insult."[54]

Hostile relations among the inhabitants of such a tiny village who share many blood relations have been brought about by the modern preoccupation with physically bounding national identities. The relations of this one village can be seen as a metaphor for national relations elsewhere which are based on simplistic typologies and willful ignorance of historical ties. This pattern is repeated throughout the global grid of interstate borders. Allowing territorial boundaries to dictate personal and national identities is one of the sad hallmarks of twentieth-century territoriality. Examples such as the one of Leidingen show how extreme it can become, but it is hardly surprising that there has recently been a movement among scholars of International Relations to question the arbitrariness and moral legitimacy of interstate borders.[55] This questioning of modern statehood, and the legitimacy of national claims to territories, cannot proceed meaningfully without an awareness of the historical changes which have occurred in our understanding of territory itself, and especially of the conceptual relationship between territory and political legitimacy. Furthermore, the symbiosis between territoriality and the recognition of national identities in the twentieth century cannot be ignored. As the example above shows all too clearly, modern territoriality not only allows but also encourages the splintering and separation of identities which formerly were complexly intertwined. This process politicizes both territory and identity in ways which threaten the security of both.

This chapter explores the development of the administration of political space. Territoriality, upon which secession depends, is only a recent form of political control of space. Earlier periods solved problems of political identity and sovereign control in different ways. Secession, then, is not only a logical outcome of modern territorial structures, but also an outcome which is all but propelled by the momentum of international politics and the imperative of controlling the relationship of the sovereign inside with the outside other. In the following chapter, I examine the role of identity politics in maintaining the inside/outside boundary and theorize strategies for encountering and politicizing the other which preclude the exclusivism of secession as a means of securing identity.

Notes

1. R. B. J. Walker, "State Sovereignty and the Articulation of Political Space/Time," *Millennium: Journal of International Studies* 20, no. 3 (Winter 1991): 445, 445-461.

2. Onora O'Neill, "Justice and Boundaries," in *Political Restructuring in Europe: Ethical Perspectives*, ed. Chris Brown (London: Routledge, 1994), 78.

3. Walker, "State Sovereignty," 460.

4. James Mayall, *Nationalism and International Society* (Cambridge: Cambridge University Press, 1990), 51.

5. Kamal Shehadi, *Ethnic Self-Determination and the Break-up of States* (London: Brassey's, The International Institute for Strategic Studies, Adelphi Paper No. 283, 1993), 30.

6. See Reinhart Koselleck, *Futures Past: On the Semantics of Historical Time*, trans. Keith Tribe (Cambridge, Mass.: MIT Press, 1985).

7. Jens Bartelson, *A Genealogy of Sovereignty* (Cambridge: Cambridge University Press, 1995), 4.

8. See Steven Grosby, "Territoriality: The Transcendental, Primordial Feature of Modern Societies," *Nations and Nationalism* 1 (July 1995): 143-162.

9. Bartelson, *Genealogy of Sovereignty*, 41.

10. I am not the first to notice and interpret the strange etymology of the term. See William E. Connolly, *The Ethos of Pluralization* (Minneapolis: University of Minnesota Press, 1995), xxii; and Thomas Baldwin, "The Territorial State," in *Jurisprudence: Cambridge Essays*, ed. Hyman Gross and Ross Harrison (Oxford: Clarendon Press, 1992), 209.

11. *The Oxford English Dictionary*, 2d ed., s.v. "territory."

12. U.S. Constitution, art. 4, sec. 3.

13. Ian Brownlie, *Principles of Public International Law*, 4th ed. (Oxford: Oxford University Press, 1990), 108.14. SCOR 383rd. Mtg., 2nd Dec. 1948, 41. Cited in James Crawford, *The Creation of States in International Law* (Oxford: Clarendon Press, 1979), 37-38.

14. SCOR 383rd. Mtg., 2nd Dec. 1948, 41. Cited in James Crawford, *The Creation of States in International Law* (Oxford: Clarendon Press, 1979), 37-38.

15. See Benedict Anderson, *Imagined Communities: Reflections on the Origin and Spread of Nationalism* (London: Verso, 1993).

16. Dante, *Monarchy*, trans. Donald Nicholl (Westport, Conn.: Hyperion, 1979), 13.

17. Dante, *Monarchy*, 15.

18. Dante, *Monarchy*, 17.

19. Anderson, *Imagined Communities*, 19.

20. See Isaiah Berlin, "The Originality of Machiavelli," in *The Proper Study of Mankind*, ed. Henry Hardy and Roger Hausheer (London: Pimlico, 1998), 269-325. In 1972, Berlin found over 3,000 items in a bibliographic search on Machiavelli.

21. *Virtù* can be translated as "strength," "ability," "courage," "manliness," "ingenuity," "character," "wisdom," or even sometimes "virtue." Robert M. Adams, translator's note to Niccolò Machiavelli, *The Prince*, ed. and trans. Robert Adams (New York: Norton, 1977).

22. Adams, translator's note to *The Prince*, xvii.

23. Niccolò Machiavelli, *The Prince*, ed. and trans. Robert Adams (New York: Norton, 1977), 6.

24. Machiavelli, *The Prince*, 7.

25. Quentin Skinner, *Machiavelli* (Oxford: Oxford University Press, 1981), 7.

26. Skinner, *Machiavelli*, 16.

27. Sir Thomas More, *Utopia*, trans. Peter K. Marshall (New York: Washington Square Press, 1965), 1.

28. Bartelson, *Genealogy of Soveriegnty*, 121-122.

29. In a link with the past, More specifically criticized the enclosure of common agricultural areas, which was just beginning to take place in England at the time. Lands that were formerly cultivated collectively were being enclosed and claimed by private landowners—to the detriment of many of the poorest. See John Freeman, "A Model Territory: Enclosure in More's *Utopia*," in *The Territorial Rights of Nations and Peoples*, ed. John R. Jacobson, Essays from the Basic Issues Forum, Studies in World Peace vol. 2 (Lewiston, N.Y.: Edwin Mellen Press, 1989), 241-267. However, More also describes some startlingly advanced ideas about relations between the genders, crime and punishment, and political economy.

30. More, *Utopia*, 28.

31. More, *Utopia*, 29.

32. More, *Utopia*, 58.

33. It could be argued, for example, to employ More's framework, that Saddam Hussein did not conform to More's requirements for just intent toward the territory, but Hussein's own arguments were that he did in fact have historical title to the area of Kuwait. This argument could easily have been restated in terms of the needs of the Iraqi people for the sustenance of greater oil reserves. The finer points of applying legal standards to balance the needs of the Utopians and the needs of the prior inhabitants are not raised by More, but the real point in this analogy is that More could not have written about territorial conquest the way he did if he had lived in a world like the one that reacted so violently to the invasion of Kuwait.

34. Liah Greenfeld, *Nationalism: Five Roads to Modernity* (Cambridge, Mass.: Harvard University Press, 1992), 30.

35. This perspective could also reflect a growing awareness of the "openness" of the world afforded by the discovery and colonization of the New World. If so, it is still far from the territorial sovereignty that later developed. John H. Herz argued that this period actually marked the beginning of the rise of the age of territoriality as anarchy could be continually pushed beyond the frontier, allowing for strict control of the territories of the European states. See John Herz, *International Politics in the Atomic Age* (New York: Columbia University Press, 1959), 68.

36. Adam Watson, *The Evolution of International Society: A Comparative Historical Analysis* (London: Routledge, 1992), 189.

37. Hugo Grotius, *De Jure Belli ac Pacis*, trans. Francis W. Kelsey, ed. James Brown Scott (1925)(1.1.14), 44.

38. Thomas Baldwin, "The Territorial State," in *Jurisprudence: Cambridge Essays*, ed. Hyman Gross and Ross Harrison (Oxford: Clarendon Press, 1992), 212. Baldwin provides a very competent historical analysis of the idea of territoriality; however, he inexplicably assumes that the territorial state was a medieval idea that Enlightenment political theorists mysteriously failed to discuss. The modern territorial state has so captured the twentieth-century intellect that it cannot explain the absence of territoriality in an era that had yet to conceive of it.

39. Thomas Hobbes, *Leviathan*, ed. C. B. Macpherson (London: Penguin, 1985), chap. 17, 228.

40. Hobbes, *Leviathan*, 187-188.

41. Watson, *Evolution of International Society*, 182.

42. The Treaty of Westphalia. *Peace Treaty between the Holy Roman Emperor and the King of France and Their Respective Allies*, Munster, October 24, 1648, sec. 76, trans. British Foreign Office. Available from http://www.tufts.edu/fletcher/multi/ texts/historical/ westphalia.txt. Accessed 25 April 2003.

43. The *united* was used as a simple adjective in the Declaration of Independence and thus not capitalized. In the opening lines of the Constitution thirteen years later, however, the usage has changed to "We the People of the United States."

44. The decolonizations of the twentieth century could be seen as similar events that actually took place during the age of territoriality. I would argue that these decolonizations were more about modern self-determination of subject peoples than was the American Declaration of Independence. The American revolutionaries would have, if given a choice, remained British as long as they could have had the full complement of political rights guaranteed to free Englishmen. This situation is very unlike the anticolonial movements of the post-World War II period.

45. Cited in Greenfeld, *Nationalism*, 417.

46. These words by the founding fathers seem especially ironic in light of the recent trend by the U.S. Congress to restrict and control immigration and immigrants.

47. Daniel C. Turack, *The Passport in International Law* (Lexington, Mass.: Lexington Books, 1972), 137.

48. David Campbell, *Writing Security: United States Foreign Policy and the Politics of Identity*, rev. ed. (Manchester: Manchester University Press, 1998), 36-37 (emphasis in original).

49. U.S. Immigration and Naturalization Service, *A Guide to Naturalization* (M-476) (rev. 12/00). Available from http://www.immigration.gov/graphics/series/natz/English.pdf. Accessed 25 April 2003, 25.

50. U.S. Immigration and Naturalization Service, *A Guide to Naturalization*, 28.

51. Tomke Lask, "'Baguette heads' and 'spiked helmets': Children's Constructions of Nationality on the German-French Border," in *Border Approaches: Anthropological Perspectives on Frontiers*, ed. Hastings Donnan and Thomas Wilson (Lanham, Md.: University Press of America, 1994), 63-73.

52. Lask, "Constructions of Nationality," 65.

53. Lask, "Constructions of Nationality," 65.

54. Lask, "Constructions of Nationality," 66.

55. See *The Territorial Rights of Nations and Peoples*, ed. John R. Jacobson.

Chapter 4

Begging to Differ: Patriots, Nationalists, and Minorities

The previous chapter examines the changing role of territory in its political historical context and highlights the development of the particularly modern conception of territoriality. This phenomenon, sharpened to perfection by the events and perspectives of the twentieth century, has compelled a perilous balance between the recognition and legitimation of political identities and the sovereign control of a physical territory. Not only must a national group maintain sovereign control to be legitimated as an international actor, but the actual drawing of the borders, the defining of the state's inside and its outside, creates schisms and clashes between groups which have taken on the status of minority or majority with the stroke of a cartographer's pen. Before territorial sovereignty became the badge of legitimacy, identities did not need to serve as political markers. Under contemporary international law's twin principles of self-determination and nonintervention, politics has inevitably come to rely upon the identification of the boundaries of the state and the proper delineation of its national membership. This arbitrary hardening of political boundaries has resulted in a paradoxical political dynamic. The contingent and boundless processes of social identity formation have been wedded to the static mythology of the sovereign territorial state. It should come as no surprise that the match is not made in heaven. This chapter shows that the modernist conception of securing identity through territory is a misguided goal. Identities cannot be secured without damaging the very diversity and richness that makes them valuable. Paradoxically, the "secured" identity is a stifled and dying one, while the identity which allows itself the constant challenge of recognizing and accepting otherness is vibrant and resilient. Naturally, these conclusions have broad implications—not only for secessionist politics, but for the territoriality of state security practices in general.

"Outsiders" Inside—Internal Insecurity

The making of group identity and security through the state creates a system that privileges the groups which identify with state power. The identity of the group which is in the most advantageous position (for reasons of historical contingency) will claim the national identity of the state itself—promulgating its particular histories and conceptions of security needs and social values. Those within the state who have identities which differ from the privileged national identity of the state will automatically be in a "minority" position and thus have "insecure" identities which are unexpressed in political ways. Yael Tamir argues that even if the political ideology of the majority advocates a nationally neutral system of redistribution and welfare, the identity of the decision makers and bureaucrats will reflect a set of social values which cannot be kept out of the public sphere. Thus, minorities "feel alienated from the public sphere, less able to understand its cultural origins, less capable of playing according to the 'rules of the game.'"[1] Minorities are free to familiarize themselves with the dominant national culture, she continues, but they will be devoting time and energy to trying to understand what comes naturally to members of the majority. The expression of minority identities will not be equated with that of the nation as a political whole, and they will become relegated to the status of a cultural and historical anomaly, useful for the promotion of tourism.

The smelting of sovereignty and territoriality out of which the modern state was forged has very serious implications for identity formation. R. B. J. Walker says of territorial sovereignty:

> [it] fixes an account of where politics occurs, and what political life itself can be. It identifies who can be made secure: the political community inside state boundaries. . . . And it denies the possibility of alternative arrangements on the ground that only through the state do we now seem capable of resolving all those contradictions—between universality and diversity, between space and time, between men and citizens, between Them and Us—that were once resolved by the subordinations and dominations of feudal hierarchy, monotheistic religion, and empire.[2]

Not only is the description of political life fixed in this "in" or "out" way, but this structure has become so entrenched that we now lack the ability to imagine any other—nonbounded—types of political community. This description highlights the particularly modern difficulty faced by groups which lack the privileging apparatus of the state—effectively those groups called "minorities." Ironically, though, this plight by no means restricts the definition of minority groups to the categories of ethnic minority identities currently in common linguistic use, since the minority/majority status of every national group is contingent on the placement and maintenance of state borders. The territorial sovereignty of the modern state exerts an irresistible pull through the certainty and stability of its defined scope of influence. The effective limitation allows those within the state to feel secure in their restricted, delineated space. So powerful is this need for definition and certainty, and so clearly does the state seem to provide for the need, that we are now unable to conceive of secured identity and legitimacy without the rubric of the territorial state. But there is a structural flaw within this cozy setup.

In our rush to create definitions of, and defenses against, the outside "other," we have overlooked the "other" that we ourselves are, and will continue to become. The statist presumption of identity as territory allows only an external location for the insecurity of otherness. This presumption has allowed the state to operate as the provider of identity and describer of security needs. To acknowledge that threats to identity may occur within the state is to abandon the reasoning behind the construct of the territorial (nation) state itself and to recognize the impossibility of legitimate, secured identities within its realm. Yet, it is the very nature of the state construct itself which gives rise to the internal "threat" of minority identities by pointing toward secession as the only means of legitimating their identities. All too often, minorities have been left little choice but to seek a separate territory within which they can re-create the state processes of identity legitimation and securitizing. This includes the constant process of identity creation through the retelling of national histories and the continual participation of the group in its culturally distinct traditions and observances. This need for identity creation and affirmation has become part of the scholarly fascination with nationalism and national movements. While nationalism is typically associated with ethnic identities, any group which makes a political claim for sovereign independence draws on a collective affirmation of the collective self of the group.

The mistake of postwar theorists and state leaders was to assume that national loyalty and patriotism were identical forces and that they were conveniently bounded by existing, or adjustable, state borders. The perfect match of bounded territories to homogeneous peoples has never existed, and the ability of states, as political entities, to foster cohesive identities has been greatly overestimated.[3] The nation-state as a project was never more than an ideal model. Even so, the failure of this project has not resulted in a reconceptualization of the doctrine of self-determination into a nonstatist ideal. When the League of Nations' plan for protecting minorities in the wake of World War I resulted in miserable failure, state leaders began to focus on assimilation and accommodation. Many states contain minority groups which do not agitate for independence, while others contain groups with active separatist segments within generally stable minority identities. Finally, there are separatist movements so fully developed that they lead to partition, secession, or wars. Despite the recognition that minority identities can potentially coalesce into secessionist movements, such identities have inevitably defeated all attempts to locate objective predictive criteria.[4] The bonding of people into group identities has such a profoundly subjective basis that actual kinship or common descent need not exist. As one commentator put it, "it is not *what is* but *what people perceive as is* which influences attitudes and behavior. And a subconscious belief in the group's separate origin and evolution is an important ingredient of national psychology."[5] Hence, artificially emphasized histories are a potent piece of the nationalist repertoire and can be found in almost every example of nationalist rhetoric. Erik Ringmar argues that it is only through narrative that we can actually make sense of our individual or collective selves. Thus, the identity of "we" is "neither a question of what essences constitute us nor a question of how we conclusively should be defined, but instead a question of how we are seen and a question of which stories are told about us."[6] The telling of histories is then a tool for creating a present which makes sense for the identities in question. This dynamic operates in two directions—we both create ourselves through our own telling and are created through the stories of others. Certain options are foreclosed to collective groups by the nonrecognition of nonmembers.[7] Making collective and intersubjective use of historical narrative is how national identities are formed. This process can be and often is consciously manipulated.

A recent well-known example of the potency of the nationalist project is the conflict in the former Yugoslavia, where different religions and different imperial jurisdictions were revived from historical lapses to form the basis of the sharp delineations of a formerly integrated people into three. The fact that the three peoples had formed peaceful friendships and intermarriages for years (which could just as easily have served as the basis for forging a strong single national identity) came to no consequence when the identity-shaping rhetoric of nationalist leaders began to take hold. The bloodiness and brutality of nationalist wars have prompted collective confusion from the academic community, which shrugs, perplexed, that it cannot account for irrational primordial passions. Nationalism rejects common denominators and objective criteria. What has become increasingly clear, however, is that where matters of identity are concerned, the dry administrative claims of the state become inconsequential. The prize at stake is very precious indeed because without it the social context of group identity fails and the individual as previously constituted vanishes. As one former resident of Sarajevo, currently living in London, has described it, she now comes from "nowhere" and has no national identity—or rather, an obsolete one. The child of a Serb and a Croat, she condemns all sides for demolishing the multicultural city that created who she is. The identity which comes from belonging to a national group, the most potent form of collective identity, has forever been lost to her.[8]

While the obliteration of a national identity constitutes a cultural tragedy for human diversity, it is crucial to recognize that the loss of an identity (through violent war or forcible assimilation) is not equivalent to the adaptations a distinct group may make over time which cause it to seem quite different from its earlier manifestations. All identities change and grow in new directions in response and in relationship to the course of historical events. In other words, although we make use of stories of a singular past in the creation of our group "selves," and revere traditions derived from "ancient" times, we cannot actually keep a group identity static, or "secured," as is so often attempted. The flow of time cannot be frozen in place at the point considered most representative or expressive of a particular culture. For example, as compelling as the charms of rustic life can be, few late moderns have the desire or the fortitude to truly eschew the developments of the last two hundred years of Western technology and join the Amish in their devotion to the preservation of a distinct and isolated identity. It requires the strictest codes of social isolation and resistance to innovation within to maintain the kind of continuity demonstrated by the Amish and similar communities.[9] Notwithstanding our reluctance to seriously live "in the past," nationalist sentiment often causes members of distinct groups to "re-live the past" in order to stoke the passions of an earlier—and thus now decontextualized—conflict. Of course, not all minority identities take on a militant nationalist agenda, but there is an intrinsically urgent drive behind groups which search for political recognition. Once a group has recognition, both internally and externally, it has substance and existence in the realm of international law and politics. It is an "actor" and therefore provides a legitimate identity for its members. Unfortunately, there are no rules about which groups may be eligible for political recognition. The doctrine of self-determination is ominously silent about the nature of the "self" concerned, leaving the question of membership in the community of states a perilously open one.

Patriots, Nationalists, and Minorities

In a recent discussion of modern nationalism, Thomas Franck states that the certainty of old categories of identity is no longer valid and that many of us must now rethink our identities. Franck takes upon himself the task of sorting through the complex meanings of commonly misunderstood terms: nation, state, people, ethnie, tribe, nationalism, and patriotism. According to Franck, much of what we consider to be nationalism today is actually patriotic loyalty to the state, since "[i]n the twentieth century, the state has had pride of place in the construct of personal identity."[10] The point is that this type of nationalism recalls the late eighteenth century and the nation-building practices of the United States and France, which focused around the abstractions of liberty and equality rather than essentialist qualities such as race. A century later, Franck argues, the nationalisms of Germany and Japan and other recent cases "tended to define their enemies as those of different (and usually inferior) gene pools or religiocultural ancestry. . . . [they] have turned inward in paroxysms of xenophobia."[11] This is the nationalism of contemporary notoriety, which can be placed at the scene of many an international crime. While Franck oversimplifies and thus confuses the difference between civic and ethnic nationalism, his main argument—that modern nationalist movements seek separate states for all the wrong reasons—is a point worth making.[12] Regardless of how one feels about the proper political policies of a multiethnic state—even if one believes that assimilation under the concepts of a civic ideal is actually another name for a form of cultural imperialism—there is something troubling about the widespread nature of adamant claims for political independence. The self-determination which separatists claim is their goal and their right can never actually be achieved because identities (both individual and collective) are highly subjective and cannot be purified. The whole concept of self-determination—as far as it concerns sovereign statehood—is based on a dangerous myth. Franck terms the concept of a pure national state as nothing less than "apartheid" and notes that it has become surprisingly "fashionable" again:

> [I]t has become socially and politically correct to aver that political and social organization should be based on the principle of "likes-with-likes" whether "likes" be defined in linguistic, ethnic, racial, religious, historical, cultural, or other terms. . . . It does not seem much to matter to the force of a secessionist claim whether it is based on a demonstrable genetic-cultural-historical reality, or, more likely, is pure romantic invention.[13]

The point is, that even if a separatist claim is based on a harsh reality of oppression it also relies on a patently false assumption—that political rule by one's own cultural group (however defined) is a good and fair thing and is a fundamental right. The right of belonging to a cultural group is one thing, but it should and must not be confused with an inherent right to the political constitution of a state. To argue otherwise would be to assume that membership in national groups should be maintained by objective criteria for the common good. Such an assumption curtails the very freedom which was fought for in the first place.

Isaiah Berlin said of national self-determination:

> It is a cry for room in which men can seek to realize their natures, quirks and all, to live lives free from dictation or coercion from teachers, masters, bullies and persuaders and dominators of various kinds. No doubt to do entirely as one likes could destroy not only one's neighbors but oneself. Freedom is only one value among others, and cannot be realized without rules and limits. But in the hour of revolt this is inevitably forgotten.[14]

Absolute freedom is neither possible nor desirable—because there is no common understanding of its meaning amongst humanity, how can any single interpretation of the value of freedom be privileged over all others? The independence sought by separatist groups is a kind of freedom which inevitably entails limitations on the freedoms of those who do not fit membership criteria or who demonstrate nonconformity within the group. The only form of "protection" an independent state would guarantee to members of a cultural group already residing in a liberal democracy is the freedom to impose their own criteria of membership and thus transform themselves from the minority to the majority. This is not protection for the newly created majority identity because it will continue to be subjected to multiple interpretations both from within and without. The "protection" of state sovereignty, then, is nothing less than the pleasure of drawing boundaries by military means rather than social and legal ones. This "just solution" which separatists claim as their right is, then, neither just nor a solution. In cases where the minority is genuinely oppressed and prohibited from expressing and creating its cultural identity, the blame lies with the state apparatus, and the right the minority may exert operates in favor of restructuring the state to allow for autonomy and cultural protections. In other words, there are no national rights to independent states; there are only rights of protection of national (and multiple) identities within and across states. Any other assumption supports state-by-state apartheid, as Franck described. It is also fallacious to assume that a state border will end the oppression or hostility between national groups. In many ways, it is likely to exacerbate it. How many Yugoslavs, Israelis, and Northern Irish must be lost before the fallacy of self-determination is realized?

One suggestion, which many theorists agree upon, for easing the strain of national groups struggling to gain an international voice is the creation and encouragement of international institutions which expressly provide fora for substate and transstate identity groups. Franck and Will Kymlicka both favor increased franchisement for minorities and nongovernmental organizations, but from vastly different perspectives. For Franck, an international forum for substate identities would act as a pressure valve and ease the force behind many separatist movements, thus resisting the trend toward the "two thousand-state global system." Kymlicka, on the other hand, finds that the idea has merit as one of the only ways in which minority groups may represent their interests and receive justice, since states so often ignore minority issues. Kymlicka further critiques Franck's support as contradicting his earlier representation of nationalism as being irrational, asking "wouldn't we be pandering to this irrationality by giving them representation at the United Nations or other international bodies? Wouldn't representation give legitimacy to their nationalist aims and self-identity?"[15] In doing so, however, he conflates national secessionist aims with the need for legitimating national identity. This is precisely the mistake which impels the separatist craze Franck fears. National identities for minorities and majorities, wherever they might be, are in constant need of legitimation. But the institution of the state itself is a chimerical means of providing it. One of Franck's very first points was that there seems to be a global identity crisis in this post–Cold War era. Majority (or hegemonic) identities are in crisis in unsuspected ways. Russia is no longer the other superpower, and therefore what it means to be Russian has been called into question on a profound level. Further, with the splintering of the Soviet Union, there are now Russian minorities in former Soviet states and satellites whose identity is suddenly one of political disadvantage. This pattern is merely one example. The white Anglo-Saxon identity of the United States is no longer "politically correct," and the nation struggles to find an identity which can be articulated by all while allowing expression for the multiple cultures currently swirling around in the melting pot. Kymlicka's critique then falls away because the point of the proposal for international recognition of national identities is not to legitimate separatism, but rather to legitimate national identities themselves, regardless of their political status. The separation of national legitimacy from national statehood is crucial and long overdue. Political legitimacy through mutual recognition of equals is the only way to satisfy the true needs of self-determination. To this end, any such forum must include representatives from all national identities—including those associated with the national majorities of their home state. Only in this way can the voices of the minorities be legitimated as equally valid with those of the majorities. Such legitimation stands to benefit national identities all over the globe of whatever proportional status.

Kymlicka's critique contains another interesting point. He disagrees with Franck that minorities bear long grudges and often no longer face discrimination in democratic states. Indeed, he says, "I would argue that it is often members of the majority who exhibit an irrational commitment to an unrealistic and obsolete identity, refusing to accept the reality that they live in a multi-nation state."[16] This statement is undoubtedly true in many respects, but it also contains the germ of a counterargument. The best way to counter the irrationality of the blind majority which cannot recognize the needs of the minority is to work to raise the status of the minority identity to a fully legitimate one. In other words, Kymlicka's minority groups are necessary to force the majority to confront its multinational reality. Of course, it puts the minority in a difficult position with no quick fixes and no easy answers, but surely a struggle for recognition is more peaceful and more rewarding than a possibly military and certainly hostile struggle for sovereign independence. The way to handle the failure of majority groups to legitimate minorities in their midst is to continue to confront them with the reality of difference—not "difference as otherness," in the words of Iris Young, but relational difference, which admits of the mutual and integral relationships among identity groups.[17] In other words, majorities and minorities *need* each other in order to be who they are, and also to fully confront the fact of legitimate differences among human beings. Kymlicka himself obliquely refers to this when he refers to the value of minority nationalism and how it "enhances the autonomy of its members." The benefits of membership in a cultural group are significant in ways which often go unrecognized by the majority group. In fact, the ideal of the autonomous self, espoused by liberalism and urged by Franck, is only possible if the individual has the ability to make choices about his or her identity. Identity choices are only possible and appreciated where there is an awareness of alternatives. As Tamir argues, "individuals will be unable to exercise their right to make cultural choices unless they live in a culturally plural environment."[18] Not only do multiple cultures provide the individual with an awareness of choice and help define his or her own identity, but they mitigate against cultural chauvinism and the tendency of the majority to assume that it has a claim on the sole true image of utopia. Those whose identity rests upon a certainty of conviction which rejects doubt are, in the words of Isaiah Berlin, "victims of forms of self-induced myopia, blinkers that may make for contentment, but not for understanding of what it is to be human."[19]

The contingency of multiple cultures and identities, then, is of critical importance. Minorities, as those who bring the reality of relational otherness before the complacent majority, are crucial for the full realization of the identities of all individuals. The idea that sovereign state separatism is a solution for minority oppression neglects the necessary ambiguity of the identity dynamic, the constant reappraisal and re-creation of the individual and collective self that requires contact with and respect for difference and that alone provides real recognition. Another way to describe this dynamic is to use the phrase put forward by Anthony Appiah and Amy Gutmann, *interactive multiculturalism*. A society that is interactively multicultural allows all its individuals to be exposed to multiple cultural possibilities, and no single culture predominates within any individual identity.

> A society is interactively multicultural to the extent that individuals experience the creative effects of the mingling of different cultures. A culture need not be universally or equally appreciated by all individuals to be valuable. But, other things being equal, cultures are more valuable to the extent that more people have access to them.[20]

The important point here is that cultural identities should all be seen as equally valid and accessible public resources. One need not fully participate in a cultural identity to reap the benefits of its presence in society. An Irishman may adore Manchurian cuisine and the music of West Africa. If he can have access to these cultural accoutrements without leaving Dublin then his Irish identity is not threatened or diminished but enriched. In addition, the identities of immigrant groups or historic minorities are not warped by being thrown into constant relief against the cultural practices of the majority, rather they are enhanced, made fuller. The Francophones of Québec, as is argued below, are not the same as the French of France. They have had more than two centuries of life and interaction on a different continent and under very different circumstances. Their French heritage and language is an important component of who they are today—but it does not mean that they are identical culturally to the citizens of contemporary France, anymore than Anglo Americans are interchangeable with contemporary Britons. This unpredictable cultural palette is not something that should cause concern. Rather, it should be hailed for allowing greater access and therefore more meaningful freedom for individuals in their continual processes of identification. Cultural identities do not have to conform to a single uniform ideal within the boundaries of a state for the civil institutions of that state to be a success and to be stable. The American ideal metaphor of the melting pot is actually profoundly illiberal in its aim to erase difference and create a homogeneous and single whole. Such a result is both unobtainable and undesirable because it requires that individuals forsake (or repress) their complex and uncertain identities for something fixed as the ideal. Even were it possible, it would result in a great loss of freedom for all rather than the protection of a single national identity.

Identity in International Relations Theory

Even in this era of national uprisings and minority activism, International Relations theory has been slow to focus on the nature of identity and the importance of culture. The traditional theoretical structures of the discipline—sovereignty, statehood and anarchy—mitigate against epistemological commitments to ambiguity and multiple perspectives. International Relations theory has tended to regard issues of identity as stable and given, and questions of nationalism have been ascribed to a historically determined primordialism about which nothing can be done politically. This approach yields unhelpful and morally barren results, as described by David Campbell regarding the reaction of the West to the crisis in Bosnia:

> [T]he representation of the timeless quality of the conflict is disenabling of our understanding of the cause of fighting, and thus detrimental to future attempts to deal with such instances. If ethnic and nationalist conflicts are understood as no more than settled history or human nature rearing its ugly head, then there is nothing that can be done in the present to resolve the tension except to repress or ignore such struggles. In this view, the historical animus has to be enacted according to its script, with human agency in suspension while nature violently plays itself out.[21]

If national identity is indeed primordial, the structure of international society becomes fiercely determinist and the need for political and social science at all becomes questionable. Given that nationalist conflicts threaten the basis of international society, it is difficult to justify the discipline's hitherto "hands-off" approach to questions of identity. In lamenting the late arrival of questions of identity and culture into the realm of IR, Yosef Lapid attributes the problem to one of worldview. Citing John Shotter, Lapid states that "we have a choice: either to think of it as based in invariances (fixed things) and to treat change as problematic, or, to think of it as in flux (as consisting in activities) and to treat the attainment of stability as a problem."[22] The theoretical commitments of the discipline have been focused for too long on treating change as problematic, neglecting even the possibility of a choice between the two perspectives. But ironically, perceiving the nature of the world to be one of flux allows for more engagement with the dynamics of identity formation since identity and culture are most coherent if perceived as constructed and interactive.

If traditional International Relations theory was one of static structures with the variables being the interaction and balance of power and interests, then contemporary International Relations theory has evolved into a considerably broader enterprise. Far greater interdisciplinary overlap is considered permissible in the field today, and scholars are taking notice of the discourses of sociology, anthropology, and psychology, among others. The question of who we are and how our identity is defined have been and are of grave relevance to international politics. As Marysia Zalewski and Cynthia Enloe point out, a person's identity as a European Jew in the 1930s and 1940s was a matter of life or death, but also a matter of whose definition of German was allowed to operate.[23] Identity politics have relevance today especially in the political wake of the Cold War. Since the consequences of identity are so great—from privilege to deprivation, from hostility to friendship—it is crucial for International Relations scholars to account for the process of identity formation and its connection to the state. In addition, it is important to see identity as a two-way process; one that involves both the perception of the self and the projection of the other. So, "we need to think of identity politics as a process in which both the person seeking to answer 'Who am I?' and others who want to influence the answer are pushing and pulling each other, though often with unequal resources."[24] It is awareness of the discrepancy between the identity of the self and the identity perceived by the other encountering the self that provides scholars with the opportunity not only to understand identity dynamics but also to encourage more effective political discourse on identity. As simple as this discrepancy seems, it has often been overlooked in the theoretical race to eschew ambiguity and provide stable "working definitions." Such definitions are the very antithesis of identity itself. That is not to say that identity must involve confrontation between two sides, but rather that it is negotiated in the encounter of the self with others. Thus, the need for defining and encountering the other does not vanish when a national group establishes an independent state, regardless of the seeming tangibility of the physical border. The process of identity negotiation and the politics of group membership continue within the borders of sovereign states vis-à-vis minorities within and foreigners without. This process cannot stop, for when it does the self (individual or group) ceases to be—or rather, the self cannot be located in the world without the criteria of what it is and what it is not. This dynamic does much to explain the drive for human contact: it is self-knowledge. "Selves and cultures come to know themselves, construct their identities, in relation to a world beyond themselves. A sense of the world—a cosmological scheme, a vision or a representation of the world—sustains the culture or self, constituting its particular conceptions of what it means to be human (and a human community) in the world."[25] In other words, the more closely the self encounters others, the more finely tuned will be the perception of the self and the perception the other has of the self. The more one encounters strangers and different others, the more facets there are to the identity of the self. And also, there will be a greater likelihood of the self having grown to understand the need for and respect of difference.

Applying these dynamics to International Relations theory requires close attention to the discourses of these identity encounters. In this sense, every public or diplomatic statement plays a role in the constitution of identities, and consequently in the political strategies which follow. Language is a powerful political tool which can elaborate structures of meaning through subtle metaphors. Feminists have made primary contributions to International Relations literature on identity through their studies of the gendering of issues through language, particularly in the areas of defense and strategic studies. National security decisions in most countries have inevitably been made by men, and a profoundly gendered discourse has resulted. For example, during discussions by American nuclear physicists on the impact of deploying a specific type of counterforce attack, it was perceived by the group to be effeminate and unacceptable when one of them exclaimed that they were actually discussing attack models which would result in millions of human lives gone instantaneously. The male physicist told his story to Carol Cohn. "Wait," he said,

"I've just *heard* how we're talking—*Only* thirty million! *Only* thirty million human beings killed instantly?. . . Silence fell upon the room. Nobody said a word. They didn't even look at me. It was awful. I felt like a woman."[26] Cohn elaborates:

> This story is not simply about one individual, his feelings and actions; it is about the role of gender discourse. The impact of gender discourse in that room (and countless others like it) is that some things get left out. Certain ideas, concerns, interests, information, feelings, and meanings are marked in national security discourse as feminine, and are devalued. They are therefore, first, very difficult to *speak*, as exemplified by the physicist who felt like a woman. And second, they are very difficult to *hear*, to take in and work with seriously, even if they *are* said. For the others in that room, the way in which the physicist's comments were marked as female and devalued served to delegitimate them. It is almost as though they had become an accidental excrescence in the middle of the room. Embarrassed politeness demanded that they be ignored.[27]

Thus, things considered to be weak and unacceptable are discussed in terms of feminine metaphors while the prevailing acceptable culture is masculinized.[28] This pattern of silencing the prospect of alternatives is then repeated during international hostilities in terms of the enemy to be defeated (cowardly, feminine) and the members of the national armed forces (brave, masculine).[29] Thus, the importance of language in the creation of identities and the negotiation of the encounter with the other must not be underestimated, and the implications far exceed gender politics. Analyses of the discourses among groups is the methodological key to understanding identity politics generally. These methods are difficult to employ since "sexuality, masculinity, concepts of racial otherness are hidden not just in an empirical sense but in an epistemological sense."[30] A comprehensive interpretation of identity politics therefore requires an understanding of linguistic categories which work "backstage" in ways we all take for granted, but which must be exposed and debated for international *relations* to be understood.

Meanwhile, International Relations as a field has long taught and reproduced theoretical patterns which do not integrate easily with issues of identity. Notwithstanding the recent spate of attention on identity as a hot topic, the path is still largely untrodden in terms of applying theoretical lessons of identity politics to the large body of IR practice in both teaching and policy making. Zalewski and Enloe discuss how the traditional three paradigms into which the great majority of International Relations literature falls—Realism, Pluralism, and Globalism—are largely devoid of any meaningful discussion of the impact of identity dynamics. While Realism has exerted a powerful influence on thinking within the discipline since before the Second World War, its assumptions of sovereign statehood in an anarchic system and the relative search for power work to suppress the subtle workings of identity politics. Further, since conflicts are expected and integrated into Realist theory, there is little incentive to study the hidden relationships behind them. Second, Pluralism has shifted the focus away from the state and created intellectual space for the concepts of interdependency and transnationalism. While this would seem to be a positive step toward the understanding of identity issues, Pluralists have maintained a positivist epistemology that discourages any attempt to poke beneath the surface of politics to find the cultural meanings. Finally, Globalism also introduces actors beyond and within the state, but it tends to operate within a homogenized worldview based on a "capitalist global structure," and thus remains blind to the possibility of multiple perspectives. To summarize: "realists are far too committed to states and military-political affairs; pluralists are far too committed to the empirical nature of transnational processes; structuralists/globalists are far too committed to economics and classes to allow much room for the consideration of questions of identity in international relations."[31]

These mainstream theories are all hampered by their positivist ontologies. They are based on certain assumptions of objectivism and of fixed meanings. The most important outcome of this approach is the belief that theory is generated by the observation of reality and is not a participant in its (social) construction. No useful study of identity can be made if it presupposes the prior existence of an identity and then posits a descriptive theory regarding that identity as an object. Thus, it is no surprise that IR theory has come so late to the social science theory-fest on the construction of identity and has been so helpless in the face of rampant clashes of culture. Traditional ontological commitments have proved a stumbling block to analyzing multiple perspectives and cultural encounters. Postpositivist theories have finally begun to counteract this blind spot of International Relations. The hallmark of such theories is their express realization that theoretical perspective affects greatly the designation and interpretation of fact. Postpositivist theory is able to question the entrenched assumptions of identity and value and thus gives voice to the silenced and a more responsive answer to moral concerns. Positivist theories have prioritized certain issues and marginalized others, thus excluding many of the questions that are of profound relevance for relations in the international sphere. Zalewski and Enloe explain that the resistance to admitting issues of identity as relevant in the study of IR has actually hampered a sophisticated investigation into key questions:

> The assumption is made that sexual identity or gender identity can have nothing to do with the causation and enactment of war. But although these are just assumptions they do a great deal of work in defining what is and is not relevant to consider. When this ideological commitment is linked with a limited epistemological understanding of the construction of reality, it becomes easy for scholars within international relations to think that such things as the politics of identity can have no real importance to our understanding of the international system.[32]

Such assumptions, as I have already discussed, are not only intellectually confining but also leave us with few options for a normative policy perspective in the face of frequent separatist violence.

Identity with Difference

The simple step taken by Postpositivist scholars in recognizing the implication of theoretical contributions in the construction of reality is actually a giant step in terms of its repercussions for social science. Once this step is taken, the road is paved for a deeper understanding of how identities and differences operate in the political sphere. These dynamics have been deeply explored by political philosopher William Connolly in his seminal study *Identity\Difference: Democratic Negotiations of Political Paradox.* Connolly attributes the need for difference as a component of identity to the human problem of responsibility for evil in this world.

In the Christian tradition, we have refused to allocate blame to god—therefore finding evil in differences that threaten us. Once god has been exempted, evil can be located only in human agency, and those whom we perceive to be nonconforming with the traits of the dominant (moral) identity are evil through responsible choice. This is what Connolly calls the First Problem of Evil. The Second Problem of Evil stems from the development of universal truth so that any idea that questions this universal becomes a profound and intolerable threat. This is "the evil that flows from the attempt to establish security of identity for any individual or group by defining the other that exposes sore spots in one's identity as evil or irrational."[33] Connolly attempts to tease out the features of the dynamic of the second problem of evil in late modern society. Although god is no longer discussed in terms of cultural security, the pattern of ascertaining a responsible human agent for evil remains. This is especially cruel since "no identity is the true identity because every identity is particular, constructed, and relational."[34] Yet, we continue to privilege our own identities as true and capable of purity, and we continue to search for human others upon which to focus the blame, our Nietzschean *resentiment* for the sheer arbitrary helpless contingency of the human condition. Connolly believes that a general perspective, which resists totalitarianism, is possible through a continual resistance to binary oppositions. Binary oppositions pertaining to identity might include, for example, good/evil, inside/outside, or secure/insecure. Although critics of such a postmodern stance claim that any general approach—such as the assumption that binary oppositions are problematic—must presuppose truth, Connolly replies that the concept of truth does not necessarily contradict his approach since truth does not have to be singular. "[T]here is no necessity that what must be presupposed as true at one moment must then be validated as unquestionable at the next or that what must be presumed in one gesture is unsusceptible to self-problematization in another. . . . The point is to refuse to curtail thinking in the name of guarding the faith."[35] The recognition that there can be many truths opens the door to a perception of the other that does not necessitate fear of difference as an existential threat.

In fact, as discussed above, difference is absolutely necessary to an identity. "These differences are essential to its being. If they did not coexist as differences, it would not exist in its distinctness and solidity."[36] This requirement of difference is precisely what makes identity such an insecure experience—it is constantly subject to the resistance of others to the categories ascribed to them. Connolly describes the paradox of identity by saying that an identity may be secured only through the repression of otherness, and any recognition of the validity of difference requires the sacrifice of the secure identity.[37] Given the constant presence of difference and ambiguity in the late modern age, any attempt to secure an identity must fail or require tremendous efforts of repression. Connolly's approach resonates as an explanation of the drive to ethnically cleanse territories perceived as national properties. This is the application of the paradox of identity by means of military violence to crush difference out of existence. But such attempts to secure a national identity must fail, for identity can never be truly secured—not by violence, not by state action, and certainly not by territorial sovereignty. Identity cannot be secured because it requires a constant engagement with the other and a constant mediation with difference. It is the intertwining rather than the opposition of identity and difference that needs to be recognized in politics today. Recognizing the need of the self for the definition and understanding provided by the other gives rise to respect—even among those who are at war with each other. The recognition of otherness as valid and necessary allows for acceptance rather than the need for annihilation. It is the need to annihilate relative truths in favor of a single absolute *real* truth, which still haunts the modernist legacy.

Connolly does not reject the need for or existence of stable social forms. In fact, social institutions form another paradox: humans require common social forms to function, but any kind of social institution requires some subjugation and cruelty. In other words, for every standard of the normal or the common there will be innocent individuals or groups which fall outside of it. But Connolly sees politics as a means of stretching and confronting these gaps and ambiguities, and in his eyes, "a society that enables politics as this ambiguous medium is a good society because it enables the paradox of difference to find expression in public life."[38] He also makes the point that since it is clear that there is no natural utopian plan for human existence which we can simply discover and implement, the best system we might attempt is a "politics of agonism" which recognizes difference and accepts it as valid. The first step in this system is to cease the insistence on harmony, since it tends to produce dogmatic results, and to give up any belief in one's own identity as primordial or deep. Connolly posits that "[i]f I take my identity to be chosen or deep *essentially*, I am likely to take you to share those traits too. There is a powerful pressure to interpret differences in your conduct through the categories of bad faith, false consciousness, innocence, deviation, sickness, and evil."[39] It is precisely this result that he wishes to avoid; but he cannot do so by advocating a singular counter-truth. Connolly's goal for politics is that it become the "medium for the enunciation of suppressed alternatives and the contestation of entrenched commonalities."[40] Thus, he does not seek to bring everyone to his own conclusions—it will be enough if there is space in the political realm for the expression of difference. And the political realm which permits multiple interpretations and locations is not one which is "fractured," contrary to contemporary pundits, but rather it is one which more truly protects the freedoms of both individuals and groups.

There is much to be gleaned from Connolly's understandings of the operation of identity formation. The most important lesson perhaps is the need to embrace ambiguity and recognize the validity of different perspectives. In terms of political science research, the prevailing assumptions of the historical stability of national identity must be questioned and the underpinnings exposed. Despite the presentation of a united front, every national identity contains a multiplicity of practices within it. If these multiplicities are teased out and realized, it promotes a politics of awareness and recognition rather than one of exclusion and protection. Although it is analyzed textually in detail in the next chapter, the case of Québec's secessionist agitation serves as an introduction to the contradictions inherent in the operating concepts of statehood and national identity.

Assuming Identity—The Case of Québec

Many who have proposed theories of secession as a right have done so on the assumption that group identities are a valuable good and should be protected when under threat. But what exactly are identities? Certainly they cannot be protected or preserved without some understanding of how they operate. Although they are an inseparable part of each human being, and therefore necessarily bound up in our conceptions of the good, can identities be secured? Is it desirable to do so? Because national (and other) identities are stabilized collectively through shared understandings of particularity and a perceived common past, the security of an identity (whether individual or collective) cannot take place without the control of its history. In other words, we must essentialize a certain history of ourselves or our nation to maintain it as an unchanging good. However, the processes involved in making such a (truth) claim give off a distinct odor of totalitarian "cleansing" and the worst excesses of religious zealotry. Such nation-building processes do not allow for contradictory—or even various—versions of the collective history to flourish. It is this hidden side to the securing of identity that brings an ironic resonance to liberalism's support for the "right" to group identity. How can collective identities be guaranteed? They can be so only if they are assumed to be fixed. This chapter is far from an argument for a global assimilationist project. Rather, it seeks to demonstrate the hidden contradictions in the commonly accepted understandings of national identity and the "rights" attached to its maintenance.

In teasing out the arguments of those making claims for a right of cultural preservation, it is revealing to look at a case which is actually made on these assumptions. The fixedness of identity is never overtly discussed, and this is exactly why the arguments seem coherent at first. A prime example is the liberal/political discussion concerning the secessionist movement in Québec. While there has been some popular resistance to the very idea of a secession taking place in wealthy, liberal democratic North America, most liberal theories cannot offer an explanation of why the Québécois should not be able to freely decide to become independent. After all, Québec does have a distinct identity within Canada, and it has a history as a well-defined semiautonomous province, so why not? Aside from the basic notion of the social contract and consent, the secession of Québec has also been supported on the grounds of self-determination and the right to a cultural identity. Kai Nielsen argues, for example, that the case of Québec is very clear: "The society or nation that is Quebec can rightly form a nation-state if it chooses. . . . This comes in this circumstance essentially to majority determination. That decision can be made and that state formed without violating anyone's rights."[41] In a rather odd conception of rights and majority voting, Nielsen seems to suggest that it is perfectly unproblematic to allow a distinct minority of a state population to secede on the basis of a simple majority vote, thus creating a further minority (made up of those who voted no as well as those with a different national identity) in the new state. Apparently, as long as the newly created minorities are protected in their turn, no wrong has been done. According to Nielsen, any other conclusion is "individualism gone mad."[42] One may argue that in the case of Québec the distinctness of the Francophone identity is under such consistent assault from Anglophone culture that any unfairness for the non-Francophones caught up in the new state is overshadowed by the need to give the Québécois identity its chance. One may argue this way and have a point. But Nielsen actually denies any unfairness to anyone at all on the basis of a simple majority vote. This is simple democracy at its most simple. These arguments clearly imply that the identity of the Québécois is something concrete enough to be physically delineated in the form of a state. Ironically, since he argues on the basis of protecting the distinctness of the Québec identity, Nielsen shows a careless disregard for how identities are made and kept. As R. E. Ewin points out in his critique of Nielsen, "[t]he issue of Quebecois secession requires that the Quebecois be considered, not merely as persons, but as a people. What makes them a people means that we cannot simply ignore the history of how they came to be where they are and go ahead and treat the issue as one dealing with Canada as a momentary time-slice."[43] Ewin's point here is that group relations are complex and contextual over time and space, and arguing that there is a prima facie right to secession, as Nielsen does, seriously underestimates the importance of this dynamic.

The dangers of a simplified theory that fails to account for the formation of identity came into brutally clear focus in 1995 when the referendum on Québec yielded the extremely close result of 51 percent/49 percent at the polls.[44] While these numbers perhaps make for a well-balanced parliamentary debate on a matter of civic importance, they are harbingers of doom where national identity and the state are concerned. The obvious counterfactual suggests itself. What would have happened if the numbers had been reversed and 51 percent voted "oui"? As it stands there are large numbers of disenchanted separatists feeling that their "rights" have been denied. They do not live in the state they would choose. But if the new state had come into being on the basis of a majority vote, would the result have been any more fair? Framing the issue of Québec's secession as a matter of a majority vote silences the voices who have a more nuanced outlook on the matter. The decision is cast as yes or no, but those who find themselves in these two camps have many reasons for their decision. Those who make a decision not to secede are cast as the outsiders, the nonnationals, those who have no feelings for the culture that is at stake. Even French speakers who love and respect Québec's unique culture do not belong. The "outsiders" in Québec are actually a plurality of diverse people—not the simple Anglophone obstructionists, but immigrants, businessmen, native Indian tribes, and Francophones who fear disaster. The choice of secession does not allow these identities to flourish with their own validity. Many of these people feel that Québec is their home—but the polarization of the "inside" or "outside" vote leaves them alienated.

What is really at stake here is not the right of a group to have and maintain an identity. It is the means by which they feel entitled to do so. Why is it that the Québécois—who have many protections against assimilation—feel entitled to a state? Nielsen himself concludes that "states are necessary evils, essential instrumentalities for security and the very possibility of something approximating a commodious life."[45] But this is not a conclusion which should be lightly made. Or, rather, having concluded that states are necessary for the good life, Nielsen should provide an argument supporting his connection between a state and a cultural/national identity. What rights does a state ensure for a national group beyond those they are entitled to as members of a democratic federation? Is the ability to make foreign and defense policy so crucial in this era of transnational interdependencies?

Nielsen continues:

> It is indeed true that a people can have a sense of nation without having a nation-state, but what is also true is that this national consciousness, and the identities that go with it are, under modern conditions, only secure when people with these national identities gain control of the conditions of their existence by having the power that goes with having their own state: a state which protects and actively furthers these national aspirations. Multi-cultural or multi-national states have not worked very well.[46]

Nielsen's assertions place the majority of the world's peoples in a position to feel that their national identities are under threat. It is no slip of the pen that causes Nielsen to associate the need for a national state with modernity. The modern evocation of the territorial sovereign imperative has already been discussed. But instead of accepting this framework as an undeniable given, one which is obvious and immovable, the role of the modern state should be examined closely and critically. Does the state provide the security that we think it does? Furthermore, there is a hidden subtext in this argument which is easy to overlook. People with a sense of national consciousness want the "control" and the "power" that go (or are perceived to go) with a modern state. They will feel insecure if "their state is controlled by foreigners."[47] If this argument ultimately hinges on power and control, it should not be allowed to masquerade as an issue of fundamental human rights. We all have needs as social beings, and meeting these needs requires an identity which allows us to feel part of a continuous whole. But how can liberal philosophy sustain the argument that our collective national identities require the exertion of power and control—particularly a monopoly on the use of force, which is the difference a state makes—to be validated? The important point here is that "power" and "control" are not to be exerted *on* the self, but *by* the self against others. This is the goal of national identities in search of a state because this is what an international border provides—the power to make decisions which affect the "other" by defining and controlling it. When Nielsen argues that a people need control over their own destiny, he neglects to fully parse the implications of that operation. How can a group control its destiny without causing serious ramifications for nonmembers of the group who happen to be in its path? Indeed, if Québec secedes, the effects will reach far beyond its territorial borders. It is this search for "national" control of destiny which has led to the fiercest territorial conflicts of recent years.

There might be some justification for this perspective if national identities were sharply and irrevocably fixed and determinable, and membership could never be an issue. But such a view would require that nations perceive themselves almost as separate species—unmixable and with permanent, objective, identifying characteristics. This would remove national identity from the social and place it squarely in the realm of the biological. The reality of the matter is infinitely (and thankfully) more complex than that. Instead, inclusion in national groups is subjective and changeable, and the self-perception of the group as a whole is contingent on the time and space of global social relations. Modern cultures, as Tamir describes, "need not necessarily be the linear continuation of long historical traditions beginning in the rural practices of small, closed communities entrenched in an ethos of the soil. They can be urban, open, and democratic, even populistic."[48] Given the multiple options for interpreting a national culture, the criteria for membership are based on choice.

The important criteria of membership, then, is not any kind of fixed feature or activity but rather participation in the ongoing practices and interpretations of a particular culture, since "at any given time, different cultural interpretations compete for recognition within each nation. Membership in the cultural community would then be expressed by participating in this debate, rather than by following one specific interpretation."[49] Cultural membership on the basis of participation allows for multiple loyalties and identities which reflect the true possibilities of modern lifestyles. Individuals may identify with the group into which they were born, or associate more closely with one of several cultural groups of which their extended family is made, or feel truly "multicultural" on the individual level. In addition, a person might "go native" through marriage or business or educational associations. This diversity of valid possibilities allows for a confusing but appealing contingency in the making of the self and the collective. But it also provides a kind of freedom in its very indeterminateness. How free is the individual who resides in a (liberal?) national state where his identity is "protected" in a way which locks him forever into his group and that group's interpretations of acceptable and unacceptable behavior? If we assume that "foreigners" and "outsiders" are a fixed and definite group, then our own national identities as "insiders" are also finite, determinable, and limited. How else is the national identity to be protected but by creating constraints on the freedom of its members to leave? In fact, there are social constraints on the freedom of the Francophones of Québec who wish to remain unified with Canada. Their national loyalties—hence their identities as Québécois—are as suspect as the rest of those who voted "non" on the referendum.

By refusing to allow for the possibility of alternative views from within their ranks, by presenting an independent Québec as the only possible desirable goal, Francophone separatists are creating "outsiders" within and among themselves. This policy creates internal borders and makes foreigners out of those living within the (proposed) state.[50] Such insistence on clear dichotomies of choice rely on what Iris Young calls "difference as otherness," a logic of identity which sees groups as "mutually exclusive, categorically opposed."[51] This logic does not allow for the overlap and mutual constitution of identities, but rather sees them as necessarily opposed. Not only is this a deeply antagonistic perspective, but it is demonstrably incorrect. Identities seep and blend and bounce into and against one another. To view them as impermeable harmfully simplifies a delicately complex and unpredictable process. Thus, "the attempt to demarcate clear and permanent boundaries between things or concepts will always founder on the shifts in context, purpose and experience that change the relationships or the perspectives describing them."[52] The separatist Francophone identity is both dependent on and intermingled with the various other groups of Québec: Anglophones, native Indians, and immigrants. Further, the Francophone identity itself contains ambiguous members—those who are nonseparatist, among others. Instead of the logic of difference as otherness, Young suggests a relational conception of difference in which "a group exists and is defined as a specific group only in social and interactive relation to others," so "group identity is not a set of objective facts, but the product of experienced meanings."[53] In this sense, group membership is always ambiguous and never capable of absolute definition. This is not to say that there are no recognizable social groups, or that group identity is not a necessary aspect of individual and collective existence. Young describes the positive aspects of separatism as calling attention to the particularities of the dominant group and forcing them to confront their own supposed cultural neutrality. It also provides a disadvantaged group with a focal point for political solidarity, giving it increased ability to achieve steps toward relief from oppressive policies. However, ultimately, separatist politics depend upon an exclusivist logic of identity—one which attempts to surround and secure a "pure" identity—and must result in a continued cycle of absolutist rather than compromising politics.

Identity politics, and especially those of separatism, hinge on the ability to control one's history. As Friedman acutely points out, since "history is the discourse of identity, the question of who 'owns' or appropriates the past is a question of who is able to identify him- or herself and the other at any given time and place."[54] Thus, the question in Québec hinges on how the different groups perceive both themselves and the members of the other group(s) in historical context. The separatist identity clings to a concept of Frenchness based on descent from the French settlers of the seventeenth century. The domineering policies of the British after wresting control of the colony from France in the eighteenth century provoked a nationalist rebellion as early as 1837, which was suppressed. French Canadians, then, draw on a history of alienation and repression in the constitution of their identity, which is formed in opposition to the concept of the English and Englishness. In fact, the French Canadians and Anglo Canadians of today are distinctly different from their continental cousins across the Atlantic. Canadians of both cultural groups have developed in relation to one another such that the Francophones would not be who they are without their history of living on a primarily Anglophone continent, and the Anglophones are distinctly different from their British counterparts who have lived without the experience of more than two centuries with a strong internal Francophone minority.

Indeed, it would be difficult to identify the French of the early Québec period as French at all. When Papineau led his rebellion in 1837, thus reflecting a developed sense of "national" identity in Québec, the unity of the European French identity was itself highly questionable. It was not until after the French Revolution that the state of disunity of the French identity became clear, and the leaders began to implement educational changes to eliminate the variety of patois and local customs that had caused many in the south of the country to see the French as foreigners. "If one's home happened to be in the south, then one could get to France by traveling toward Loire and Seine."[55] Even in the mid-nineteenth century, there were still an impressive number of citizens who did not speak French: twenty-four out of the eighty-nine departments contained a majority of communes that were not French speaking. In fact, many Frenchmen "did not know that they belonged together until the long didactic campaigns of the later nineteenth century told them they did, and their own experience as conditions changed told them that this made sense."[56] So what becomes of the precious and threatened "Frenchness" of the Québécois? If modern France was not even recognizable as a nation to its inhabitants until the early part of the twentieth century, what is the source of the historic identity of the Francophone Canadians? It is just that—they are Canadians as well as Francophones. The development of contemporary Québécois identity cannot be divorced from its history on the North American continent—including the history of contentious relations with the British Empire and Anglophone Federalist government. In attempting to preserve their identities as *separate* rather than *different*, the secessionists in Québec (and in general) deny the debt they owe to others (Anglophones, immigrants, and Native Americans) for the identity they wish to keep "pure." By denying the contribution of the other, separatist identities thus deny a part of themselves.

In the next chapter, I analyze the textual narratives of secessionist groups with the purpose of exposing the mechanisms used in unifying identities as part of the justification for separation from the other. This analysis of the performativity of language in the creation of identity relations is a necessary illustration of the relevance of the above discussion of territoriality and identity in the secessionist imperative.

Notes

1. Yael Tamir, *Liberal Nationalism* (Princeton: Princeton University Press, 1993), 149.

2. R. B. J. Walker, "Security, Sovereignty, and the Challenge of World Politics," *Alternatives* 15 (1990): 14, 3-27.

3. Walker Connor, *Ethnonationalism: The Quest for Understanding* (Princeton: Princeton University Press, 1994), 69-70.

4. For example, Donald Horowitz, with his extensive coverage of various ethnic conflicts, in Ethnic Groups in Conflict, only achieves a classification system rather than any truly predictive criteria. See chapter 2, Why the Patient Cannot Be Cured.

5. Connor, *Ethnonationalism*, 197 (emphasis in original).

6. Erik Ringmar, "On the Ontological Status of the State," in *European Journal of International Relations* 2, no. 4 (1996): 453, 439-466.

7. An obvious illustration of this is also the most brutal example: namely, the unwillingness of the Nazis to concede to Jews any role other than that of pestilence that must be eliminated—which left Jews little choice in creating their own story beyond the roles of martyrdom and victimhood.

8. Conversations with the author, Spring 1995.

9. Even then, they cannot be impervious to the urban ways of the "outsiders" living all around them, and for their own physical protection even the Amish have had to make concessions to the modernized existence of others around them, such as adding electric lights and blinkers to their buggies when driving amongst automobile traffic.

10. Thomas M. Franck, "Tribe, Nation, World: Self-Identification in the Evolving International System," *Ethics & International Affairs* 11 (1997): 161, 151-169.

11. Franck, "Tribe, Nation, World," 165.

12. See Will Kymlicka, "Modernity and Minority Nationalism: Commentary on Thomas Franck," *Ethics & International Affairs* 11 (1997): 171-176. Kymlicka argues that both America and France used exclusivist (illiberal) methods of ethnic nationalism to unify the nations linguistically and culturally.

13. Franck, "Tribe, Nation, World," 167-168.

14. Isaiah Berlin, "The Bent Twig: A Note on Nationalism," *Foreign Affairs* 51, no. 1 (October 1972): 28, 11-30.

15. Kymlicka, "Modernity and Minority Nationalism," 176.

16. Kymlicka, "Modernity and Minority Nationalism," 175.

17. Iris Marion Young, "Together in Difference: Transforming the Logic of Group Political Conflict," in *The Rights of Minority Cultures*, ed. Will Kymlicka (Oxford: Oxford University Press, 1995), 158.

18. Tamir, *Liberal Nationalism*, 30.

19. Isaiah Berlin, *The Crooked Timber of Humanity* (New York: Alfred A. Knopf, 1991), 14.

20. K. Anthony Appiah and Amy Gutmann, *Color Conscious: The Political Morality of Race* (Princeton: Princeton University Press, 1996), 175.

21. David Campbell, "Violent Performances: Identity, Sovereignty, Responsibility," in *The Return of Culture and Identity in IR Theory*, ed. Yosef Lapid and Friedrich Kratochwil (Boulder: Lynne Rienner, 1996), 173-174.

22. Yosef Lapid, "Culture's Ship: Returns and Departures in International Relations Theory," in *The Return of Culture and Identity in IR Theory*, ed. Yosef Lapid and Friedrich Kratochwil (Boulder: Lynne Rienner, 1996), 6.

23. Marysia Zalewski and Cynthia Enloe, "Questions about Identity in International Relations," in *International Relations Theory Today*, ed. Ken Booth and Steve Smith (Cambridge: Polity Press, 1995), 281.

24. Zalewski and Enloe, "Questions about Identity," 282.

25. Naeem Inayatullah and David L. Blaney, "Knowing Encounters: Beyond Parochialism in International Relations Theory," in *The Return of Culture and Identity in IR Theory*, ed. Yosef Lapid and Friedrich Kratochwil (Boulder: Lynne Rienner, 1996), 81.

26. Carol Cohn, "Wars, Wimps, and Women: Talking Gender and Thinking War," in *Gendering War Talk*, ed. Miriam Cooke and Angela Woollacott (Princeton: Princeton University Press, 1993), 227.

27. Cohn, "Wars, Wimps, and Women," 231.

28. Zalewski and Enloe, "Questions about Identity," 290-291.

29. For a fascinating analysis of the Vietnam War in these terms see Jennifer Milliken and David Sylvan, "Soft Bodies, Hard Targets, and Chic Theories: US Bombing Policy in Indochina," *Millennium: Journal of International Studies* 25, no. 2 (1996): 321-359.

30. Zalewski and Enloe, "Questions about Identity," 293.

31. Zalewski and Enloe, "Questions about Identity," 297.

32. Zalewski and Enloe, "Questions about Identity," 301.

33. William E. Connolly, *Identity\Difference: Democratic Negotiations of a Political Paradox* (Ithaca: Cornell University Press, 1991), 8.

34. Connolly, *Identity\Difference*, 46.

35. Connolly, *Identity\Difference*, 60-61.

36. Connolly, *Identity\Difference*, 64.

37. Connolly, *Identity\Difference*, 66.

38. Connolly, *Identity\Difference*, 94.

39. Connolly, *Identity\Difference*, 117.

40. Connolly, *Identity\Difference*, 121.

41. Kai Nielsen, "Secession: The Case of Quebec," *Journal of Applied Philosophy* 10, no.1 (1993): 30, 29-43.

42. Nielsen, "The Case of Quebec," 30.

43. R. E. Ewin, "Peoples and Secession," *Journal of Applied Philosophy* 11, no. 2 (1994): 229, 225-231.

44. Actually, the results were even closer: 50.58 percent voted to stay in the Canadian federation, while 49.42 percent voted for independence.

45. Nielsen, "The Case of Quebec," 30.

46. Nielsen, "The Case of Quebec," 32.

47. Nielsen, "The Case of Quebec," 33.

48. Tamir, *Liberal Nationalism*, 51.

49. Tamir, *Liberal Nationalism*, 51.

50. See Roxanne Lynn Doty, "The Double-Writing of Statecraft: Exploring State Responses to Illegal Immigration," *Alternatives* 21 (1996): 171-189.

51. Iris Marion Young, "Together in Difference," 158.

52. Iris Marion Young, "Together in Difference," 159.

53. Iris Marion Young, "Together in Difference," 161.

54. Jonathan Friedman, "The Past in the Future: History and the Politics of Identity," *American Anthropologist* 94, no. 4 (1992): 854, 837-859.

55. Eugen Weber, *Peasants into Frenchmen: The Modernization of Rural France, 1870-1914* (Stanford: Stanford University Press, 1976), 98. Weber explains that in patois a river did not have the definite article because it was treated as a person, hence "toward Loire and Seine," 93.

56. Weber, *Peasants into Frenchmen*, 113.

Chapter 5

Secessionist Performances, Narrating Otherness

Chapters 3 and 4 expose the impossibility of stabilizing identity and territorializing politics; this chapter examines the logical expression of these social assumptions in the narratives produced by the leaders of secessionist movements. Analysis of these texts shows the extent to which secessionists take their identities as both historically and territorially circumscribed. In the framing of their historical origins, secessionists demarcate social and territorial boundaries to present a separate state as the only plausible institutional manifestation of their nationhood. This chapter explores in detail the secessionist narratives of three contemporary separatist movements: the Québec Sovereigntists, Padania's Lega Nord, and The Kanaka Maoli of Hawaii. The point of this textual combing is to demonstrate the consequences of modernist assumptions about political identity and territory—the assumptions upon which secessionist claims are based—and to reveal the linguistic processes of the politicization of identity that all such claims must involve. Secessionist narratives employ reiterated accounts of counteridentity to bolster the social and cultural boundaries of the secessionist group against the majority identity of the state. The point is to frame statehood as the only plausible institutional manifestation of these boundaries. The assertion made here is that this social boundary drawing cannot occur without socially forcing the exclusion of groups within and without the secessionist identity. By definition, secessionists must try to exert rigid control over the identity of the group—they must police the boundaries (socially and territorially) of the separatist nation to justify its separation from the state. But also by definition, secessionists must be antipluralist; if secessionists allow a multicultural conception of their identity to take hold, their argument for separateness is doomed to fail.

It is crucial to note that these analyses are not meant to be an exercise in the comparative approach. The goal here is emphatically not to compare each case to a template looking for compliance and divergence with some arbitrary standard of legitimacy or definition. Neither causality nor validity of claims is the point here. Rather, the aim is to show that there is a secessionist logic underlying these documents and speeches that springs from the constraints imposed by perceptions of the modernist international order. Ironically, in their attempts to differentiate themselves, secessionist leaders inadvertently reveal the infinite contingency of social identity. The very diversity of claims—from the Frenchness of Québec to the industrial prowess of Padania, to the pure bloodlines of the Kanaka Maoli—upon which secessionists base their difference, even while pursuing similar rhetorical devices, illustrates the endless array of potential focal points for identity politicization. These three examples were chosen for ease of access and current application; the choice is acknowledged to be somewhat arbitrary and thus should not be taken as an indication that these cases belong together as examples of single or contrasting categories within secessionist narrative literature. However, that is not to say that certain resemblances are irrelevant. These particular cases are interesting, for example, because they happen to be located within Western liberal democratic states. It is a common misunderstanding that separatism and ethnic conflict occur in unstable, underdeveloped, or repressive countries. This understanding of secession also assumes the accuracy and utility of causal analysis as a problem-solving method. But the stubborn existence of secessionist groups in North America and Europe presents a delicious irony: economic stability and political freedoms are no protection from the secessionist imperative. The politics of identity and difference operate throughout liberal as well as totalitarian societies. Apart from their location within the broad social category of the West, the other singular common feature of these three cases is that they insist upon the ultimate goal of sovereign independence.

It is hoped that careful reading of these secessionist stories will highlight the process of the linguistic performance of secessionist politics—how the histories of the groups are told in ways that create, validate, and maintain them as political entities. Secessionists offer a separate discourse of political identity to counter what they perceive to be the oppression and marginalization by the dominant discourses of the majority. But in offering their counternarrative, secessionists reproduce the patterns of social power and influence that spurred their separatism in the first place. In other words, secessionist narratives show in stark relief the ongoing processes of social differentiation deployed by discourses of power in any society. In their telling of a separate identity, these narratives are re-creating the process that excluded them in the first place. So, this chapter does not attempt an analysis in search of causal patterns for secessionist activity. Such approaches have already been attempted, and they rely on assumptions that directly contradict those of this book.[1] Specifically, a broad comparative approach must assume that there are ahistorical and acultural patterns to political behavior that can be discerned if the sampling is wide enough and deep enough. Under a comparative approach, no attempt is made to distinguish historical revolutions from modern guerrilla or terrorist warfare, or to understand secession as a historically dependent phenomenon. In direct contradiction, this book maintains that secession can be understood only as a by-product of the modern system of territorialized political identities and that the processes of creating and maintaining social and political boundaries must be understood before its effects can be dealt with meaningfully.

Legalizing the Nation

By definition, secessionists attempt to create a state based on a single identity group. Even if the group contains variations within it, there must be a rationale for political separation. Self-determination requires a political "self" that must be recognizably separate. The more serious the claim for secession, the more strongly the argument must be made that the secessionists' interests cannot be recognized and protected by the state as a whole. Therefore, these are not neutral or universalist political movements with open arms for all who wish to join. They are specifically aimed at defining and protecting an "inside" group, and no matter how loudly they proclaim that they will protect minorities and remain open to naturalized citizenship, the very basis of their claim to statehood is national identity rather than political freedom. Even before the secessionist state materializes, its very purpose calls into question critical issues of civil and human rights. The nationalist foundations of such states are described by Robert Hayden as *constitutional nationalism*, in which states are created with "a constitutional and legal structure that privileges the members of one ethnically defined nation over other residents."[2] As Hayden explains, this structure does not necessarily result in overt discrimination; rather, it is based on a vision of the state as the embodiment of self-determination for a particular nation, and thus the sovereignty of the state resides with the members of that nation and no one else. While Hayden takes the new republics of the former Yugoslavia as his example, his description also applies to secessionist movements, since they are based on obtaining sovereignty for a specifically defined national group and not an identity-neutral body of citizens. The language Hayden discusses from the constitutions of the former Yugoslav republics strongly resembles that of secessionist texts since they are effectively trying to achieve the same thing—legal entrenchment of political identity. For example, the preliminary section of the Croatian constitution mentions among its "Basic Sources" the "thousand year national independence and state continuity of the Croatian nation" and the "historical right of the Croatian nation to full state sovereignty."[3] The document continues, asserting that Croatia is "established as the national state of the Croatian nation and the state of the members of other nations and minorities that live within it."[4] While such language may not seem at odds with the tenets of a liberal democratic state, it actually enshrines the principles of ethnic nationalism into the state's founding document. Hayden further stipulates that the term "Croatian nation" in this context has an ethnic rather than a political meaning in the native tongue. So the state is legally created as the embodiment of a national group with closed social boundaries. He also discusses similar passages in the constitutions of Slovenia, Serbia, and Bosnia-Herzegovina, but his most important point is that European democracy and the principle of self-determination are incompatible.

The tragedy of Yugoslavia, as Hayden explains, was that the chauvinist politics of the seceding republics were accepted as democratic by Europe and the United States on the basis of the principle of self-determination. But failing to recognize the inherent contradiction between democracy and national self-determination as a political ideology only perpetuates the continued agitation of separatist groups with exclusionist (and sometimes cleansing) tendencies. Indeed, the states created out of the former Yugoslavia all continue to deal with serious ethnic divisions and claims, some more peacefully than others. Self-determination in the constitutional national-ism sense is not the neutral guarantee of political freedom mentioned in United Nations declarations and covenants. It "establishes and attempts to protect the construction of a nation as a bounded unity: a sovereign being with its own defining language, culture and perhaps 'biological essence,' the uniqueness of which must be defended at any cost."[5] This kind of uniqueness is not the harmless neutrality of open citizenship, but rather the harbinger of institutionalized repression of identity. For example, some of the citizenship laws enacted in the former Yugoslav republics grant special rights to ethnic members of the nation who are nonresident, effectively giving them citizenship by virtue of ethnic heritage alone. These laws are accompa-nied by exceptionally rigid naturalization laws for nonnational residents (some of whom have resided in the country many years) who wish to become citizens.[6] Thus, "Constitutional nationalism . . . builds a massive structural flaw into the polity that it is meant to define, since the permanent exclusion of minorities will likely make them at best indifferent and at worst hostile to the state."[7] Such efforts to identify and protect a separatist state are then likely to engender further secessionist agita-tion from their own minorities who have been newly defined outside of the sover-eign nation.

Secessionist activities tend to generate further political separatism since they are based on two incompatible principles of international law: the concepts of national self-determination and the sanctity of state territorial boundaries. Because national self-determination involves a continual process of discrimination between members and nonmembers, it always contains within itself the seeds of further conflict. By defining its territorial sovereignty on the basis of the sovereignty of the people who are members of a specific nation, constitutional nationalists—and secessionist movements—deny equality to people who are not members of the legalized nation. The results can only be further unrest by groups who have been "minoritized" by this excluding process. Also, since the international political model remains one in which territorial states are the only legitimate actors, any organized alienated groups will logically seek the goal of an independent territorial state for themselves. It is no simple coincidence that each of the secessionist cases analyzed below contains the germ of further agitation from internal groups which will become *minoritized* if the movements succeed.

Language as Politics

Before the introducing any secessionist texts, it is important to clarify the impact of narrative itself as a political act. Regardless of the many forms in which they may be told, the historical narratives of national groups have powerful effects upon both the tellers and the listeners. Secessionist leaders exert a kind of power in their telling of the nation. As Michael Toolan puts it:

> narrators are typically *trusted* by their addressees. In seeking and being granted rights to a lengthy verbal contribution . . . narrators assert their authority to tell, to take up the role of knower, or entertainer, or producer, in relation to the address-ees' adopted role of learner or consumer. To narrate is to make a bid for a kind of power.[8]

The power of the narrator is especially enhanced in the telling of national history, a story with a claim of existential importance. Secessionist leaders exert political authority as narrators of the nation, telling the national identity as distinctive and worthy of statehood. Secessionist stories tell the past as distinctive and glorious, and the future as one of sovereign independence. But in doing so, they suspend the nation between past and future—as something that is somehow never realized in the present. As William Connolly writes:

> A nation is something that has been or will be but never is at any actually existing moment. Its most fervent advocates today imagine it to be something that has been lost, must be (re)instated, or both. Its promise as future unity is thus defined less by positive exemplification than by marking a set of constituencies who deviate from it.[9]

In the cases below the addressees are primarily those who will be included within the identity-generating narrative, but they are also those who will become marginal-ized as outsiders within the secessionist state. Stories of nationality explicitly claim the authority to draw boundaries around social groups. They both unify and divide as they provide historical criteria for the inclusion of some and the exclusion of others from the national group. These narratives constitute acts of power. They "act upon people" in two ways: "either by informing them and so modifying their perceptions or by defining them and so modifying the ways in which they are perceived by others."[10] National narratives produce a double effect: one may have one's own perceptions modified at the same time that others perceive a modified view of one. Secessionist narratives operate in exactly this way—telling stories of the struggles of a separate people who will finally triumph when they achieve sovereign statehood. At the same time, the texts define the membership of a seced-ing group and by implication create a category of all others as *not* of that group.

Thus, secessionist narratives exert considerable power; they are *acts* with political effects.

As J. G. A. Pocock describes in his discussion of the politics of speech, no one's speech is strictly his or her own. Because language is so contextual and institutionalized, it is not possible to utter a statement with a completely pure meaning. Further, no statement can be purely attributable to its author. Our language, both in utterance and understanding, is made up of words that have been formed "by sedimentation and institutionalization of the utterances performed by others whose identities and intentions may no longer be precisely known."[11] Our words, then, are only "borrowed" from countless others who have used and contributed to their meaning in the past. Language acts "have been preinstitutionalized; they must be performed by institutionalized means . . . . [I]nstitutionalization makes my language available to the person to or about whom I speak for purposes of reply and refutation; he can, as we put it, answer me in my terms."[12] The application of this concept to the secessionist situation indicates the extent to which secessionists are both impelled and limited by the institutionalized setting in which they exist. This setting is one in which the language of politics is institutionalized in terms of territorial sovereignty. If they wish to be recognized as legitimate political actors, secessionists must literally speak in terms of sovereignty and the nation-state. The international sphere has been narrated with the language of sovereignty, democracy, territorial states, and national self-determination. Each of these words has an institutionalized contextual meaning that has come to limit the way in which a people may perceive themselves and be perceived. In the institutionalized practice of the international sphere, a people who see themselves as distinct have only two choices: that of being a sovereign nation with a territory or that of remaining a "minority" within the sovereign state of another distinct people.[13] Given the starkness of these options, it is not surprising that despite their ambiguity, terms such as "sovereignty" and "self-determination" are interpreted by secessionists in their most absolute sense.

The politics of speech must be understood as a two-directional action. According to Pocock, the intersubjectivity of language determines that there can never be an act of self-definition that is entirely pure. Identities can be located only by reference to others. Charles Taylor calls this a crucial feature of the self: "One is a self only among other selves. A self can never be described without reference to those who surround it."[14] This is critical to our understanding of the politics of self-determination.

> Now clearly [a nation] cannot say "we" without redistributing a number of other human beings among the categories "we," "you," and "they". To do this to people can have very considerable consequences for them. . . . Liberation, even, that image of such potency in the contemporary sensibility, involves an act of power over others: a speech-act by which I define myself is performed in another's universe and redefines him as well as me.[15]

Self-determination must also involve *other-determination* and thus constitutes an attack on the others' political understanding of themselves. This is not to argue that social boundaries and identity definition are harmful per se, but rather that institutionalizing these boundaries within the territorial sovereignty of the state perpetuates the politics of identification by exclusion rather than by encounter with the Other. Secessionist groups cause a redefinition not only of the boundaries of the parent state, but also of the social boundaries of the rest of the world. When Croatia and Slovenia seceded from Yugoslavia, they redefined themselves as national groups with international standing, and the rest of the international community was redefined as containing the actors "Croatia" and "Slovenia." Furthermore, the national identities recognized as sovereign were redefined from those of a world in which "Croatian and Slovenian" were subsumed under "Yugoslavian" (and the rest of the world could claim a non-Yugoslavian identity), to one in which being non-Yugoslav did not rule out the possibility of being Croatian or Slovenian (and the rest of the world recognized itself as not just non-Yugoslavian, but also non-Croatian and non-Slovenian). All this still leaves out the difficulties of redefinition for the many members of nonsovereign groups within the newly defined areas.

Performing the Nation

Identities are necessary to all of us, so why should secessionist identity narratives pose any problem? Even while secessionist narrators assert their authority to tell us of their nation's history and cause, we (the nonsecessionist listeners) also exert authority in our willingness to accept (or not) the validity of the narrative. Toolan concludes that "the ultimate authority for ratifying a text as a narrative rests not with the teller but with the perceiver/addressee."[16] This suggests that success lies in convincing secessionist rhetoric, but there is a performative element as well. Performing the text—making it true through repeated acting in accordance with its logic (just as an actor makes real the script)—relies upon a normative exchange. Even if the text is recognized as valid the addressee must grant recognition of the moral point of the narrative—the right to sovereign statehood. This is the crucial distinction between narrative and nonnarrative accounts, as Hayden White argues. Narrative necessarily refers to and creates a normative context for the subject. Thus, narrativity "is intimately related to, if not a function of, the impulse to moralize reality, that is, to identify it with the social system that is the source of any morality that we can imagine."[17] Secessionists do not narrate their identities as bland chronologies or even as neutral statements of fact, they write grand epics and ancient histories to create moral authority for their claims to a separate state. These texts are *performative* in the sense that they are discursive practices that produce the effects they name.[18] By continually asserting the terms of their identity, secessionists perform that identity. These performances become more meaningful and more authoritative to the extent that they are repeated and compelled. As Judith Butler explains: "Performativity is thus not a singular 'act,' for it is always a reiteration of a norm or set of norms, and to the extent that it acquires an act-like status in the present, it conceals or dissimulates the conventions of which it is a repetition."[19] Repeated identity performances, then, have the cumulative effect of normalizing their own assertions. The less we question these norms (i.e., the more hidden their performativity), the more successful they become at achieving authority as natural or ideal. This establishes a critical link between performative speech and norms that is helpful in revealing the concealed processes that produce political conventionality. As Cynthia Weber explains:

> Key to understanding the difference between performance and performativity is their connection to normativity, understood as the ongoing citational processes whereby "regular subjects" and "standards of normality" are discursively co-constituted to give the effect that both are natural rather than cultural constructs.[20]

The performative subject cannot be engaged in the citation of norms without being herself created by them. Neither can these norms be resisted or rearticulated except by a subject who has been produced by the norms. This constitutive circle is what Butler calls "The paradox of subjectivation." Where does this leave the reader of secessionist narratives? The task here is both to reveal and to question the extent to which norms of national identity have been essentialized through performative texts. In revealing the underpinnings of secessionist identity performances, we can see that the ideals that secessionists strive to authorize have arisen from the political norms of the current international system. In this sense, we are all implicated in secessionist identity performances even while we reiterate the performances that legitimate our own selves.

An Act Respecting the Future of Québec

On October 30, 1995, the government of the Canadian province of Québec held a provincewide referendum on the question of secession. The word "secession" was not mentioned; rather, the question was posed as one of sovereignty under the terms of a bill, called Bill 1, An Act Respecting the Future of Québec. The bill, subtitled as "Declaration of Sovereignty," included a preamble, a text, and an appendix discussing the schedule of political separation under the terms of the June 12, 1995, agreement among the three secessionist parties. The effect of a yes vote on the bill would have committed the government of Québec to attempt to negotiate a treaty of economic and political partnership with Canada. One year after such negotiations would have begun, the Québec government would have had a mandate to declare Québec's sovereignty, either under the terms of the partnership treaty or after having determined that the negotiations had failed. As is now well-known, the 1995 vote ended with the narrowest of margins in favor of rejecting sovereignty. Nevertheless, the text of Bill 1 provides a rich example of an identity-essentializing narrative performance.

The preamble of Bill 1 consists of about two and a half pages of the reasons why Québec is a nation and why it should be sovereign; the passage ends in a declaration of sovereignty. The preamble is the stuff of great drama—narrated like a Greek tragedy, it contains a monologue of the history of the people, interspersed with songlike choral interludes. It begins:

> **I.** *The time has come to reap the fields of history. The time has come at last to harvest what has been sown for us by four hundred years of men and women and courage, rooted in the soil and now returned to it. The time has come for us, tomorrow's ancestors, to make ready for our descendants harvests that are worthy of the labours of the past. May our toil be worthy of them, may they gather us together at last.[21]*

This opening paragraph provides a clear set of clues about the assumptions and goals of the bill's supporters. It is heavy with territorial import. The agricultural metaphor of toil, sowing, harvest, and reaping creates a strong tie between the Québécois and the territory of Québec. Moreover, there is an element of obligation implied in the references to the ancestors who have labored so hard for four hundred years. It is the honorable choice, the words imply, to vote yes and bring to a culmination all the work of the "ancestors." In fact, this preamble speaks only to the national group of Francophones and excludes both immigrants and English speakers whose ancestors have not "toiled" for independence.

After this opening chorus, the preamble continues to further describe the group for whom the referendum is specifically designed. They are "the pioneers" who had "come from a great civilization" and who "maintained the heritage of France." Despite the "conquest" of 1760, the determination of these pioneers' descendants to "remain faithful to a destiny unique in North America" continued. "Neither attempts at assimilation nor the Act of Union of 1840 could break their endurance." These passages cement an image of the heroes of the narrative: the gritty, hard-working settlers who fought to keep their French identity, despite deliberate assaults on their very Frenchness. This version of Québec history establishes a record of protest against domination, of the constant struggle not to succumb to assimilation, no matter the cost. It describes a clash of cultures in which an embattled minority of French speakers emerges victorious. To the (unnamed) authors' credit, they do acknowledge a debt to non-French peoples: "the First Nations" who further "enriched" their great civilization, the English community "that grew up at their side," and the immigrants "all have contributed to forming this people which became in 1867 one of the two founders of the Canadian federation." But if the native peoples, the English, and the immigrants did contribute to the formation of the Québec people then why does this version of Québec's history exclude their stories?

The preamble continues with a series of points justifying the right of the people of Québec to choose their future. "Because the heart of this land beats in French"— the words resonate. "Because we inhabit territories delimited by our ancestors," and "because for four hundred years we have cleared, ploughed, paced, surveyed, dug, fished, built, started anew, discussed, protected, and loved this land that is cut across and watered by the St. Lawrence River." The insistence on four hundred years of history persists in excluding all who do not spring from the loins of the first French pioneers. Here is the performative "We" in clear relief—the "We" that enacts and creates the Québécois norm. The many histories, longer and shorter than four centuries, that went into the making of today's Québec are written out of the script. The description of the nature of the land and the work done on it shows a surprising deafness to the history and rights of the tribes of the "First Nations." In the story told by this preamble, the land simply had no existence before the pioneers came and called it "Québec." The text here asserts a counterdiscourse to Canada's dominant English—Frenchness will be privileged in Québec. At most, the narrative allows that the natives and the non-French-speaking peoples can claim to have "contributed" to the making of the nation—a helpful, but not formative, role. Meanwhile, those who can comfortably belong to this specific French "We" are exhorted by "the legacy of the struggles and courage of the past" to "take charge of [their] own destiny."

The preamble's attempts to include "all those men and women who inhabit it" among the people of the land of Québec are contradicted by the emphasis on French as the source of uniqueness. The non-Francophones are those who currently feel most threatened by the prospect of an independent Québec. They perceive their interests in self-expression to lie in a multicultural Canada rather than in a French nation that promises to uphold their rights. They also perceive their legal status to be at risk from a change of state governance. More specifically, the native peoples are parties to a treaty with the federal government of Canada respecting their rights and usage of reservation lands. This treaty covers a very large portion of the northern half of Québec province. A secession by the province, the native peoples have warned, would be regarded as a unilateral (and therefore void) change in the terms of the treaty and would not be valid in their eyes. They would, moreover, claim a secession of their own to maintain control over their lands. In the referendum on this bill that took place in October 1995, the English speakers and immigrant population, about 18 to 20 percent of Québec's total, voted solidly no. These people were not convinced by the story of the preamble—the story that excluded them and spoke to a particular national group, privileging it in the founding document of the proposed state. The story the preamble tells, of an obligation to claim sovereignty over the land because "it is this land alone that represents our pride and the source of our strength, our sole opportunity to express ourselves," is a story that performs a particular subject. The people who claim "our pride," "our strength," and "our sole opportunity" for expression, are the "descendants" only of the French. They are the people whose Frenchness has been a baton passed by each generation, who feel that their very selves are imperiled unless they can be guaranteed the materialization of a sovereign (French) state. The language of self-preservation and expression in the preamble speaks only to Francophones. It is only they who feel so fiercely the connection between their cultural preservation and a secessionist state. Native peoples, immigrants, and English speakers, by contrast, cannot identify with the embattled metaphor since their identities are not tied to the story of a French cultural struggle. In fact, these non-French identities fare far better in multicultural federal Canada where they are subsumed in a plurality of identities, and where the state is no longer overtly linked to a particular (subfederal) national identity.

The preamble's second chorus sings:

II. *We know the winter in our souls. We know its blustery days, its solitude, its false eternity and its apparent deaths. We know what it is to be bitten by the winter cold.*

Here seasonal metaphors set the tone for a passage that discusses the difficult times in the history of the Québec people. The images of winter, blustery cold, and "apparent death" narrate the hopelessness and despair of the Québécois, of their thwarted dreams and aspirations to build their own sovereign nation. The story then takes a turn with the entry of Québec into the federation with Anglo-Canada "on the faith of a promise of equality" and "respect for our authority in certain matters that to us are vital." This description of the province entering willingly into a federative union implies that it had a choice, but the territory of Québec had been lost by France in a war with Britain. Thence it became a British territory to be governed as Britain saw fit, which eventually included unifying it with the rest of Canada as one administrative unit. The French-speaking province wished from the beginning to be recognized as "distinct" and vociferously withstood all attempts at assimilation. Although current federal policies requiring bilingualism privilege Francophones beyond the proportion of their numbers within the federation, they continue to long for a status beyond that of one culture among a multitude. They wish to be recognized as "unique," a "distinct society" and an autonomous national group.

At this point, the preamble introduces Anglo-Canada as the villain and tells a tale of betrayal: the arrangements within the federation "did not live up to those early hopes. The Canadian State contravened the federative pact, by invading in a thousand ways areas in which we are autonomous." Attributing a unitary motive of trickery and deceit to the federal government, the preamble declares, "We were hoodwinked in 1982 when the governments and Canada and the English-speaking provinces made changes to the Constitution, in depth and to our detriment, in defiance of the categorical opposition of our National Assembly." These words maintain an assumption of bad faith on the part of "English-speaking" Canada, narrating a conflictual relationship between Francophone and Anglophone, performing distrust. This belies the previous assurances of welcome given to the Anglophone minority of Québec. There can be no clearer statement of othering than that of *We were hoodwinked* by *Them*, the English-speaking provinces. Although the writers and supporters of Bill 1 clearly have no wish to alienate their own non-French minorities, they cannot refrain from narrating Québec the way they see it—as an oppressed nation struggling to break free of the cultural chains of the federalist state. For Québec, anything but total independence is an insult to its greatness. The other stories tied to the history of this province cannot be told without marring the purity of the movement for the liberation of the French "Us."

In the story told by the Québécois, the very presence of the province in an English-speaking country is one of constant threat. Thus, the *We* "reached a decision never again to restrict [themselves] to mere survival but from this time on to build upon [their] difference." And this difference cannot flourish in a plurality but must have the freedom to be pure: "Because we have the deep-seated conviction that continuing within Canada would be tantamount to condemning ourselves to languish and to debasing our very identity." The identity performativity of these words produces profound social divides. These words act upon the people of Québec to create two groups: those who are the "We" of French pioneer ancestry and who therefore *must* vote for independence as an act of self-preservation, and those who are the "Them" of Canada, of plurality, of multiculturalism, who will be excluded from this story of Québec no matter how they vote. By producing the identities it describes, such identity performative language creates and perpetuates social fault lines that are not easily repaired. These groups will remain at odds in Québec for as long as the issue of secession continues to be active, and would certainly have difficulty quietly assimilating within an independent state.

The third and final choral interlude of the preamble reads:

III. *For the men and women of this country who are the warp and weft of it and its erosion, for those of tomorrow whose growth we are now witnessing, to be comes before to have. And this principle lies at the very heart of our endeavour.*

Images of woven fabric and of present and future set the tone here for a segment that elucidates the characteristics which will make the new nation great. It will be the very expression of the identity of the Québec people, an existential necessity regardless of the economic cost. "To be comes before to have." Contextually, this passage could only imply that *being* cannot be expressed in any way other than through a fully independent state.

The preamble continues with a section about the distinctness of French language and culture. "In order that the profound sense of belonging to a distinct people be now and for all time the very bastion of our identity, we proclaim our will to live in a French-language society." The recurring phrase "distinct people" and its dependence on French language and culture reveals assumptions about the nature of the identity cherished by the Québécois. It is an identity that is seen as distinct and therefore as pure. The *will to be French* evinced in this document stems from a shared feeling that Frenchness is something definite, recognizable, fixed, and therefore capable of being adopted as a political agenda. Why else would there be a desperate need for a state? The assumption of the supporters of Bill 1 is that Frenchness is necessary for the identity of the Québec people, and that political sovereignty is necessary to guarantee Frenchness. This is a hidden—but nonetheless present—agenda of constitutional nationalism here

The need to acknowledge the presence of non-French people in Québec surfaces, immediately following the strong declaration of the need for a French identity. But again, the non-French elements of Québec are relegated to the place of supporting roles, definitely not part of the star attraction. The non-French peoples are described as "varied and new contributions" through which "our culture takes on fresh color and amplitude." This is not an acknowledgment that modern Québec's identity is produced through continued contact and mutual absorption of various cultures; it is a statement of toleration under the wing of the French Québec nation. Thus, the purity of Frenchness is preserved, and also enlivened, through contact but not mingling with other cultures. The Québécois see that "It is essential that *we* welcome *them* in such a way that never will these differences be seen as threats or as reasons for intolerance."[22] The non-French cultures are to be made "welcome"—they will be guests, tolerated—part of the state of Québec, but not part of its special Frenchness. Although the nature of the state envisioned by Bill 1 is that of a liberal democracy, it is a mistake to see it (and indeed, liberal democracies in general) as culturally neutral. The whole raison d'être for an independent Québec is one of nationalism and identity. And although the rights of the English-speaking community "will be maintained" and also the rights of the First Nations will be "safeguarded," that does not erase the fact that the state in charge of maintaining and safeguarding them will be one that has an official national identity of Frenchness. This identity is actually mandated under the terms of the bill in the section entitled *The New Constitution*. Clause 7 reads: "The new constitution shall state that Québec is a French-speaking country and shall impose upon the Government the obligation of protecting Québec culture and ensuring its development." Institutionalizing the protection of a national culture in the state's constitution is the hallmark of a nationalist state.

One year after the 1995 referendum, the former leader of the Parti Québécois, Jacques Parizeau, contributed several articles to the newspaper *Le Devoir*. These were translated and published in Toronto by *The Globe and Mail*. In these articles, the secessionist leader clarifies his postreferendum stance and his continued insistence on a vision of a sovereign Québec in the future. In a piece titled "Who Are We? Where Are We Going?" Parizeau reiterates that "We" the people of Québec must have sovereignty: "Québec's sovereignty appears to me necessary for the Québec nation. It must be responsible for itself."[23] Defining it as a simple equation of rights and interests, he states: "Defending one's interests, promoting them, isn't just an option, it's absolutely natural." But Parizeau deliberately simplifies the complex question of *whose* interests and *how* they are to be determined. With the clarity of a purist, he sees the social conflict as normal and acceptable. The behavior of those who voted against secession is "perfectly comprehensible. They prefer to remain part of the Canadian majority rather than becoming a minority in Québec. Their interests dictate this attitude." There is nothing to condemn them for; *their* interests are not *our* interests—the We, the French. For Parizeau this is acceptable, because the We will prevail and the referendum will finally be won: "Afterwards, they will adapt." Thus, with stunning simplicity, the foundations of the secessionist standpoint are laid bare. The *Us* of the nation must have sovereignty to preserve our fixed and definable identity. Others who are not of this identity may contribute to the life of the nation as long as they choose to also preserve and adapt to it. Any other nonnational groups will be allowed to continue as institutionalized minorities with special "protections." However, the identity of "The Nation" will be enshrined in the state.

Parizeau himself answers the question of what is the Québécois nation with the response: "It is constituted essentially of Francophones (whatever their origin), sharing a culture unique to them." In other words, anyone may be a Quebecker—as long as he or she speaks French and joins in the French Québec culture.[24] As for those other elements of the society, the native groups and English speakers, "once sovereignty is achieved they should, at their own pace, integrate themselves into the Québécois nation." The irony of this sentiment seems completely to have escaped Parizeau, who writes it with apparent seriousness. The Québécois must not be assimilated into English-speaking Canada—this is an insult to their very identity, yet English-speaking Canadians should, to be Quebeckers, assimilate into French-speaking Québec. This is natural. Having writhed under the cultural constraints of bilingual Canadian federalism, the Francophone leader feels no compunction about advising the members of Québec's minorities to capitulate. Of course, Parizeau himself does not see it as a question of exclusivity, but of open welcome to membership in the Québec culture: "We need to be responsible for ourselves. There is nothing racist or xenophobic in saying it: A Quebecker is whoever wants to be one. Case closed!"[25] What he does not allow for is the possibility that many people wish to be both Quebeckers and Canadians, or Quebeckers and Native Americans, or Quebeckers and representatives of various immigrant groups. The secessionist view of national culture is an absolutist one—you may be either "in" or "out" according to the terms with which secessionists have defined the nation.

This analysis does not presuppose malicious intent upon the drafters of any particular secessionist text. Rather, these texts are the logical outcome of a political ontology of national being. The Pandora's Box of secessionism is actually more like a Russian doll. Having been denied a fulfilling sense of recognition for their identities, secessionists feel the need, in turn, to create pure political spaces for themselves where their identities may be sheltered and protected. This space of constitutional nationalism, in turn, threatens the identities of members of non national groups—many of whom have made their homes in the country for centuries, and some actually indigenous. Unfortunately for secessionists, if a population does not feel the ties of a common identity, no matter how recently constructed (or reconstructed), they will have difficulty creating a new state. This is especially the case now when global economic interdependence has greatly increased the possibilities for regional prosperity based on global markets, as is illustrated most clearly in the next set of narratives.

The Northern League

The activities of the Northern League (*Lega Nord*) of Italy represent an interesting blend of radical secessionism and practical politicking. The Northern League itself is both a political party with an influential presence in the Italian parliament and a political movement for independence for the north of Italy. The thirteen regions of the north have been given the national name "Padania" after the god of the Po River, which runs through the area. Padania has a flag (a green Celtic star on a white background) and a national symbol (a medieval warrior with sword raised, commemorating the struggles of the North Italian communes for self-rule in the twelfth and thirteenth centuries). There is a parliament of Padania, which has 200 members elected from a field of 1,175 candidates. Identification cards and currency have been designed, but are not in general use. These activities are largely due to the efforts and motivation of one man, Umberto Bossi, the founder of *Lega Nord*. Tapping into the economic frustration of heavily taxed businessmen of the north, Bossi attacked Rome both with pleas for a federalist structure in which the north would have autonomy and with threats of secession if this did not occur. The political activities of the Northern League in Rome's parliament have sustained local support for years with an emphasis on federalism and devolved power. However, direct support for secession has depended on specific hard-hit areas of the Padanian provinces rather than broad popular approval.[26] Despite having been coy about the possibility of secession in his speeches to the Italian Chamber of Deputies in Rome, Bossi took steps to set up a government for Padania. He announced the approval (by the Constituent Assembly of the Regions of the North) of a provisional "Constitution of the North" on March 24, 1996. On May 4, 1996, the Parliament of the North changed its name to the Parliament of Padania, and began the business of forming a government of Padania. Eight days later, the Padanian parliament chose its first prime minister, Giancarlo Pagliarini, and appointed a Committee for the Liberation of Padania. On September 15, 1996, a ceremony announcing the Declaration of Independence and Sovereignty of Padania was held on the banks of the Po River. The State of Padania currently exists in virtual limbo—no longer a simple political party, but also not a recognized state with an international presence (despite its symbolic efforts and "foreign office"). Its public relations documents indicate a certain ambivalence between the contradictory goals of sovereign independence and a federalist restructuring of the Italian state. Most of the population of Padania considers itself to be Italian, but that does not seem to bother Bossi, who declares, "History is made by minorities, not the majority."[27]

The Declaration of Independence and Sovereignty of Padania is a narrative that performs an identity for Padanians on several levels. On its face, it acts as a document for the purpose of declaring that Padania is a separate state. But through its language and style, it evokes an image of Padania as one of a distinguished company of secessionist revolutionary nations destined for democratic greatness. The opening passage of the declaration is taken more or less directly from the American Declaration of Independence of 1776:

When in the course in [sic] human events it becomes necessary for one Peoples
[sic] to dissolve the bands which bind them with another, to establish themselves
as an independent and sovereign community, and to assume the role assigned to
them by the Natural Law of Self-Determination among the nations of the Earth,
respect for International Society and all of humanity requires that they should
declare the reasons which impel them to the separation.[28]

The Padanian version of this passage has been slightly altered to fit more securely
into the twentieth-century system of international legal norms. Thomas Jefferson's
text made no reference to the "Natural Law of Self-Determination" (a post-World
War I form of usage), but instead refers to "the Laws of Nature and of Nature's
God." Nonetheless, the verbal similarities must be intended to imply a similarity in
the moral worthiness of the cause. Padania is no less deserving of sovereignty than
were the American colonies. Indeed, even the motivations are similar: rebellion
against heavy taxation. However, the slight differences in language between these
two passages reveal the vast differences in effect between the two documents on the
whole. While the American document is largely one of complaint and invective
against the monarch, referring to the Lockean doctrine of equality to support its then
novel claims for popular sovereignty (see chapter 1), the Padanian declaration
strives to locate itself within a context of sovereign states based on historical
national rights. The Padanian declaration, like the American one, accuses the central
government of abusive colonialist policies toward its people; its main claim to
legitimacy derives both from the concept of national self-determination and the
identification of Padania as a historical nation belonging to Europe and the tradition
of democracy.

The declaration strives to produce a distinctive "We" in the people of Padania:
"Since time immemorial, we live, we build, we work, we protect, we love these
lands handed down to us by our forbearers, bathed and quenched by the waters of
our great rivers." To lay valid claim to the principle of self-determination, a people
must be distinct. Thus: "Here we have invented an original way of living, of
developing the arts, and of working. . . . We therefore constitute a natural, cultural,
social, and economic community founded on shared values, culture, and history,
and on harmonious social, moral, and economic conditions." Not only is Padania
a historical entity (regardless of the fact that its name is of recent vintage), but its
independence is necessary for the security of the cultural identity of its people:
"Padania is our pride, our precious resource, and our only chance for freely and
fully expressing our individual natures and our feeling of community." These are
the performative words of secessionist speech acts in operation—the differentiation
of a people, and the declaration that they cannot live under the rule of any other
people but themselves. The definition of the people in Padania's case is almost
entirely based on prior administrative territorial delineations. And since there is no
distinct language to help distinguish the differentness of Padania, grounds must be
elaborated for the distinctness of its people from those of the south of Italy. In other
words, not only must the Padanians declare that they exist as a people, but they also
must clarify how different they are from the people with whom they now share a

political system. This is a crucial part of every secessionist movement. Without this process of *social* and *cultural* othering, there can be no justification for the *territorial political* othering they hope to achieve.

In Padania's narrative, southern Italy, symbolized by the Italian state, is depicted as a colonialist power bleeding the wealth of Padania dry. In contrast to honest, hard-working Padania, "the history of the Italian State has become the history of colonial oppression, of economic exploitation, and of moral violence; The Italian State has, over time, systematically occupied Padania's economic and social system through its parasitic bureaucratic apparatus; The Italian State has systematically annihilated every form of autonomy and self-government of our Towns, our Provinces, and our Regions." But again, unlike the American Declaration of Independence, which refers to the British people as "our brethren," the writers of the Padanian declaration find it necessary to make a national case beyond the one of colonialist exploitation. The Italian state, they claim, "has deliberately attempted to suppress the languages and the cultural identities of the Peoples of Padania through the colonization of the public education system." Also, the laws of the Italian state are not only unfair, but are "applied with racist criteria" and enforced by "Roman-style prefects and law enforcement officers applying the most hateful forms of Statist colonialism." These grievances finally lead to the necessary conclusion: "We are profoundly convinced that the continued presence of Padania within the confines of the Italian State would lead to gradual extinction of all hope of rebirth and the annihilation of the identities of its Peoples." Thus, despite the fact that the Italian state still exerts legal authority over Padania, the narrative of its secessionist leaders attempts to perform a social chasm between residents of Padania and the rest of Italy.

The advocates of Padanian secession adopt contradicting metaphors to validate the need for independence. The first image is one of history, the continuity of the present-day Padania with the communes of the medieval Northern Italy, as symbolized by the medieval warrior of the national symbol. This image tells a story of Padania as a continuous entity whose ancestors struggled and toiled to build a prosperity that the current people are bound to protect. But in direct opposition to that, the narrative also tells a tale of Padania as a new baby being birthed by the secessionist leaders and embodying new hopes for the inclusion of Padania in a federation of European regions. Thus, the assertion, "Padania will become a political and institutional focal point for the construction of a Europe of the Regions and of the Peoples"; and the proclamation that "the hour has finally arrived to set forth on the great enterprise of giving birth to this new Country which we baptize today with the name Padania." On September 15, 1996, Umberto Bossi enacted the baptismal metaphor by pouring a jug of Po River water into the Venice lagoon after having read the Declaration of Independence to a crowd of one hundred and fifty thousand.

Having read out the declaration, Bossi and his supporters have the heavy task of creating a sense of nationhood among the residents of Padania if they are ever to be taken as a serious secessionist movement. A document titled "Padania: The

Foundations of a Nation" provides further details of the points hinted at in the declaration.[29] This text also indicates the extent to which the secessionist leaders of Padania are aware of the performative potential of their language and the intentional re-presentation of history. In a section called "Reclaiming Our History," the author condemns the tactics of the Italian state in attempting to create an artificial nation by confusing the people into believing that states and nations are the same thing: "Italian officialdom professes to teach us Padanians that we should regard ourselves mentally and emotionally closer to the inhabitants of the southernmost islets off Sicily, than to, say, those of neighboring Southern Switzerland, sharing the same mode of speech with Lombardy. How can we build a Europe of the Peoples on such an artificial basis?" The people of Padania, the text goes on, are more definitively a nation than the Italian state, "which for 135 years has attempted in vain to define itself as a Nation." Moreover, according to this history, Padania has long had close ties to the rest of the continent of Europe, looking northward rather than toward Rome from the sixth century onward.

In the Middle Ages, the history continues, Padania was the site of the development of the Free Communes, which developed "profound differences in civil life and social organization" from the rest of the Italian peninsula, and which "reached the heights not only of industry, commerce, and finance, but also of culture, indeed, of Western civilization." Moreover, the description of the entire territory of the Italian state as the "Italian peninsula" is an erroneous and "thinly veiled attempt to instill the idea that the 'Nation-State' is eternally defined by nature itself." A glance at the map, the Padanian historian tells us, would show that only 130,000 square kilometers of Italian state territory are peninsular. The remaining 120,000 "are clearly part of the European continental land mass." Therefore, Padania is geographically as well as historically pointed toward Europe, and its "geographical position in the center of Europe has made it a strategic area for communications, and also for warfare." Thus, Padania's history must be narrated to resituate it as different, not only politically from the modern Italian central state, but also historically as an entity that was never a natural part of the rest of the Italian territory. Old ways of understanding and speaking of Italy must be swept away, and "When we hear people talk about the 'northern part of the Italian peninsula' in reference to the Alpine-Padanian regions, we must object to the incontrovertible abuse of this expression."

In a segment of the *Foundations of a Nation* document titled "The Padanians Rise to Consciousness," the Padanian narrator attacks even the notion of linguistic compatibility by claiming that the language of the Padanian area is not a dialect of Italian, but rather an entirely different language group: "According to distinguished scholars, the Romance languages (neo-Latin dialects) are divided into two large groups: Western, including Gallo-Romance and Iberic idioms; and Eastern, including Italian and Romanian." The border between the two language groups apparently (conveniently) runs right along the southern border of the would-be state of Padania.[30] But, the author continues, knowledge of this linguistic border "is rigorously forbidden in Italian schools so as to make people believe that our modes of speech are dialects of Italian." With the Padanian Declaration of Independence, it became crucial to enact a unique culture for secession to take place. Since the doctrine of self-determination is lauded as the linchpin of the right of Padania to sovereignty, the Padanian *self* must be determined. Economic prosperity has never been the appropriate theme for narrating a unique culture, and so the Padanians must proclaim their cultural difference as historical, geographical, and linguistic. The Padanian narrator emphasizes that the culture of the north is not simply its tax base: "the Padanian identity cannot be explained a priori as the reaction to the oppressive tax burden, the mafia, uncontrolled immigration, the arrogant bureaucracy, the inefficiency of the Italian State . . . etc. . . . The reality is that we Padanians identify Rome and the unitary Italian State as the carrier of all these threats to the progress and stability of OUR life in civil society."[31]

This litany of the faults of Rome cleverly strengthens the colonialist metaphor, while serving to outline the cultural differences by implication. Without saying so explicitly, the Padanian historian implies identity through negativity. Whatever Rome *is* (oppressive, corrupt, out of control, arrogant and bureaucratic, inefficient), Padania *is not* (liberal, incorrupt, controlled, polite and decentralized, efficient). Thus, being subject to all the evils of Rome will taint the good Padanian regions. But does inefficiency in the central government thereby create a unique culture among those people who wish to impose efficiency? Is this what self-determination is meant to achieve? The retelling of Padanian history illustrates that a unique culture can be "found" among people of the same language, religion, and geographic region. Moreover, once this unique culture is asserted, its leaders can easily argue that separation is necessary for survival, as in this case: "The Italian State, the Italian rule-by-party/vote-pandering system is a beast afflicted with incurable ills which thrives on forcibly and deceptively holding together Peoples of different civic traditions." Thus, not only will Padania fall ill with the same fatal disease if it is not set free, but it also should be free based on the purity of its "civic tradition."

The medical metaphor of the Italian state as sick and on the verge of infecting Padania continues throughout the document. The Italian state is "impotent," it has "been infected" by the "cancer of the Mafia," and it uses its "transmission mechanism" to infect Padania as well. Furthermore, the demographics of the south of Italy combined with Padania's negative rate of population growth have created a "risk of moving down the path to extinction." The purity of Padanian identity is also threatened by the laxity of Italian immigration control and the "massive non-European immigration," which "causes serious problems of public order" and "endangers the identity of our Peoples." Secession is once again called upon to protect the dubious idea of cultural and racial purity, regarding migration and immigration as invasion: "The point is that a People have the human right not to be invaded by other Peoples, thus risking to become foreigners in their own land." Only if a culture believes in its own inviolable purity and distinctiveness can it ever become a "foreigner" in its own land—by refusing to accept and embrace difference as a necessary contribution to its *self*.

The Padanian focus on the fact that the immigration is "non-European" is no accident—it is part of a tactic of identifying Padania with Europe (efficient, wealthy, successful) and distancing the south of Italy as something "other" than European (lazy, poor, corrupt). In a section of the Padanian narrative called "Padania Towards a Europe of the Peoples and of the Regions," a specific vision is set forth of Padania as a unique regional voice within Europe. But the Europe envisioned by Padanian leaders encourages local authority in the regions and avoids "mere transfer of power from the bureaucratic State capitals to the super-bureaucratic institutions of Brussels." In a decentralized Europe of the Regions, Padania would shine as a local power and become further differentiated from its southern neighbor. The Padanian European vision is one in which southern Italy is isolated by its inefficiency and corruption. For the Padanian narrator, localism "is a European-wide phenomenon which the retarded and provincial Italian State, culturally and economically mired in the backwaters of Europe, cannot and wishes not to see for evident reasons of self-interest." Ironically (since the Italian state is a full member of the European Union), the Padanian version of Europe—the true Europe, the one of regional autonomy—excludes the south of Italy.

Thus, Padanian secessionists envision their role as European regional power in a Europe which somehow, oddly, excludes Italy. The distancing tactic employed in this Padanian text resembles the phenomenon formulated by Edward Said as *Orientalism*. The Orientalist perspective "refers to pervasive patterns of representation of cultures and societies that privilege a self-confidently 'progressive,' 'modern' and 'rational' Europe over the putatively 'stagnant,' 'backward,' 'traditional' and 'mystical' societies of the Orient."[32] In the Padanian narrative, the "Orient" is southern Italy. While Padanian historical narrative cannot give southern Italy a past within the Ottoman Empire, it links the south with all of the same undesirable characteristics usually associated in the European mind with the Orient. This othering tactic is not necessarily limited to the Ottoman/Christian dichotomy, but includes a whole symbolic geography of Europe which distinguishes among axes between eastern and western churches, communist and noncommunist states, and northern and southern cultures. As Milica Bakić-Hayden and Robert Hayden point out, a rhetoric similar to orientalism

> has been preserved and applied in regard to another orientation of post-war symbolic geography, one in which an underdeveloped, poor south is contrasted with a developed, rich north. This modern economic geography of the world reflects and continues an older European political geography in which "undisciplined," passionate" peoples of southern Europe (e.g. Italy, Spain, Greece) were contrasted to the industrious, rational cultures of the north.[33]

So even though most of the region historicized as Padania in this narrative has been referred to as "Italian" for centuries, there is a conscious and overt need on the part of the secessionist leaders to dissociate Padania from Italy and its Oriental (negative) connotations. This dissociation extends even to the pope—Padanian documents refer to the medieval history of the region and describe papal rule as a "conservative, sometimes oppressive regime," which had a stagnant economy (unlike the north) and "worst of all, the Papal State acted as a barrier (both political and cultural) between the South of Italy and Europe."[34] Thus, Padanian texts vividly illustrate the political uses of historical narratives and the norm-creating potency of the performative language used to declare and enact a separate people. By definition, because of the requirements for state recognition and the understanding of self-determination, secessionist movements cannot be neutral. They must rely upon narratives of othering and difference, and also, by definition, exclusion of that difference. But as the situations of Québec and Padania have shown, not only do these attempts to separate and purify identities make for hostile and violent politics, they are also futile since even so-called distinct and unique cultural identities must be created in an interactive process with the Other.

The Kanaka Maoli

The population of Hawaii literally embodies the contradiction between a purifying preservationist narrative of secession and the inescapable mutuality of human interaction. In the two centuries since the isolation of the indigenous peoples was breached by the arrival of Europeans, a diverse ethnic mixture has come to populate the islands, including, along with the native Kanaka Maoli, Caucasian, Japanese, Filipino, Chinese, Portuguese, Vietnamese, Korean, and other Pacific Island peoples. The Hawaiian spirit of *aloha* has permeated the cultural mix and resulted in the ready acceptance of intermarriage and mutual respect among the different cultures, to such an extent that few individuals would claim unmixed heritage of any sort, and pure Kanaka Maoli have practically vanished. Therefore, it is all the more surprising that there is a strong (if tiny) secessionist movement astir in this multiculturalist archetype, and that it is overtly based on racial criteria. No one denies that the history of Hawaii has been one of exploitation and dishonest dealings by the United States. Beginning in 1893 when the Hawaiian monarch was overthrown by resident Americans in cooperation with the U.S. military, the United States acted unilaterally and unlawfully by annexing Hawaii (1898) and turning it into a territory of the United States (1900). Further, in 1946, when Hawaii was designated by the United Nations as a non-self-governing territory and placed under the authority of the United States, the option for full independence was never given, and the 1959 vote on the question of Hawaii's immediate statehood included U.S. military personnel and others who had resided on the islands for only a year. In 1993, the U.S. Congress finally passed a law known as the Apology Resolution, which officially apologized for the illegal overthrow of the Kingdom of Hawaii and recognized that "the indigenous Hawaiian people never directly relinquished their claims to their inherent sovereignty."[35] Given the discrimination and sociocultural disadvantages which accompanied U.S. territorial administration and statehood, many of Kanaka Maoli descent feel entitled to reparations. These range from better funding for the Office of Hawaiian Affairs, to some form of autonomy over public lands, to fully fledged sovereignty.

Sovereigntists—those aiming for separation from the United States—claim that Hawaii is currently in a state of occupation but is undergoing a transition phase toward restoration of the original Hawaiian nation. On January 16, 1994, a coalition of sovereignty organizations gathered in Honolulu to endorse a document called *The Proclamation of Restoration of the Independence of the Sovereign Nation State of Hawai 'i.*[36] Apart from declaring independence, the proclamation authorized the Council of Elders to act as Hawaii's provisional government and to take steps toward restoration and the development of a constitution. The proclamation narrates a story of injustice—the invasion and suppression of an indigenous people. It consistently speaks for "We, the Kanaka Maoli" who reestablish their sovereign nation and "join the World Community of States." Its very title emphasizes that this people do not claim self-determination to create a new state but to restore a historical one. "We have resided here forever, from time immemorial. We have displaced no other people. We, the Kanaka Maoli, are the original inhabitants and occupants of these Islands." Kanaka Maoli historical narrative does not list character traits or language differences to demonstrate the distinctness of this people. Rather, the Kanaka Maoli define themselves strictly and simply by genetic relationship. "The current citizens of the Independent and Sovereign Nation of Hawaii consist of all those who are descendants of the Kanaka Maoli prior to the arrival of the first westerners in 1778, and [those who are descendants of persons] who have lived in Hawaii prior to the illegal overthrow, invasion and occupation of January 17, 1893." This is constitutional nationalism in its clearest form, and especially striking in a population famous for the breadth of its genetic mix. The strictness of this definition of nation does not allow political space for those who have some Kanaka Maoli heritage but do not identify themselves with the national movement, or for people with a Hawaiian lineage more recent than 1893. Although possibly fourth or fifth generation, these "habitual residents of Hawaii" must apply for citizenship by means of naturalization, according to the proclamation. Thus, the Kanaka Maoli identity narrative performs a simple and sharp delineation, blunt in the in the finality of its exclusion.

One of the primary reasons for restoring sovereignty is the feeling by the sovereigntist Kanaka Maoli that their culture is in danger of being wiped out. The proclamation declares that the new state will revive the traditions of the pre-1778 nation: "We, the Kanaka Maoli, today embody within our governmental structure traditional customs and culture of the 'Aha Kuka O Na Kupuna (Council of Elders), based on mutual respect, traditional practice, and family order. Their consultation on many decisions is highly regarded as the basis of all authority and principle, as handed down through generations of teachings." The assumption underlying these sentiments is that ancient traditions can and must be resurrected and preserved from the destructive forces of modernity. In other words, the ancient Kanaka Maoli culture is something knowable and reproducible in the late twentieth century; and further, it is Hawaii's only salvation. "We must protect our sacred 'aina [land] from such invasion and exploitation, to liberate it from alien destructive forces, and preserve and protect our Cultural Heritage for future generations, from the devastation of extinction." Designating the land as something "sacred" immediately establishes a relationship with it that has religious connotations in terms of purity and reverence. In conjunction with designating the land of Hawaii as sacred, the Kanaka Maoli have associated non-Hawaiians (aliens) with destruction, and their own native traditions with preservation. Such clearly drawn social boundaries preclude the possibility that nonnative Hawaiians might wish to love and protect and claim Hawaii as their home also. This narrative establishes the Kanaka Maoli not only as a people with cultural traditions in need of respect and protection, but also as the sole legitimate arbiters of the fate of Hawaiian territory. Only they can protect the sacred land. The proclamation describes those non-Kanaka Maoli who now "illegally occupy our Territory" in no uncertain terms as "Those who disregard the Principles and Rule of the Law of Nations, Justice, Integrity, Morality of Character, and Humanity, by force and acts of aggression." Institutionalized national exclusivity of this sort leaves no space—on the land and in the society—for all the various non-Kanaka Maoli who call Hawaii their home.

Exactly one year after the proclamation was read out, the Kapuna (elders) met to sign the national constitution.[37] As a document detailing the type of law and government a society will have, how its powers will be both mandated and circumscribed, a constitution is essential reading for theorists of political narrative. The Hawaiian Constitution provides a deeply othering text. It begins with a preamble describing the members of the nation not as "We the People," but as "We the Kanaka Maoli Nationals and Descendants." As a people who have been "subjected to the international crimes of Genocide and Crimes Against Humanity," the preamble asserts, the Kanaka Maoli have a right to self-determination and to "freely determine to restore Our political, economic, social, and cultural rights."[38] The difficulty is that the new Hawaiian state, as envisaged in the constitution, creates legal discrimination against non-Kanaka Maoli citizens, regardless of whether they have resided in Hawaii since 1778 or wish to become naturalized. There are officially two separate types of citizenship defined in the Hawaiian Constitution, and they are endowed with different rights. The Kanaka Maoli are referred to as "Nationals" and defined in Article XV as "any person who by birth or national origin and ancestry is a descendant of the original inhabitants who prior to 1778 exercised sovereignty over the Archipelago of Hawaii." The second definition, "Citizens, Naturalized," covers anyone not descended from the original inhabitants and is defined as "all persons who qualify and choose to become citizens of the Nation." The qualifications are left open for enactment by the Legislative General Assembly.

The differences between these two classes of citizens are apparent throughout the constitution. The constitutional structure of the proposed Hawaiian government is based on a tripartite system with legislative, executive, and judiciary branches. The proposed Hawaiian Legislative General Assembly contains two parts, the Na Kapuna Council and the Citizen's Assembly. The former shall consist only of

Kanaka Maoli nationals, while the latter shall consist of fifty-six nationals and fifty-six citizens. The duties of the Na Kapuna Council include laws relating to "the preservation of Hawaiian cultural values" or "maintaining cultural values." Consent by the Legislative General Assembly may occur concerning the passage of bills on cultural values, but it is not necessary as "the Council law shall have supremacy." The executive administration consists of "the Head of State, a Deputy Head of State, and all Ministries established for the purposes of executing the laws and business of the Nation." The office of the Head of State or Deputy Head of State shall *only* be held by a person "who is a Kanaka Maoli National and Descendant." Third, the judiciary consists of National Tribunals as the Legislative General Assembly sees fit, and one Supreme Tribunal. All judges are to be selected by the Na Kapuna Council, and "Every judge shall be a Kanaka Maoli National." Thus, the Hawaiian Constitution describes a state in which there are two classes of citizens with one, the "Nationals," definitively privileged over the other in exercising governmental power. Of the three branches of government, one (the judiciary) is entirely closed to nonnationals; one (the legislature) restricts membership to one half of one of the two chambers; and the third (the executive) allows nonnationals only as appointed to the ministries with the consent of the Na Kapuna Council. Again, secessionists perform an identity differentiation that perpetuates the patterns of power and oppression that they have found unacceptable in the "majority" identity.

Despite its references to international law and human rights, the Hawaiian Constitution contains some legally alarming provisions. Not only do non-Hawaiian descendants have limited access and representation in government, but they are constitutionally locked out of the communal land tenure system which is part of the envisioned restoration of the Hawaiian regime. "Prior to 1778, the Kanaka Maoli Nationals lived in a communal land tenure system, and every National had the right and privilege to receive and acquire the use of land." Once the "transition" to an independent Hawaiian state has been made, all national land will be held in trust "for the Kanaka Maoli Nationals" by the new government. Thus, not only will all private ownership of land vanish but only individuals of the proper lineage may apply for use of the communal land. Institutionalized discrimination of this sort will not make reparation for past wrongs; it can only generate friction among the various groups that make up Hawaii's richly various culture.

Secessionist Narratives and the Uses and Disadvantages of History

An examination of several secessionist texts soon uncovers the assumption shared by them all—that the nation in question had a common (and ancient) history and that it was glorious and deserving of preservation through the continued reverence and traditions of the national population today. But what is also clear is that history can be narrated in many ways, and that the politics of secessionist identity performance require it to be told in an exclusivist, boundary-drawing fashion. The secessionist nation ("We") performs its identity against nonnationals ("Others") in ways which neglect the necessity of the nonnational for the identity of the nation. Historical narrative is the tool used for this social and political boundary drawing, and as such its meanings have become as contested as the territorial space to which it so often refers. Nietzsche recognized and criticized this use and abuse of history, considering it an encumbrance on human abilities.[39] Mankind cannot live, or have an identity, without a memory, but, Nietzsche might argue, the essence of truly living occurs in the space between remembering and forgetting. In other words, we must remember in order to know who we are, and forget in order to become what we may be. The disadvantages of historical narratives, for Nietzsche, are that they focus on the past to an extent which limits the possibilities of the present and the future. In terms of the secessionist texts discussed here, historical narratives have been used to limit the terms of identity of the particular groups and to call on the members of these groups to fulfill their historic destiny by fighting for independent statehood. The vision is one of constraint (by perceived historical imperatives) rather than freedom. Because their French-ness, their Northern Italian-ness, or their Hawaiian-ness was narrated historically in certain circumscribed ways, these secessionist groups now maintain that their current and future identities must perpetuate these patterns. But Nietzsche's critique equates such historical identities with death; they are the identities of the dead, and therefore to maintain the pattern of the past is to *mortify* your own present identity, excluding the possibilities of the living present.

Nietzsche provides a useful schematic of humanity's three types of relationships to history and how history is necessary for life. These uses of history contain recognizable echoes of secessionist narratives. He describes the first relationship as *Monumental History*, which involves the belief that "the great moments in the struggle of the human individual constitute a chain, that this chain unites mankind across the millennia like a range of human peaks . . . that is the fundamental idea of the faith in humanity."[40] But, Nietzsche argues, it is this demand for eternal greatness that causes great conflict. Monumental history inspires foolish courage and fanaticism. "As long as the past has to be described as worthy of imitation, as imitable and possible for a second time, it of course incurs the danger of becoming somewhat distorted, beautified and coming close to free poetic invention; there have been ages, indeed, which were quite incapable of distinguishing between a monumentalized past and a mythical fiction."[41] Monumental history clearly plays a role in secessionist narratives in the way that the past is told as a story of grand struggle and the mythical ancestors whose toil and oppression shall not have been suffered in vain. Secessionist movements do not confess to the faults in their own national histories: to the violence against indigenous peoples, or the exploitative use of cheap immigrant labor, or the long intervals of peaceful integrated living amongst different groups. National histories must be exalted as sacred and worthy of political enshrinement through sovereign statehood.

Nietzsche's second category of man's relationship to history is that of *Antiquarian History*. The antiquarian historian is a preservationist, painstakingly recording the conditions of his existence for the generations to come. This kind of history builds on the sense of communal continuity: "the contentment of the tree in its roots, the happiness of knowing that one is not wholly accidental and arbitrary but grown out of a past as its heir, flower and fruit, and that one's existence is thus excused and indeed, justified."[42] But Nietzsche finds antiquarian history to be problematic in its extreme restrictedness of vision. Everything old and of the past is taken to be worthy of equal reverence, while everything new is rejected. He compares antiquarian history to a tree's awareness of its roots. It judges its roots by the size of its visible branches, but if "the tree is in error as to this, how greatly it will be in error regarding the rest of the forest around it!—for it knows of the forest only that in it which obstructs or favors it and nothing beside."[43] Antiquarian history, too, is a recognizable part of secessionist political discourse. The attempt to re-create the past as the only system worthy or valuable, and the rejection of change (and the present) as destructive and threatening bear all the hallmarks of Nietzsche's typology. This is perhaps most clearly reflected in the wishes of the Kanaka Maoli to resurrect all of the ancient patterns of governance, including the land tenure system, because these patterns were theirs historically. The Kanaka Maoli are exhibiting great reverence for the roots and are neglecting the impact of their actions on the rest of the forest.

The third relationship is one Nietzsche describes as *Critical History*. This is the necessary mode, because if man is to live fully, he "must possess and from time to time employ the strength to break up and dissolve a part of the past: he does this by bringing it before the tribunal, scrupulously examining it and finally condemning it." This sweeping away of the past is necessary to liberate mankind from the burden of history. Furthermore, no group is immune because "every past . . . is worthy to be condemned—for that is the nature of human things: human violence and weakness have always played a mighty role in them."[44] But, Nietzsche warns, critical history is difficult and dangerous, since it is always hard to know when to stop—the complete denial of the past results in a denial of one's own participation in the chain of human history, and therefore also of the responsibility of being human. According to Nietzsche, the best we can do is maintain knowledge of our inheritance and try to combat it with the cultivation of a new instinct, a new habit. The logical outcome of critical history is in fact the downfall of nationalist identities, since a thoroughly scrupulous look into any nation's past will crumble its monumental and antiquarian pretensions. This is what E. J. Hobsbawm meant when he wrote that a serious historian of nations or nationalism could never be a dedicated nationalist: "Nationalism requires too much belief in what is patently not so."[45] In other words, nationalism requires a belief in the objective existence and purity of an identity and a belief that this identity can be preserved stably over time. It is critical history that is missing from (indeed which vitally threatens) secessionist historical renderings. Rather than examining their histories as burdens and restraints on their present, secessionists must persist in the veneration of the past, in both monumental and antiquarian terms. Such uses and abuses of history fail to create a "new origin" that will bequeath a less violent and weak legacy upon the future. What Nietzsche's categories urge is that we realize our identities as socially constructed and therefore historically indebted, but also that we recognize the contingency of history and use that contingency to open the critical space required for living a creative (as opposed to mortified) politics.

The critical relationship is a frightening way to engage with history, but it is a necessary one if the cycle of violent encounters is ever to ease. As Michel Foucault commented in his discussion of the Nietzschean typology, "The search for descent is not the erecting of foundations: on the contrary, it disturbs what was previously considered immobile; it fragments what was thought unified; it shows the heterogeneity of what was imagined consistent with itself."[46] For Foucault, history can be seen as productive only to the extent that it exposes the discontinuities (or contingency) of our existence, thus disturbing the myths of monumental history and the reverence of antiquarian history. As Foucault elaborates:

> Where the soul pretends unification or the self fabricates a coherent identity, the genealogist [critical historian] sets out to study the beginning—numberless beginnings whose faint traces and hints of color are readily seen by an historical eye. The analysis of descent permits the dissociation of the self, its recognition and displacement as an empty synthesis, in liberating a profusion of lost events.[47]

It is this critical vision of history which secessionist politics obscures and obstructs in its attempt to lay claim to a purity in the present and the worthiness of the past. But it is this critical history that is so necessary to the generative rather than preservative form of politics. This is not a call to forget, or disrespect history—but rather an urging to dig more deeply into history to lessen its hold on the living present. Nietzsche urges us to confront our inherited nature through our knowledge of it, and thus to grow the seeds of new habits and patterns for the future. The possibilities and new habits liberated by the political space formed by critical history provide the basis for the speculations of the final chapter of this book.

Notes

1. See Viva Ona Bartkus, *The Dynamic of Secession* (Cambridge: Cambridge University Press, 1999).

2. Robert M. Hayden, "Constitutional Nationalism in the Former Yugoslav Republics," *Slavic Review* 51, no. 4 (1992): 655, 654-673.

3. Hayden, "Constitutional Nationalism," 657.

4. Hayden, "Constitutional Nationalism," 657.

5. Hayden, "Constitutional Nationalism," 663.

6. Hayden, "Constitutional Nationalism," 666-667.

7. Hayden, "Constitutional Nationalism," 669.

8. Michael J. Toolan, *Narrative: A Critical Linguistic Introduction* (London: Routledge, 1988), 3.

9. William Connolly, *Why I Am Not a Secularist* (Minneapolis: University of Minnesota Press, 1999), 95.

10. J. G. A. Pocock, "Verbalizing a Political Act: Towards a Politics of Speech," in *Language and Politics*, ed. Michael Shapiro (Oxford: Blackwell, 1984), 28.

11. Pocock, "Verbalizing a Political Act," 31.

12. Pocock, "Verbalizing a Political Act," 31.

13. I place quotation marks around the word *minority* because the term is only relevant as long as international practices continue to identify states with national groups.

14. Charles Taylor, *Sources of the Self: The Making of the Modern Identity* (Cambridge: Cambridge University Press, 1989), 35.

15. Pocock, "Verbalizing a Political Act," 39.

16. Toolan, *Narrative*, 8.

17. Hayden White, *The Content of the Form: Narrative Discourse and Historical Representation* (Baltimore: The Johns Hopkins University Press, 1987), 14.

18. Judith Butler, *Bodies That Matter: On the Discursive Limits of Sex* (London: Routledge, 1993), 13.

19. Butler, *Bodies That Matter*, 12.

20. Cynthia Weber, "Performative States," *Millennium: Journal of International Studies* 27, no. 1 (1998): 81, 77-95.

21. *Bill 1: An Act Respecting the Future of Québec* (Introduction Québec Official Publisher, 1995).

22. Emphasis added.

23. Jacques Parizeau, "Who Are We? Where Are We Going?" trans. P. Van de Wille, *The (Toronto) Globe and Mail*, 30 October 1996.

24. The terms Québécois and Quebecker are the Francophone and Anglophone versions, respectively.

25. Jacques Parizeau, "The Objective Is Sovereignty, Not Partnership," trans. P. Van de Wille, *The (Toronto) Globe and Mail*, 19 December 1996.

26. Benito Giordano, "A Place Called Padania? The Lega Nord and the Political Representation of Northern Italy," *European Urban and Regional Studies* 6, no.3 (1999): 221, 215-230.

27. Alexander Stille, "The Fall of Rome?" *George*, September 1997, 102-108.

28. Declaration of Independence and Sovereignty of Padania, 15 September 1996. Available from http://www.seveso.org/English_version/declaration_of_independence_of_padania.htm. Accessed 16 June 2003; on file with the author.

29. Padania: The Foundations of a Nation. Available from http://www.seveso.org/English_version/padania_the_foundations_of_a_nation.htm. Accessed 16 April 2003; on file with the author.

30. The orthodox view appears to contradict this assertion, placing all of Italy together within the romance language category. See *Atlas of the World's Languages*, ed. Christopher Moseley and R. E. Asher (London: Routledge, 1994), 247; *The Atlas of Languages: The Origin and Development of Language throughout the World*, ed. Bernard Comrie, Stephen Mathews, and Maria Polinsky (London: Bloomsbury, 1997), 40.

31. Emphasis in original.

32. Edward Said, *Orientalism* (New York: Vintage, 1979) cited in Milica Bakić-Hayden and Robert M. Hayden, "Orientalist Variations on the Theme 'Balkans': Symbolic Geography in Recent Yugoslav Cultural Politics," *Slavic Review* 51, no. 1 (Spring 1992):1, 1-15

33. Said, *Orientalism* in Bakić-Hayden and Hayden, "Orientalist Variations," 4.

34. *Fighting for the Freedom of North-Italy.* Available from http://www.seveso.org/English_version/Introduction_to_Lega_Nord.htm. Accessed 16 April 2003; on file with the author.

35. United States Public Law 103-150 (November 23, 1993).

36. *Proclamation of Restoration of the Independence of the Sovereign Nation State of Hawaii* (16 January 1994). Available from http://www.hawaii-nation.org/proclamall. html. Accessed 16 April 2003; on file with the author.

37. *Hawai'i Constitution* (16 January 1995). Available from http://www.hawaii-nation.org/hawaii-nation.html/constitution.html. Accessed 16 June 2003; on file with the author.

38. The claim of genocide against the Kanaka Maoli has never been made legally, and would be difficult to substantiate, but the use of the term has great shock value in confirming them as victims of great evils and therefore entitled to serious reparations.

39. Friedrich Nietzsche, "On the Uses and Disadvantages of History for Life," in *Untimely Meditations*, trans. R. J. Hollingdale (Cambridge: Cambridge University Press, 1983).

40. Nietzsche, "Uses and Disadvantages of History," 68.

41. Nietzsche, "Uses and Disadvantages of History," 70.

42. Nietzsche, "Uses and Disadvantages of History," 74.

43. Nietzsche, "Uses and Disadvantages of History," 74.

44. Nietzsche, "Uses and Disadvantages of History," 76.

45. E. J. Hobsbawm, *Nations and Nationalism since 1780: Programme, Myth, Reality* (Cambridge: Cambridge University Press, 1990), 12.

46. Michel Foucault, "Nietzsche, Genealogy, History," in *Language, Counter-Memory, Practice*, Selected Essays and Interviews, ed. with introduction by Donald F. Bouchard, trans. Donald F. Bouchard and Sherry Simon (Oxford: Basil Blackwell, 1977): 147, 139-164.

47. Foucault, "Nietzsche, Genealogy, History," 145-46.

Chapter 6

*In*conclusion: Forgetting
and the Theory and Practice of the Self

The previous chapters discuss the internal contradictions of the relationship between the territorialization of politics and the contingency of identity formation. As this journey through several secessionist texts has shown, groups must emphasize their differences to make secession a credible option. In drawing the necessary social boundaries, secessionists must carve a political space for their national identity which is exclusive—thus, secessionist movements inevitably display troubling tendencies toward discrimination and concepts of ethnic purity, which easily lead to violence against perceived others. This is not because national identities are inherently violent, but because the territorialization of any identity establishes an exclusive claim to space which provokes contestation by those defined outside the nation. These dynamics have been institutionalized through the apparent customary requirements of international society. Secessionist activity, as a phenomenon which grows out of the twentieth-century territorial nation-state and its inherent tensions, occurs within (and is defined by) certain institutional limits. These are: the international legal framework which upholds both self-determination and territorial integrity, the political framework which allows only states to have an international voice, and the social framework which privileges majority identities over minority ones according to arbitrary boundaries. These institutional limitations all work to encourage secession as the only viable option for unrecognized (internationally illegitimate) identity groups. Unfortunately, secession turns out to be a Pyrrhic victory, for it re-creates and perpetuates the tensions and incoherencies already enmeshed in the nation-state, often inflaming the violence of cultural encounters.

The problem of secession—and secession is a problem rather than a solution—is that it occurs as a logical outcome of the structure of the international system today. As discussed in chapter 3, political identity in the last century has become more closely associated with territorial claims and control than ever before. Jacques Derrida calls this phenomenon a *"primitive conceptual phantasm* of community, the nation-State, sovereignty, borders, native soil and blood."[1] This phantasm is outdated, Derrida argues, because of its reliance on *ontopology*. Ontopology is defined as a social axiom "linking indissociably the ontological value of present-being [*on*] to its *situation*, to the stable and presentable determination of a locality, the *topos* of territory, native soil, city, body in general."[2] David Campbell argues, in his discussion of the Bosnian war, that ontopology assumes "that the political possibilities have been limited by the alignment between territory and identity, state and nation, all under the sign of 'ethnicity,' supported by a particular account of history."[3] Because we have identified (and thereby limited) politics as a function of power exerted over territory, we have all but required any group craving political recognition to exert a claim to specific territories as well. Thus, the system ensures that "secession" will continue to lurk beneath the surface as the only pathway to political viability for certain determined groups. If identity was a neat, pure, and stable thing this would present less of a problem. Indeed, there would be little reason for the violence of the conflicts we see now amongst groups struggling to "cleanse" their identities of those who might "taint" them or keep them from being recognized. Stable identities would be instantly recognizable, and thus would require no protection—they would have no "others" in the sense discussed here. Difference among us would be a nonconstitutive thing—and obviously we would also be lacking in much of the adaptability and learning capacity that makes us human.

Because we are all profoundly affected (created) by the presence of others, and our identities are thereby contingent through a process of constant negotiation with others, the territorialization of politics presents a major problem. Not only does it provide a constant temptation for unrecognized groups to create their identities through seizing territorial control by whatever means are available to them, but the territorialization of politics also is based on the false assumption of uniformity among those who do reside within "legitimate" territorial states. Territories do not come "stranger-free." There is no way to territorialize preexisting, homogenous, comprehensive group identities in neat state packages. Such identities cannot exist—and even if they could, locking them into a fixed territorial space (which must maintain strict control over movement inward and outward) can hardly be the most desirable or liberty-driven of outcomes. Social identities cannot be locked in to a place—or out. What appears to be the historical rootedness of groups is due to the "performative" nature of identity. Performativity, as described and applied by Campbell, includes both the creative and the stabilizing effects of discursive identity formation.

Rather than viewing identity—which is an inescapable prerequisite of being—as either given by intentional human activity or granted by natural extra-human forces, the idea of performativity draws attention to "the reiterative and citational practice by which discourse produces the effects that it names."[4]

Performativity, then, points to the enormous power of language to create, through repeated terms and relational understandings, a sedimentation of meaning which, though contingent, appears historically settled. In other words, when secessionists claim that they "are a nation," their words (in stories, speeches, political actions, and declarations) generate narrative performances which, repeated unproblematically, produce nationhood (in a joint conceptual sense) over time. Secessionists can legitimate their nationhood through an ex post facto constitutive decision. Any sovereign entity can be traced to a foundational moment in which its legitimacy was simply declared and then became actual through the continued absence of contestation.[5] It is thus that secession performs a Derridean *coup de force*—a legitimating act which "receives its interpretive justification as true after the fact," as does, for example, the declaration of independence of a new nation.[6] Yet, even if it was never contested, secession as an identifying act would not be a neutral choice. "Self-cession" is self-removal, but it is also an "other-removal" by definition. By creating social and territorial boundaries around the declared nation, secessionists both delineate and remove the "other." Self-cession is also a call for self-cleansing.

If secession is only a symptom of these inherent conflicts and not a solution to them, what then? How can identities flourish in a political space which does not depend on territorial legitimacy or definition? What alternative form of political legitimacy is possible given the tensions between territory and identity? Can democracy operate under conditions different from those of the modern territorial state? These questions can be approached only through the continuous process of international politics. There can be no perfect unitary model which stops all the conflicts and creates universal harmony. But certain possibilities are not necessarily unforeseeable. The future will be an outcome of this present, and the particular choices it creates can already be recognized in the variations on political space that currently exist. What is crucial for our understanding of future possibilities is an awareness of the shifting meanings of our most important political concepts today. Anyone who undertakes a conceptual history must realize that not only do concepts "teach us the uniqueness of past meanings," but they also "become the formal categories which determine the conditions of possible history."[7] As Koselleck puts it:

It is only concepts which demonstrate persistence, repeatable applicability, and empirical validity—concepts with structural claims—which indicate that a once "real" history can today appear generally possible and be represented as such.[8]

Concepts, then, allow us to recognize certain histories as possible, to trace their paths through past and present meanings, and furthermore, to allow for future possibilities. The importance of Koselleck's statement extends not only into our understanding and reading of history, but also into our understanding of our choices for the future. The political concepts we are currently operating under will be the conditions of a possible future. We are not bound to maintain our contemporary understandings of these concepts, but they will be the basis of our future understandings of the conceptual signifiers. Just as the words *territory, sovereignty* and *state* had very different meanings in 1648 than they do at the turn of the second millennium, so these same terms, these same concepts, will carry different meanings in the future. We cannot set goals for the universal achievement of world peace according to a single model and expect to see them reached. But we may make possible now the changes in conceptual meaning which will help to compensate in the future for the obvious failures of the past. In this vein, anything which problematizes the ontopology of the state is to be encouraged as a step in a helpful direction. The authors examined in this chapter all question, or make it possible to question, ontopological structures and are thus useful in exploring alternative ways of performing future politics. By allowing our concepts of identity and statehood to grow beyond the ties of territory, our concepts of the national and the international to grow beyond the state border, and our concepts of law and recognition to grow beyond sovereignty, we provide the link both to a "real" history and to the conditions of possible futures.

Within and Without the State

I refer to the nation-state in various ways in this text, and although I have tried to problematize this concept, its very presence—unquestioned—perpetuates its meaning as a solid unchanging uniform thing. In actual practice, however, it has already become commonplace to point out the variations on the nation-state theme. Not only are all nation-states in the world today territorial (if not political) homes to individuals of more than one ethnocultural group, but the political structures of each state provide countless interpretations of voting, citizenship, representation, legitimacy, and the role of the state. International Relations has traditionally been silent about the "domestic" political systems of states, but in fact these variations are highly relevant for our understanding of new forms of political space, and thus for the future of the concept of the international.

Various theorists have examined the changing nature of the state and discussed the need for new political perspectives, some of which will be treated below. But any discussion involving the nature of political space would be incomplete without a nod to the theorist who first fully articulated the concept of the political. Carl Schmitt merits the dubious distinction of being at once a brilliant critical politico-legal theorist and an unrepentant antidemocrat with close ties to the Nazi Party. Yet, his theories on politics nonetheless bear further scrutiny. His definition of the political highlights the division of political space into sovereign units, but his insistence on the identity-constitutive nature of politics serves also to undermine the legitimacy of state boundaries. He is a theorist, then, who both underpins and undermines ontopology, and for that reason, he is worth a look.

As a modernist-realist, Carl Schmitt saw the political in terms of the friend/enemy distinction. The nature of the political, he pointed out, is rarely discussed, but it must depend upon a particular set of distinctions, as do the concepts of morality (good and evil), aesthetics (beautiful and ugly), and economics (profitable and unprofitable).[9] For Schmitt, the friend/enemy distinction "denotes the utmost degree of intensity of a union or separation, of an association or dissociation," but it is also very important to separate this distinction from private dislike: "The political enemy need not be morally evil or aesthetically ugly; he need not appear as an economic competitor, and it may even be advantageous to engage with him in business transactions."[10] Schmitt carefully distinguishes the political as a *public* rather than a *private* concept, in an attempt to strip the concept of the emotions of personal friendship and enmity and define it as something more fundamental. The enemy is not necessarily hated, but "he is, nevertheless, the other, the stranger; and it is sufficient for his nature that he is, in a specially intense way, existentially something different and alien, so that in the extreme case conflicts with him are possible."[11] Although he describes the relationship in an individualistic third-person tense, Schmitt (writing in the 1920s and 1930s) refers to states in the classic modernist sense as self-contained units: "In its entirety the state as an organized political entity decides for itself the friend-enemy distinction."[12] This fixed perspective does not lessen the import of his contribution, however, since the definition of politics as constitutive is a significant breakthrough at whatever level it is applied. The major contribution of this distinction is the clarification of the meaning of politics as the process which determines the "who." In other words, politics is irrevocably bound up with identity—the two concepts cannot be separated. As Schmitt himself points out, so-called political terms such as "sovereignty," "society," "class," "constitutional," and even "state" are "incomprehensible if one does not know exactly who is to be affected, combatted, refuted, or negated by such a term."[13] Any decision or process which determines who will be included in a group and who will be excluded is thus a political one.

Although he discusses his concept of the political in the context of a theory of state relations, Schmitt recognizes that the use of the term "politics" carries strong meaning domestically in the interaction among political parties and interest groups. He sees this as the result of the "intensification of internal antagonisms [which have] the effect of weakening the common identity vis-à-vis another state."[14] Given that the determination of enemy is made by the possibility of combat, it is possible for the Schmittean friend/enemy relationship to take place within the state if "domestic conflicts among political parties have become the sole political difference [and] the most extreme degree of internal political tension is thereby reached; i.e., the domestic, not the foreign friend-and-enemy groupings are decisive for armed conflict."[15] When the friend/enemy grouping takes place within the state, the conflict is likely to end in civil war—or secession. But Schmitt does not equate politics with war, insisting that war is merely the extreme case and that a decision to pursue peaceful relations may be a good political one. The possibility of war is the exception that proves the rule of the political relationship. And conversely, if ever the friend/enemy distinction were eliminated, there would be no possibility of war and it would therefore be "a world without politics."[16] Schmitt refrains from comment about whether this result would be desirable. But he comments that if the attempt to eradicate politics (the possibility of war) were ever to become the justification for a war, it would "constitute the absolute last war of humanity":

> Such a war is necessarily unusually intense and inhuman because, by transcending the limits of the political framework, it simultaneously degrades the enemy into moral and other categories and is forced to make of him a monster that must not only be defeated but also utterly destroyed. In other words, he is an enemy who no longer must be compelled to retreat into his borders only.[17]

Writing this in the thirties, Schmitt appears almost prescient. Further, the implications of such absolutist views of politics are frightening in terms of territorializing identity. Should the conflictual nature of friend/enemy relations ever be overcome, it would involve the eradication of the enemy and thus of politics. But universal peace (the absence of politics) actually means universal identity and requires the annihilation of the other. Schmitt adopts a pretext of neutrality about the concept of the universal, but when he hypothesizes about a world state it is clear that he neither desires it nor feels that it would be possible to achieve. To begin with, a world state would only nominally be a state, based primarily on economic needs and regulation. In the absence of any global enemy, interest groups would become completely apolitical and be reduced to navigating between ethics and economics. Finally, Schmitt poses the core question of where the power for a world organization would fall.[18] In a universal state, humanity would be either totally oppressed or totally free—but in the latter case, free for what? Without politics, people would have no identity. Without the knowledge of who the other was, people would not know who they themselves were, and thus would end loyalty, friendship, and belonging—the concepts which today provide the ever-present possibility of conflict (politics). Identity has two sides and they cannot be split apart. On one side are all of the positive associations of kinship, sameness, and belonging and on the other are all of the negative aspects of strangeness, insecurity, and conflict. Politics is the means by which we maintain the boundaries, but it can also be the means by which we recognize the necessity of the other.

In his antiessentialism, Schmitt encourages the existence and maintenance of diversity, and he clearly contributes to the understanding of identity as an integral part of the political equation. But Schmitt in the end must be seen as an apologist for secession since he refuses to acknowledge the impossibility of cleansing the enemy (other) from within. Schmitt operates on the assumption that a purified collective self is the essence of the state—the "friend" in his friend-enemy equation. When difference is found within, it must be suppressed or a civil war must ensue that will re-create the sovereign boundaries surrounding the world's political friend-enemy units. These assumptions, while acting as the foundation of realist theory for many decades, have completely failed to account for or anticipate the changes in the state system. The proliferation of political spaces within and across state borders continues to present problems for ontopological assumptions. Some of the theorists who delve into these problems are discussed below.

The Future is Many

As we search for political forms which accommodate multiple and overlapping loyalties, the domestic structures of the state become highly relevant for the stability and composition of international society. In a sense, any attempt to freely speculate about the possible shapes of future political spaces requires a touch of (political) science fiction, for otherwise we can scarcely escape the intellectual confinement of our contemporary understandings. Perhaps because it has even less claim than most to ethnocultural homogeneity, North America provides a fertile theoretical ground for thoughts on a future politics of state-transcended identity and difference. Robert Kaplan provides some "futuristic" speculations about the political shape of the future based on his recent travels throughout the North American continent. Some of Kaplan's conclusions do indeed have the ring of science fiction:

> Imagine a land in which the dominant culture is an internationalized one, at every level; in which the political units that really matter are confederations of city-states; in which loyalty is an economic concept, when it is not obsolete; in which "the United States" exists chiefly to provide military protection. . . . [This land] is no longer beyond the horizon.[19]

But alarmist as this introduction sounds, Kaplan is ultimately fascinated by current developments which hint at shapes of the future and sees them as something to be embraced rather than resisted. He not only predicts the demise of traditional bordered states as we know them, but also believes that their successors are already taking shape in the north and southwest of the North American continent. The border between the United States and Mexico, he concludes, is "an artificial, purely legal construct [which] will one day revert to what it always has been: an unruly and politically ambiguous 'brown zone' of desert, several hundred miles wide, where civilizations (Spanish and Anglo, Athapaskan-speaking Indians from the Arctic, and Aztecán Indians from southern Mexico) once mingled."[20] As a consequence, there is a widespread process of integration and of "bi-nationhood" developing, as cities on both sides of the border become economically dependent on each other.

Cities in these areas of mingling cultures are playing host to a new kind of "internationalist" culture which allows multiple identities to flourish side by side without any one threatening the other. Kaplan, remarking on the size of a Chinese supermarket in Los Angeles (with its "forty aisles, each a hundred yards long, devoted to noodles, pork, taro, tofu, pea sprouts, dried shrimp, soybean paste, spicy bean cabbage, dried seaweed, rice spirits, and so on") finds himself speculating on the future of the American nation in the face of an onslaught of immigration:

> Traditionally nations rise and fall; but at the 99 Ranch Market I wondered if America might escape that fate by shedding its skin as a nation altogether and revealing an international civilization based on a single continent. . . . Why, I asked myself, worry about "the Asian threat"? The best way to contain Asian economic dynamism . . . is to absorb it, which is exactly what the United States is doing by attracting and Americanizing so many Asian immigrants.[21]

The main lesson to be learned from Kaplan's speculations is not to fret about the future. The "loss" of apparent national homogeneity is not a loss at all but a gain of new forms of the nation. These questions are particularly relevant for the wealthy nations of the West, which currently harbor numerous ongoing battles about the sanctity of their borders and the "threat" or "economic salvation" posed by large groups of immigrants in search of a better life. These issues resonate deeply with identity politics, but they are also issues of economics and perceived limitation of resources.

While the United States is often seen as a natural breeding ground for multiculturalism due to its history as a land of large frontiers and settlement opportunities, its current blend of rich diversity continues to generate struggle and conflict. The flashpoint is the question of the extent to which new immigrants must assimilate in order to become "American," and the extent to which a common American identity even exists or is desirable. While diversity and choice are deemed good, there is growing concern about the lack of a shared sense of community. Recent changes in demographic balances (resulting in pluralities rather than strong majority/minority relationships) have led Americans to "demographic balkanization" and a "powerful preference to see [themselves] through a racial prism, wary of others, and, in many instances, hostile."[22] The traditional story of immigration as an upward progress toward economic success and the accompanying social assimilation is giving way to economic "mobility traps" and a perception that there is no dominant mainstream into which immigrants may assimilate. Nevertheless, whites have long tended to lump groups into broad ethnic categories:

> It is a particularly American phenomenon, many say, to label citizens by their ethnicity. When a person lived in El Salvador, for example, he or she saw themselves as a nationality. When they arrive in the United States, they become Hispanic or Latino. So too with Asians. Koreans and Cambodians find little in common, but then they arrive here they become "Asian," and are counted and courted, encouraged or discriminated against as such.[23]

Failure to treat many immigrant identities with respect for their distinctiveness, and instead focusing on the simplest way to differentiate them from the (white European) mainstream, has contributed to this demographic balkanization and struggle along ethnic lines. However, the old broad racial categories continue to stick as the composition of the nation becomes a political issue.

Nothing reflects the entrenchment of American racial politics like questions about the U.S. Census. Since 1971, there have been only five racial categories on the census form: black, white, Asian or Pacific Islander, American Indian or Alaskan native, and other. But when the census was taken in 1990 there was a 45 percent increase in the number of respondents checking the "other" category. Birth data now indicate that the number of children of mixed race couples is increasing faster than the number of children born to single race couples, thus prompting a movement to add a new census category called "multiracial."[24] The categorization of Americans has become even more politicized with the entitlements of affirmative action, apportionment, and educational and research funding, which have been applied to redress historical inequalities in recent years. In fact, it is members of established "minority" groups who are the strongest critics of the multiracial category. They consider it a threat to their organizations and hard-won political strength since many of their members could conceivably "defect" to the multiracial category. It has even been estimated that at least 75 percent of those who currently define themselves as "black" would be able to check the multiracial box because of their mixed heritage.

Such a statistical swing would drastically affect the civil rights programs at the state and federal levels, leading many to question the validity of any racial classification at all. But without such classification, it has been argued, civil rights protections may fall prey to lurking discrimination and prejudice, which remain statistically significant in American society. However, official categories of racial classification may exacerbate racial conflict: "By creating social welfare programs based on race rather than on need, the government sets citizens against one another precisely because of perceived racial differences."[25] In addition, by offering specific categories of race for census respondents to select, the government takes a hand in restricting and enforcing the racial identities of its citizens. This is especially problematic when the identity category is as troublesome to define as race.

Many Americans do not have a clear understanding of who they are racially, as illustrated by a study in which 5.8 percent of the participants who considered themselves to be black were described as white by an interviewer. Almost one-third of self-described Asians were considered to be black or white by outside observers, and the same result was true for 75 percent of self-identified American Indians.[26] This study does not even begin to illustrate the complexity of identity in racial terms of someone with cross-cultural heritage on both sides of the family. The larger question in America's race debate is one of group membership and the extent to which an individual's identity must be articulated in terms of membership in a group (or many groups). In this sense the debate is a variation on the struggle to simplify and politicize (territorialize) national identity, and this aspect gives it broader relevance as an example of the internal politics of identity and difference that "threaten" the state. The idea that people can be counted and compartmentalized on such bases is an illusion: "To be effective, the concepts of individual and group identity need to reflect not only who we have been but who we are becoming. The more these categories distort our perception of reality, the less useful they are."[27]

The intensity of the racial classification debate appears in stark contrast to Kaplan's futuristic musings of multicultural, economically dynamic "polycentric urban pods," which appear bland and uniform by comparison. In fact, one of Kaplan's sources, a business journal editor in Orange County, California, admits that there is little local loyalty or community feeling since most people have migrated to the county from elsewhere, primarily for economic benefit. He concludes that "in the future, patriotism will be more purely and transparently economic."[28] But Kaplan himself wonders whether urban areas such as Orange County, which act as magnets for motivated entrepreneurs, can really maintain the stability they appear to present in the absence of shared notions of patriotism or civic virtue. Libertarianism thrives in such "urban pods," and the side effect of this independent-minded pursuit of the good life is social fragmentation and inequality: "the threatening and unsightly poor are kept out of sight; hence the growth of social- and income-exclusive residential areas."[29] In contrast to the individualism of Orange County, Kaplan identifies another model for the regional political space of the future—the revival of the city-state as exemplified by Vancouver, British Columbia. Geographically, economically, and socially isolated from the rest of Canada, British Columbia maintains a strong regional identity. Fueled by a large, wealthy Asian immigrant pool, the city of Vancouver is developing an "East-West hybrid culture" of economic success. But it also maintains a cohesive sense of identity which generates civic loyalty of the kind necessary for perpetuating a new type of political space.

As a Vancouver urban geographer enthused:

> This is all you need to be sovereign in the phase of history we are entering; a dynamic and highly educated population and strategic transport links. Cities and their environs already provide you with everything you need—garbage collection, schools, neighborhood whatever—but they get the least of your taxes. The bulk of your tax money still goes to the state or province and the federal government, and what do they do for you. . . . Isn't it antiquated? But that will change. In the coming decades your tax money will increasingly go to the place you really care about. . . . Though I guess we should all pay taxes to that Information Age military you are creating in Washington, D.C. They'll in effect sell us the protection we will need against terrorists and other bad people. You see, we don't need *you* [he meant America], and we certainly don't need Canada. What we need is your military![30]

Whether or not these speculations are accurate, what Kaplan and his sources tell us is that change is afoot, and even wild approximate guesses as to what shape the future may take are a more positive approach than denial and resolute insistence on the forms of the past. One of the biggest problems for Kaplan's thesis that the state structures of North America will disintegrate into a combination of urban pods and city-states is that it fails to address the question of whether the current success of these areas can be maintained without the support of the state structures within which they currently sit. The urban geographer envisioned contracting out for military protection, but national politics cover many more issues, such as health, education, welfare, environmental protection, and a strong legal system. This is not to say that these issues cannot be resolved in the future space Kaplan has in mind; it is only to point out that the question of future political spaces is a complex one and cannot ever be thought of as "solved" by a single theorist, however courageous his musings.

The fact that this discussion of Kaplan's work has apparently been restricted to local urban areas rather than states and the sphere of the "international" by no means makes it irrelevant to International Relations theory and secession. The future of such regions will certainly change the nature of international relations by changing the type of political body among which the interrelations take place. International Relations theorists would neglect such possibilities at the peril of a disciplinary descent into irrelevance. True, Kaplan's ideas are particularly based on North American conditions and therefore can be seen as culturally possible only in the Western New World. But the ties of economic interdependence and inter-cultural relations are so widespread now that no such change could be strictly *local*. Furthermore, while these forces of interrelationship and change cannot be fully controlled, they can be analyzed and accounted for in any vision of future possibility. The key is to appreciate the necessity of complexity, and to fight the tug of comfortable certainty, in attempting to understand the new politics of space and time.

Democracy *sans Frontieres*

Given the intensity with which political power is being pulled in multiple directions on a multitude of issues, both locally, as in Kaplan's models, and regionally, as economic and strategic coalitions such as the European Union and NATO illustrate, national governments can no longer claim to be the sole relevant bodies for dealing with a large number of political questions. Globalization, David Held and Anthony McGrew argue, has led to a new kind of "boundary problem," in which states' decisions affect not only their own citizens but also many others who have had no voice.[31] This raises tricky questions of accountability and responsibility which badly tangle the happy clarity of the old sovereign inside/outside divide. Held and McGrew remark that "political space for the development and pursuit of effective government and the accountability of power is no longer coterminous with a delimited political territory."[32] What, then, becomes of the post-Cold War project of spreading democracy as a means of achieving peace? This "boundary problem" is actually a crucial question of political theory—making political decisions which are legitimate and accountable. Global government is certainly not the answer to this question, and Held and McGrew are quick to point out that globalization does not act as homogenization. States still maintain unquestionable power over the big political issues concerning their territory—namely, military security and border control. But in most other areas of the political sphere, as it is currently fashionable to point out, the pretensions of states to dominance are wearing thin. In short, authority over many political questions is now being transformed by the simple collective force of world shrinkage due to the vast increase in the speed with which we conduct all of our transactions. Held and McGrew urge that "if the most powerful geo-political forces are not to settle many pressing matters simply in terms of their own objectives and by virtue of their power, then existing institutions and mechanisms of accountability need to be reconsidered."[33] To this end, they identify a "taxonomy of prospective world orders": four established schools of thought that focus on the reallocation of political power.

The first of these is the increasingly popular neoliberal school, in which economic forces cause transnational networks to develop and marginalize the influence of the state. Market forces become authoritative and consumerism pervades, causing a new identity to prevail over traditional societies. "The global spread of Western liberal democracy further reinforces the sense of an emerging civilization defined by universal standards of economic and political organization."[34] Another school of thought is liberal-reformism, which seeks to promote "a new global civic ethic based upon 'core' values that all humanity could uphold." Liberal-reformists, in the tradition of the great liberal ideals of the nineteenth century, with their "faith in progress and human rationality . . . have argued that creating a peaceful and democratic world order is far from a utopian project but, on the contrary, a necessity in a world of growing interdependence."[35] Rather than relying on the market to push democratic standards, liberal-reformists would make states more accountable through reform of international institutions. Third, in contrast, there are those who adhere to the "radical project," emphasizing a bottom up means of change in world order. Radicals do not rely on individualism or rationality, but believe in alternative mechanisms such as social movements which "challenge the authority of states and international agencies as well as orthodox definitions of the 'political.'" Thus, the radical version of humane governance is based on "a multiplicity of 'communities of fate' and social movements."[36] Finally, Held and McGrew identify the cosmopolitan project, which aims to specify principles of accountability for "forms of power which presently operate beyond the scope of democratic control."[37] Cosmopolitans believe that citizenship and loyalty will be "mediated" through different and multiple traditions and communities and that this will increase the possibility of mutual understanding. Democratization, in the cosmopolitan project, involves not only "deepening" democracy within states and local communities, but also encouraging "cosmopolitan citizens to gain access to, mediate between, and render accountable, the social, economic and political processes and flows which cut across and transform their traditional community boundaries."[38] Cosmopolitanism, as envisioned here, centers on the legitimacy of politics and how that can be reconceived as democratic principles in a nonterritorial fashion. Held and McGrew conceive of these four schools of thought, or projects, as constituting an invigorating political debate—in contest against one another. That a multifaceted discussion of the new possibilities of nonterritorial politics is necessary seems obvious enough. What is not clear is why these "schools" should be seen as competing against one another for ultimate and exclusive success. There is nothing about the features of neoliberalism, liberal-reformism, radicalism, or cosmopolitanism as described here which shuts out the indicators of other projects or requires mutual exclusivity. Rather, one should require of Held and McGrew a vigorous defense of why global market forces, international institutional reforms, global social movements, and cross-boundary citizenship cannot all occur at once. In fact, they are all occurring today as we struggle to discern trends and order in a confusing and transitional global ethos.

It is the extension of accountability for constituencies which span territoriality that lies at the heart of the concern for new forms of a democratic order. Held examines this idea in another piece, elaborating the cosmopolitan project, in which he points out that our prior assumptions about democracy have been bifurcated by the inside/outside sovereign divide. The international system has been distinguished by "democracy *in* nation-states and non-democratic relations *among* states; the entrenchment of accountability and democratic legitimacy *inside* state boundaries and the pursuit of power politics (or maximum advantage) *outside* such boundaries; and democracy and citizenship rights for '*insiders*' and their frequent negation for '*outsiders*.'"[39] Globalization obviously threatens the legitimacy of a democratic system manifested solely within the state. Held's point in advocating a "cosmopolitan democracy" is that we must reconceive democracy as a system that applies to all the constituencies which should monitor accountability regardless of territorial boundaries and national identities. Held envisions referenda of transnational groups on issues such as energy policy and the formation of regional authorities, because cosmopolitan democracy is "based on the recognition that democracy within a particular community and democratic relations among communities are interlocked, absolutely inseparable, and that new organizational and binding mechanisms must be created if democracy is to survive and develop in the decades ahead."[40] The questions remain, What kind of mechanisms and how can they be created? Held is aware of the difficulties of asserting a specific global program, since it is arguable that globalization has sparked the renewed affirmation of particular identities and separatist tendencies. He is careful to assert that the existence of cosmopolitan communities requires neither integration nor consensus along political and cultural lines, since "part of the appeal of democracy lies in its refusal to accept in principle any conception of the political good other than that generated by the people themselves."[41] In other words, democracy is the only system which conveys legitimacy upon limitless numbers of competing "narratives of the good." What must be instituted globally for Held's vision to become meaningful is a "precommitment" to follow democratic procedures—each political entity or interest must "recognize the other as a legitimate presence with which some accommodation must be made; and each must be willing to give up exclusive claims upon the right, the good, the universal and the spatial."[42]

Covert Coercion and the Liberal Utopia

With the idea of pluralistic recognition and participation of all perspectives, and the abandonment of a single claim to the truth, the theoretical difficulties of democratic politics become more apparent. How are the multiple voices to be heard without the strong and the numerous drowning out the weak and the few? National boundaries have much less to do with the dynamics of democratic accountability than popularly acknowledged. The problem of "coercion" is one that has plagued democratic theory since its inception. Jane Mansbridge goes so far as to argue that true political legitimacy cannot exist in the real world: "If coercion is legitimated only by equal power in the decision to coerce, and if no real democracy can achieve equal power, then no real democracy—especially no real large-scale democracy—can ever fully justify the coercion it exercises."[43] Legitimacy, then, can only be approximated but never fully achieved. Coercion, in the sense of unequal deliberative power over decision making, is always present, even in the smallest groups. Thus, political accountability and representation problems are present within as well as among national identity groups. On one hand, this would seem to dissolve the importance of borders for political democratic decision making through the equally "coercive" conditions to which all participants are subject in any political process. However, it does little to attract one to the cosmopolitan project since the conditions of democracy as a whole are severely called into question. So how can the democratic process be legitimated? How can its participating identity groups be validated? Mansbridge herself considers that the coercive nature of democratic deliberation, if recognized, can drive the process of compromise and accommodation continually onward, forcing us to realize that the state of equality and justice is never actually achieved.

> Each balance of power creates a new underdog, each settlement a new group who would benefit from unsettling. Each settlement accordingly creates not only the necessary capacity for action but also the need to protect and facilitate in some way those who have lost. Because no democracy ever reaches the point at which justice is simply done, democracies need to recognize and foster enclaves of resistance.[44]

This is a crucial point—*justice is never done*—both in the sense that it is never simply achieved and that the process of trying to achieve it must continue. This is so because there can be no common perception of justice determined in a coercion-free deliberative environment. The best democracies, then, are never stable, but always poised on the point of unsettling balances, shifting alliances, and toppling the powerful. We must always be aware of the need for opposition and resistance.

As Chantal Mouffe puts it, "the relation between social agents becomes more democratic only insofar as they accept the particularity and the limitation of their claims; that is only insofar as they recognize their mutual relations as one from which power is ineradicable."[45] For Mouffe, the notion of a democratic system which is freed of power relations is a dangerous illusion. She advocates a project of "radical and plural democracy" in which "the specificity of modern pluralist democracy—even a well-ordered one—resides not in the absence of domination and of violence but in the establishment of a set of institutions through which they can be limited and contested."[46] In her critique of John Rawls's concept of just society, Mouffe asserts that any attempt to resolve with finality the question of what constitutes justice in a democratic community yields dangerous consequences. Rawls's theory of the well-ordered society has eliminated politics because a common conception of justice has been realized by "reasonable and rational citizens" who act in accordance. These citizens' mutual "differences" occur in their conceptions of the good, but these conflicting ideas are private and do not affect the public sphere. All disputes over public issues are resolved through the agreed upon principles of justice. But any dissent about what constitutes these principles of justice must be by an "unreasonable" or "irrational" person who must be forced to submit. This coercion, however, is legitimated in Rawls's society by its source in the communal exercise of reason. Mouffe concludes that "Rawls's 'liberal utopia' would, then, be a society in which legitimate dissent would have been eliminated from the public sphere."[47] Because Rawls and others who attempt to maintain a fixed definition of justice assume that an "ordered" society is one in which there is full agreement about political processes in the public sphere, they have consigned all "difference" to the private sector. But this is to profoundly miss the constitutive nature of politics itself. Democratic order is not the staid absence of dissent in the public realm, but rather the realization that "undecidability is the condition of existence of democratic politics."[48] The more contentious and indefinite are relations among participants in a society, the better the democratic project of giving voice to the plurality has been approximated.

> Instead of trying to erase the traces of power and exclusion, democratic politics requires bringing them to the fore, making them visible so that they can enter the terrain of contestation. The fact that this must be envisaged as an unending process should not be cause for despair, because the desire to reach a final destination can only lead to the elimination of the political and to the destruction of democracy. In a democratic polity, conflicts and confrontations, far from being a sign of imperfection, indicate that democracy is alive and inhabited by pluralism.[49]

The only way to properly accommodate identity and difference within political theory is to recognize the inevitability of conflict (politics) among the many selves and conceptions of the good. This conception of democracy has profound implications for the conclusions reached by most theorists of secession and has been largely ignored.

Leaving Home

Political theorist Bonnie Honig makes a crucial connection between the "inescapability of conflict" and the concept of "home." If we are to attempt to seriously integrate the concept of identity\difference into democratic theory, we must "give up on the dream of a place called home, a place free of power, conflict, and struggle, a place—an identity, a form of life, a group vision—unmarked or unriven by difference and untouched by the power brought to bear upon it by the identities that strive to ground themselves in its place."[50] Honig is not making a call for the primacy of the individual and the relative unimportance of group identities. Rather, she is emphasizing the need to recognize that "home" is a collective illusion that hides the struggle of the constituted identities taking part in it. The inter-relationship of identity and difference (as discussed in chapter 4) cannot be ignored or downplayed in any discussion of secession and international politics. Instead, this relationship must be brought to the forefront to uncover the flaws in our assumptions about the nation and the homeland and the goal of "solving" ethnic conflict. Difference is not only the self we are not; it is an actual part of our "self." Identity contains difference within it; difference is "what identity perpetually seeks (and fails) to expunge, fix, or hold in place."[51] Honig's "politics of home" reflects on the urge to reside within the illusion of a collective identity, where values are shared and difference is kept out. Democratic politics within such a *home*-land would be free of conflict because of the common identity and—thus equality—of the partici-pants. But we have already learned to be wary of complacency in politics since it refuses to acknowledge difference and thus hides the oppression of dissent. Because it must be unitary to maintain its trouble-free identity, the politics of "home" strives to withdraw from or conquer the difference within. As Honig warns:

> The dream of home is dangerous, particularly in postcolonial settings, because it animates and exacerbates the inability of constituted subjects—or nations—to accept their own internal differences and divisions, and it engenders zealotry, the will to bring the dream of unitariness or home into being. It leads the subject to project its internal differences onto external Others and then to rage against them for standing in the way of its dream—both at home and elsewhere. . . . This zealotry takes shape as a propensity either to withdraw from conflicts or to con-quer them: withdrawal (to a supposedly safe home that is elsewhere, away from all this tumult) and conquest (of that tumultuous disorder in order to build a supposedly safe home here) are two sides of the same zealot's coin. Both signal an unwillingness—on the part of constituted subjects or formed nations—to settle for anything less than a phantasmatic imaginary of home.[52]

Through this perspective, secession can be seen as both the attempt to withdraw from difference and the attempt to conquer it. Both involve the unyielding attempt to purify the identity of the collective self—a fruitless and unsavory task. Given the antidemocratic implications of this attempt, secession becomes a phenomena which no democratic theorist ought to justify. But, as mentioned several times in this book, secession is not a *problem* which can be *solved* through carefully reasoned methods and analysis. It is an *outcome* of a certain way of thinking about identity and politics. When these ways of thinking have changed, secession will no longer be relevant.

What, then, becomes of our concept of home and our obvious need for some kind of rooted identity? Honig theorizes optimistically that acceptance of the state of conflict and difference and the impossibility of the conventional notion of home is the admission of "a vulnerability that may *look like* homelessness," but actually allows a reconceptualization of home as a "coalitional arrangement."[53] Such an arrangement of home is the required first step to a true understanding of the freedoms we do have, an understanding that rejects home as "spaces of privacy and integrity that depend upon the displacement of abjection onto Others, spaces of identity that seem to require for their survival the displacement, conquest, or conversion of difference and Otherness that relentlessly intrude upon us."[54] So the response to our need for home and a rooted identity is to recognize the illusive nature of the quest. Like justice, home is a concept which can never actually be realized, and, like justice, the desire for it is never sated. But this assertion is not a call to abandon order and civil society. To the contrary, it is an urgent appeal to recognize the need for constant coalitional negotiations and the wide variety of possibilities for the social self in terms of multiple affiliations. With such an understanding of home and of the self, we are at once far less secure, and also far less bounded—that is, more free to realize the complexity of the self (both individually and collectively). This seeming homelessness is the ethical option, in terms of refusing to hide or rename attempts to eliminate difference. There is also an element of the psychoanalytical perspective in this understanding—it is what Julia Kristeva calls recognition of the foreigner within. Kristeva realizes the political possibilities of an "ethics of psychoanalysis" in the discovery of our own "disturbing otherness." If we recognize our *own* "uncanny strangeness we shall neither suffer from it nor enjoy it from the outside. The foreigner is within me, hence we are all foreigners. If I am a foreigner, there are no foreigners."[55] For Kristeva, the politics of recognizing our own internal difference might result in

> a cosmopolitanism of a new sort that, cutting across governments, economies, and markets, might work for a mankind whose solidarity is founded on the consciousness of its unconscious—desiring, destructive, fearful, empty, impossible. . . . [For] the difference within us in its most bewildering shape [is presented] as the ultimate condition of our being *with* others.[56]

Thus, theories of cosmopolitan democracy and of the politics of psychoanalytic ethics cross disciplinary boundaries to reach very similar conclusions. This should come as no surprise to political theorists, since the determination of the self, the "us" and "them," is *the* foundational question of politics.

Different Democracy

In conjunction with these discussions about the constitutive interrelationship between identity and difference, it seems clear that even if there were widespread

agreement about the value of universal peace and organization, it would be antithetical to democratic values to eliminate difference, or, in Schmittean terminology, to
eliminate the determination of friend/enemy and thus politics itself. However, taking
Schmitt's thesis from a modernist to a postmodernist stage allows us to contemplate
mechanisms for appreciating the self/other distinction on the inside as well as the
outside of the sovereign border, and thus to theorize ways of dealing with internal
difference and the nature of democratic accountability. For William Connolly
democracy has been injured by its irrevocable theorization in terms of state institutions. Political theorists have assumed the state territorial foundations of democracy
without questioning the contradictory impulses of democracy itself. The territorial
state provides the (liberating) organization of electoral institutions, but also,
Connolly asserts, the (confining) limitations of democratic "energies" which seek
to find points of identification without regard to geographical markers.[57] Rather than
seeing democracy as altered or inauthenticated by a nonterritorial reconceptualization, Connolly envisions democracy as deprived of the full manifestation of its
capabilities while it continues to be restricted to the confines of the territorial state.
These capabilities exceed the concept of democracy as a form of rule and encompass it as "an egalitarian constitution of cultural life that encourages people to
participate in defining their own troubles and possibilities, regardless of where these
troubles originate and how narrow or broad they are in scope."[58] Thus, democracy
can be seen as a social process which continually overturns settled conventions,
thrives on ambiguity, and circumvents the attempts of one perspective to claim the
final truth. In other words, *"its role as a mode of governance is balanced and
countered by its logic as a cultural medium of the periodic denaturalization of
settled identities and conventions."*[59] It is this problematizing aspect of the democratic ethos that allows it to exceed the confines of the state's political space and to
generate spaces of its own. Connolly does not argue that the dissolution of territorial
governance is imminent or desirable. Instead he argues for the "pluralization" of
democratic spaces, the allowance of new allegiances and identifications without
regard to state institutions. Such allegiances are indeed already taking place in terms
of financial structures, social movements, and media, to name a few. The point is
not to identify or name the structures of future political spaces—that would resem-
ble the type of essentialist project which contradicts the very democratic distur-
bances which fuel the changes in the first place. Connolly proposes a recognition
of the (anachronistic) limitations imposed by the state on democracy and a pluralistic response to the "democratic aspiration to have a hand in shaping corporate,
strategic, distributive, ecological, and military practices that enable, discipline, and
endanger our lives."[60]

It is important to accept the fact that no single vantage point on the shape of
pluralized democracy can be gained. The new political spaces can only be recognized and encouraged—they cannot be fully preconceived lest they deteriorate into
utopian illusions or uncompromising irrelevancies. Connolly compares today's
development of pluralized democratic spaces to the relationship between Italian
city-states and the growth of state-territorial organization in the sixteenth century.

It cannot be fully imagined:

> It is protean, unformed, and unrealistic from the perspective of fixed identities and conventional boundaries. Epistemic realists will always find it difficult to participate in the activation of new energies if they demand the solidification of future possibilities into fixed objects prior to the representation of them.[61]

Seeking solidity will prioritize certainty over ambiguity and perpetuate sameness at the cost of oppressing difference.

The big question which suggests itself upon consideration of the pluralizing ethos is to what extent can diversity be encouraged before fragmentation endangers the collective good? Connolly replies that the question assumes a misunderstanding of the interrelationship between identity and difference by identifying "extensive cultural *diversification* with the loss of cultural *connections*. . . . To pluralize, therefore, is not to fragmentize. To dogmatize is to fragmentize."[62] To illustrate his point, Connolly examines the ever-present tree metaphor of society, with a deeply rooted base from which the limbs of diversity may branch. He rejects this metaphor in favor of rhizomatic growth, which depends upon the continual interconnection of both roots and shoots, and which spreads in many directions instead of the unidirectional tree.[63] Within the rhizome metaphor, diversification indicates the flourishing strength of the plant, with multiple roots and shoots each connected with others by crisscrossing runners. The diversified pluralized culture which grows from these rhizomatic connections is helped along by a relationship among participants which Connolly calls "agonistic respect"—it is a certain reciprocal "forbearance" and "generosity"[64] in pressing and responding to claims which stems from widespread acknowledgment of the ambiguity of identity and the impossibility of an objective standard of truth. The politics of agonism are to be understood in contrast to those of antagonism. Unlike antagonism, agonism recognizes the necessity of the different other in the constitution of the self, and therefore it concedes to the other a measure of respect. Like Schmitt's friend-enemy distinction, agonists exist on level and equal terms—each necessary for the other to exist. An agonism of difference is one in which

> each opposes the other (and the other's presumptive beliefs) while respecting the adversary at another level as one whose contingent orientations also rest on shaky epistemic grounds. An antagonism in which each aims initially at conquest or conversion of the other can now (given other supporting conditions) become an agonism in which each treats the other as crucial to itself in the strife and interdependence of identity\difference. A "pathos of distance" (to borrow a phrase from Nietzsche) begins to unfold whereby each maintains a certain respect for the adversary, partly because the relationship exposes contingency in the being of both.[65]

The relationship of agonistic respect thus smooths the way for connections among the many identities in a pluralized democracy and into the multibounded political spaces beyond the state. But agonism can also have profound meaning for international relations in both its inter-*national* and inter-*state* senses. Showing agonistic (rather than antagonistic) respect for the national aspirations of an opponent allows that opponent to feel recognized (not unlike the international legal recognition that constitutes a state), and therefore removes the aspect of zero-sum politics from the game. If the starting assumption is that the "other" identity not only has a right to exist but also is intrinsic to your own "self" identity then the very definition of security politics undergoes a deep transformation and the possibility of communication and understanding (even if unaccompanied by friendship) is greatly facilitated. Secessionist politics would become increasingly irrelevant as states became less dominant as the sole validative fora and the politics of pluralizing democracy expanded through the growing organic ties of the rhizomatic structures.

*In*conclusion

While the increasingly anachronistic relationship between state and territory would seem to pose a threat to democratic politics, it only points to the conditions of possibility for the creation of new political spaces and more authentic democratic practices. We can seek now to create different meanings for the conceptual signifiers *politics, state, identity,* and *democracy.* The modernist territorial meanings for these terms that we struggle with today are becoming less and less relevant, but they contain the seeds of new *post*-modernist meanings which can make better sense for the emerging patterns of the globalized world. As stated above, future politics cannot be made to conform to a pattern or model—this would be imposing one vision over another. It would be to advocate fragmenting dogma rather than pluralizing rhizomatic patterns of relations. Because we (can) have no model, we are scarcely able to recognize contraontopological patterns. As Roland Bleiker points out,

> Discourses live on and appear reasonable long after their premises have turned into anachronistic relics. More inclusive ways of theorizing and living world(s) politics cannot surface overnight. There are no quick solutions, no new paradigms or miraculous political settlements that one could hope for. Changing the practice of IR is a long process, saturated with obstacles and contradictions. . . . It is in our daily practices of speaking, of forgetting and remembering, that slow transformative potentials are hidden.[66]

We should be wary of elegant solutions as subversive of pluralistic and agonistic politics. Politics is a messy, conflictual business; there is no quick fix. Nor, however, are there permanent structural patterns which determine the way politics must be done. A historical discourse of antagonism between nations need not dictate the precise course of the future. Enemies have become friends and friends enemies. The nations of Western Europe, engaged in total war a short half-century ago, now allow free passage across the borders internal to the European Union (EU). While there are still many modernist ontopological aspects to EU discourse, with a constant tension between the whole entity and the particular states, the leveling of economic and legal practices hints at a new willingness to break away from territorial politics. The fact that EU politics proceeds with maddening slowness is due partially to member states clinging to their shreds of power and partially also to the lack of a supreme plan or consensus. European unification does not ask (and therefore cannot answer definitively) "what is the nature of European unification?" Rather, the EU simply engages in a continual questioning and reestablishing of the semantics of *European* and of *Union*. Continual redefinition, without recourse to the determination of a historical model, allows the EU to venture beyond the familiar patterns of statehood in which regions and social movements have options for transborder recognition and cooperation. I do not wish to represent the EU as a model of contraontopology. The EU does maintain modernist conceptions of inside/outside territoriality, but the fact that the external borders are even somewhat negotiable, and that internal relations occur across state borders, hints at a willingness to conceive of new forms of political space.

As mentioned above, it is the daily practices of speaking, forgetting, and remembering that yield the full transformative potentials of alternative theorizing. Roland Bleiker discusses forgetting in Nietzschean terms—that is, one must forget history to free the future from its grasp. It is a special kind of forgetting, which allows the remembering of historically constructed identities, but also the remembering of the contingency of those constructions and therefore the forgetting of the determination of history and the recognition of alternatives for the future. As Milan Kundera says, "Remembering is not the negative of forgetting. Remembering is a form of forgetting."[67] This is the kind of forgetting which allows the blacks in America to remember slavery but forget the shame of bondage and reestablish their identities as integral to the building of the country; it allows whites to remember that they participated actively or tacitly in a system which condoned slavery, but to forget the hatred they felt for the Other and recognize that the white identity in America was constructed against the black and therefore contains blackness within it. This is the kind of forgetting which is going on currently in South Africa, Vietnam, and Chile, but it is a long, slow, and painful process, and there are always some who persist in remembering the narratives of exclusion. Their voices are a part of the ambiguity of agonistic politics, and they cannot be silenced. Secessionist narratives are a form of history which remembers without forgetting. They perform a politics which attempts to *re*-member the nation in terms of maintaining the identities (membership) of the mythical historical nation of the past. Secessionists are trying hard not to *forget*.

Examples from Western liberal democracies are in fact the "easy" cases. Conflictual and angry as relations between these groups remain, they are still relations under conditions of peace. What do we say to the groups caught in the crossfire of the Balkans? They eat, drink, and breathe ontopological convictions. How do we *practice* our *theory* of forgetting in Serbia? Listening to the nationalist mythical historical narratives stemming from all sides of the various conflicts, one pattern repeats itself: "We can never live with them after what they did to us." It is tempting to use these stories as the basis for peace. The wars between these groups have been so horrible, the quickest option to stop the fighting is also the easiest. If they cannot live with each other, then surely they should not have to. The solution most easily implemented always consists of boundaries, separation, autonomy—control over territory. But these are the solutions of history, and they are the "solutions" which made the current conflicts possible. The Dayton Agreement, with its blotchy birthmark patchwork of territorial entities held together by the thinnest threads of federal structure, is nothing if not a monument to modernist ontopological thinking. For the moment, there is peace in Bosnia, but it is doubtful that there is much forgetting.[68] Can our theories about alternatives for the future be useful in solving active conflicts? I suggest that they can, but they must be *practiced* first. Without the coercion and guidance of an ontopological teleology, the practice of forgetting and remembering is difficult. But when ethnic groups in conflict claim that their history prohibits them from coexistence, it is time to forget. Nationalist performances based on the territorial exclusion of the other must not be credited as structural imperatives for the future. Any solution must involve the slow, hard process of reconciliation and mutual recognition. The opponents need not be friends; they need only understand their mutual dependency. This requires the establishment of stable institutions which give voice and rights to all perspectives regardless of national affiliation—in other words, a free press, independent judiciary, and multiparty democracy. A new path for "war-torn societies" (Kosovo, or Northern Ireland, or Palestine) involves the refusal by peace brokers to countenance the exclusivist claims of historical nationalist identities. But more than that, groups caught in conflict must be given encouragement to engage with each other, to claim responsibility for, but also to *forget,* their histories by freeing space (both political and territorial) for different relations in the future. The relations will take shape as needed and as performed on a daily basis, but they must be nurtured and protected against the fragmentizing dogmatic tendencies of the separatist imperative.

Thus, new types of spatial politics will change our understanding of the national and the international—and International Relations theory and practice must change along with it. We cannot continue to assume that identity stops at the state's border—politics are constitutive of the self and the other. *International* politics occur wherever groups claim a national identity of the self, regardless of the institutional or spatiotemporal setting. Comprehending this dynamic is crucial for the future relevance of International Relations as a discipline—and of course for theorists of secession. As we recognize the transcendence of state boundaries and the separatist politics they engender, so we come to recognize secession as an anachronism, and eventually as history.

Notes

1. Jacques Derrida, *Specters of Marx: The State of the Debt, the Work of Mourning, and the New International*, trans. Peggy Kamuf (New York: Routledge, 1994), 82.

2. Derrida, *Specters of Marx*, 82.

3. David Campbell, *National Deconstruction: Violence, Identity, and Justice in Bosnia* (Minneapolis: University of Minnesota Press, 1998), 80.

4. Campbell, *National Deconstruction*, 24, citing Judith Butler, *Bodies That Matter: On the Discursive Limits of Sex* (New York: Routledge, 1993), 2.

5. In this sense, sovereignty is much like currency—it maintains legitimacy and strength through continued use and the absence of sustained challenges. A variation on the *coup de force* concept is William Connolly's "paradox of political founding," in which the will of the people must be created by the effect (social spirit), and the cause (good laws) would have to become effect in order to generate social spirit, and so on. The upshot of this is that political legitimacy is an illusion. See William Connolly, *The Ethos of Pluralization* (Minneapolis: University of Minnesota Press, 1995), 138.

6. Campbell, *National Deconstruction*, 26.

7. Reinhart Koselleck, *Futures Past: On the Semantics of Historical Time*, trans. Keith Tribe (Cambridge, Mass.: The MIT Press, 1985), 90.

8. Koselleck, *Futures Past*, 90.

9. Carl Schmitt, *The Concept of the Political,* trans. with intr. by George Schwab (Chicago: The University of Chicago Press, 1996 [1932]), 26.

10. Schmitt, *Concept of the Political*, 27.

11. Schmitt, *Concept of the Political*, 27.

12. Schmitt, *Concept of the Political*, 29-30.

13. Schmitt, *Concept of the Political*, 31.

14. Schmitt, *Concept of the Political*, 32.

15. Schmitt, *Concept of the Political*, 32.

16. Schmitt, *Concept of the Political*, 35.

17. Schmitt, *Concept of the Political*, 36.

18. Schmitt, *Concept of the Political*, 57.

19. Robert Kaplan, "Travels into America's Future," *The Atlantic Monthly*, August 1998. Available at http://www. theatlantic.com/issues/98aug/amfuture.htm. Accessed 12 August 2003.

20. Robert Kaplan, *Empire Wilderness: Travels into America's Future* (New York: Random House, 1998), 135.

21. Kaplan, *Empire Wilderness*, 85-87.

22. William Booth, "One Nation, Indivisible: Is It History?" *The Washington Post*, 22 February 1998, A01.

23. Booth, "One Nation, Indivisible."

24. Seth Schiesel and Robert L. Turner, "Is Race Obsolete?" *The Boston Globe Magazine*, 22 September 1996, 13.

25. Lawrence Wright, "One Drop of Blood," *The New Yorker*, 25 July 1994, 54.

26. Wright, "One Drop of Blood," 53.

27. Wright, "One Drop of Blood," 55.

28. Kaplan, *Empire Wilderness*, 101.

29. Kaplan, *Empire Wilderness*, 97.

30. Kaplan, *Empire Wilderness*, 317 (brackets in original).

31. The most stinging examples of this phenomenon occur in questions about the environment—for example, the failure of Brazil to adequately protect its rain forests, and the continued overproduction of dangerous waste by much of the developed world. For a clear discussion of how these questions relate to sovereignty and International Relations theory, see Thom Kuehls, *Beyond Sovereign Territory: The Space of Ecopolitics* (Minneapolis: University of Minnesota Press, 1996).

32. David Held and Anthony McGrew, "The End of the Old Order? Globalization and the Prospects for World Order," *Review of International Studies* 24 (December 1998): 235, 219-243.

33. Held and McGrew, "The End of the Old Order?" 238.

34. Held and McGrew, "The End of the Old Order?" 238.

35. Held and McGrew, "The End of the Old Order?" 240.

36. Held and McGrew, "The End of the Old Order?" 241.

37. Held and McGrew, "The End of the Old Order?" 241.

38. Held and McGrew, "The End of the Old Order?" 242.

39. David Held, "Democracy and the New International Order," in *Cosmopolitan Democracy: An Agenda for a New World Order*, ed. Daniele Archibugi and David Held (Cambridge: Polity Press, 1995), 103 (emphasis in original).

40. Held, "New International Order," 112.

41. Held, "New International Order," 115-116.

42. Held, "New International Order," 116.

43. Jane Mansbridge, "Using Power/Fighting Power: The Polity," in *Democracy and Difference: Contesting the Boundaries of the Political*, ed. Seyla Benhabib (Princeton: Princeton University Press, 1996), 54.

44. Mansbridge, "Using Power/Fighting Power," 58.

45. Chantal Mouffe, "Democracy, Power, and the 'Political,'" in *Democracy and Difference*, ed. Seyla Benhabib, 248.

46. Mouffe, "Democracy, Power, and the 'Political,'" 248.

47. Mouffe, "Democracy, Power, and the 'Political,'" 252.

48. Mouffe, "Democracy, Power, and the 'Political,'" 254.

49. Mouffe, "Democracy, Power, and the 'Political,'" 255.

50. Bonnie Honig, "Difference, Dilemmas, and the Politics of Home," in *Democracy and Difference*, ed. Seyla Benhabib, 258.

51. Honig, "Politics of Home," 258.

52. Honig, "Politics of Home," 270.

53. Honig, "Politics of Home," 271 (emphasis in original).

54. Honig, "Politics of Home," 272.

55. Julia Kristeva, "Strangers to Ourselves," in *The Portable Kristeva*, ed. Kelly Oliver. European Perspectives Series. (New York: Columbia University Press, 1997), 290.

56. Kristeva, "Strangers to Ourselves," 290 (emphasis in original).

57. Connolly, *Ethos of Pluralization*, 152.

58. Connolly, *Ethos of Pluralization*, 153.

59. Connolly, *Ethos of Pluralization*, 155 (emphasis in original).

60. Connolly, *Ethos of Pluralization*, 161.

61. Connolly, *Ethos of Pluralization*, 160.

62. Connolly, *Ethos of Pluralization*, 196-197.

63. Connolly, *Ethos of Pluralization*, 94. Actually, Connolly borrows the rhizome metaphor from Gilles Deleuze and Félix Guattari.

64. Connolly, *Ethos of Pluralization*, 193.

65. William Connolly, *Identity\Difference: Democratic Negotiations of Political Paradox* (Ithaca: Cornell University Press, 1991), 178-179.

66. Roland Bleiker, "Forget IR Theory," *Alternatives* 22, no. 1 (1997): 79, 57-85.

67. Milan Kundera, *Testaments Betrayed*, trans. Linda Asher (London: Faber and Faber, 1995), 128.

68. In Kosovo, to take another regional example, the agreement over the withdrawal of Serbian forces from Kosovo and the deployment of NATO troops guaranteed the "security" of returning Albanian refugees. Nothing in the agreement recognized the need for Albanians and Serbs to *forget* Kosovo's history. Nothing about this settlement indicates that relations between Serbs and Albanians will soon be "settled." All the borders—territorial and political—remain technically intact.

Bibliography

Abbot, Philip. "The Lincoln Propositions and the Spirit of Secession." In *Theories of Secession*, edited by Percy B. Lehning, 182-207. London: Routledge, 1998.

An Act Respecting the Future of Québec. Bill 1, Introduction Québec Official Publisher, 1995.

Adams, Robert M. Translator's note to *The Prince*, by Niccolò Machiavelli, edited and translated by Robert M. Adams. New York: Norton, 1977.

Agnew, John. "The Territorial Trap: The Geographical Assumptions of International Relations Theory." *Review of International Political Economy* 1, no. 1 (Spring 1994): 53-80.

Anderson, Benedict. *Imagined Communities: Reflections on the Origin and Spread of Nationalism*. London: Verso, 1993.

Anderson, M. S. *The Ascendancy of Europe 1815-1914*. 2d ed. London: Longman Group Limited, 1985.

Appadurai, Arjun. "Sovereignty without Territoriality: Notes for a Postnational Geography." In *The Geography of Identity*, edited by Patricia Yaeger, 40-58. Ann Arbor: University of Michigan Press, 1996.

Appiah, K. Anthony, and Amy Gutmann. *Color Conscious: The Political Morality of Race*. Princeton: Princeton University Press, 1996.

Archibugi, Daniele, and David Held, eds. *Cosmopolitan Democracy: An Agenda for a New World Order*. Cambridge: Polity Press, 1995.

Bakić-Hayden, Milica, and Robert M. Hayden. "Orientalist Variations on the Theme 'Balkans': Symbolic Geography in Recent Yugoslav Cultural Politics." *Slavic Review* 51, no. 1 (Spring 1992): 1-15.

Baldwin, Thomas. "The Territorial State." In *Jurisprudence: Cambridge Essays*, edited by Hyman Gross and Ross Harrison, 207-230. Oxford: Clarendon Press, 1992.

Barkin, J. Samuel, and Bruce Cronin. "The State and the Nation: Changing Norms and the Rules of Sovereignty in International Relations." *International Organization* 48, no. 1 (Winter 1994): 107-130.

Bartelson, Jens. *A Genealogy of Sovereignty*. Cambridge: Cambridge University Press, 1995.

Bartkus, Viva Ona. "Secession: An Analytical Framework Concerning the Decision to Secede." Ph.D. diss., Oxford University, 1992.

———. *The Dynamic of Secession*. Cambridge: Cambridge University Press, 1999.

Behnke, Andreas. "Citizenship, Nationhood and the Production of Political Space." *Citizenship Studies* 1, no. 1 (1997): 243-265.

Beitz, Charles R. *Political Theory and International Relations*. Princeton: Princeton University Press, 1979.

Benhabib, Seyla, ed. *Democracy and Difference: Contesting the Boundaries of the Political*. Princeton: Princeton University Press, 1996.

Beran, Harry. "A Liberal Theory of Secession." *Political Studies* 32 (1984): 21-31.

———. *The Consent Theory of Political Obligation*. London: Croom Helm, 1987.

———. "A Democratic Theory of Political Self-Determination for a New World Order." In *Theories of Secession*, edited by Percy B. Lehning, 32-59. London: Routledge, 1998.

Berlin, Isaiah. "The Bent Twig: A Note on Nationalism." *Foreign Affairs* 51, no. 1 (October 1972): 11-30.

———. *The Crooked Timber of Humanity*. New York: Alfred A. Knopf, 1991.

———. *The Proper Study of Mankind*. Edited by Henry Hardy and Roger Hausheer. London: Pimlico, 1998.

Biersteker, Thomas J., and Cynthia Weber, eds. *The Social Construction of State Sovereignty*. Cambridge: Cambridge University Press, 1996.

Birch, Anthony H. *Nationalism and National Integration*. London: Unwin Hyman, 1989.

Bishai, Linda. "Altered States: Secession and the Problems of Liberal Theory." In *Theories of Secession*, edited by Percy B. Lehning, 92-110. London: Routledge, 1998.

———. "Sovereignty and Minority Rights." *Global Governance: A Review of Multilateralism and International Organizations* 4, no. 2 (Spring 1998): 157-182.

———. "Is International Law Compatible with Peace in a War-Torn Society? Trials and Tribulations in Bosnia" *Towson University Journal of International Affairs* 36, no. 1 (1999): 17-24.

———. "Secession and Security: The Politics of Ethno-Cultural Identity." In *Security and Identity in Europe: Exploring the New Agenda*, edited by Lisbeth Aggestam and Adrian Hyde-Price, 154-172. London: Macmillan, 2000.

Bleiker, Roland. "Forget IR Theory." *Alternatives* 22, no.1 (1997): 57-85.

Booth, Ken, and Steve Smith, eds. *International Relations Theory Today*. Cambridge: Polity Press, 1995.

Booth, William. "One Nation, Indivisible: Is It History?" *The Washington Post*, 22 February 1998.

Brilmayer, Lea. "Secession and Self-Determination: A Territorial Interpretation." *Yale Journal of International Law* 16 (1991): 177-202.

Brölmann, Catherine, René Lefeber, and Marjoleine Zieck, eds. *Peoples and Minorities in International Law*. Dordrecht: Martinus Nijhoff Publishers, 1993.

Brown, Chris, ed. *Political Restructuring in Europe: Ethical Perspectives*. London: Routledge, 1994.

Brownlie, Ian. *Principles of Public International Law*. 4th ed. Oxford: Oxford University Press, 1990.

Buchanan, Allen. *Secession: The Morality of Political Divorce from Fort Sumter to Lithuania and Quebec*. Boulder: Westview Press, 1991.

————. "Democracy and Secession." In *National Self-Determination and Secession*, edited by Margaret Moore, 14-33. Oxford: Oxford University Press, 1998.

————. "The International Institutional Dimension of Secession." In *Theories of Secession*, edited by Percy B. Lehning, 227-256. London: Routledge, 1998.

Buchheit, Lee C. *Secession: The Legitimacy of Self-Determination*. New Haven: Yale University Press, 1978.

Bull, Hedley. "The Theory of International Politics, 1919-1969." In *International Relations: Critical Investigations*, edited by James Der Derian, 181-211. London: Macmillan, 1995. First published in Brian Porter, ed., *The Aberystwyth Papers: International Politics 1919-1969* (London: Oxford University Press, 1972).

————. *The Anarchical Society: A Study of Order in World Politics*. New York: Columbia University Press, 1977.

Burke, Edmund. *Reflections on the Revolution in France*. New York: Anchor Books, 1973.

Butler, Judith. *Bodies That Matter: On the Discursive Limits of Sex*. London: Routledge, 1993.

Campbell, David. "Violent Performances: Identity, Sovereignty, Responsibility." In *The Return of Culture and Identity in IR Theory*, edited by Yosef Lapid and Friedrich Kratochwil, 163-180. Boulder: Lynne Rienner, 1996.

————. *National Deconstruction: Violence, Identity, and Justice in Bosnia*. Minneapolis: University of Minnesota Press, 1998.

————. *Writing Security: United States Foreign Policy and the Politics of Identity*. Rev. ed. Manchester: Manchester University Press, 1998.

Carr, E. H. *The Twenty Years' Crisis 1919-1939: An Introduction to the Study of International Relations*. London: Macmillan, 1993 [1939].

Chaliand, Gérard, ed. *Minority Peoples in the Age of Nation-States*. Translated by Tony Berrett. London: Pluto Press, 1989.

Cohn, Carol. "Wars, Wimps, and Women: Talking Gender and Thinking War." In *Gendering War Talk*, edited by Miriam Cooke and Angela Woollacott, 227-246. Princeton: Princeton University Press, 1993.

Coker, Christopher. *War and the 20th Century: The Impact of War on the Modern Consciousness*. London: Brassey's, 1994.

Connolly, William E. *Identity\Difference: Democratic Negotiations of a Political Paradox*. Ithaca: Cornell University Press, 1991.

————. *The Ethos of Pluralization*. Minneapolis: University of Minnesota Press, 1995.

————. *Why I Am Not a Secularist*. Minneapolis: University of Minnesota Press, 1999.

Connor, Walker. *Ethnonationalism: The Quest for Understanding*. Princeton: Princeton University Press, 1994.

Cooke, Miriam, and Angela Woollacott, eds. *Gendering War Talk*. Princeton: Princeton University Press, 1993.

Coppieters, Bruno, and Michel Huysseune, eds. *Secession, History and the Social Sciences*. Brussels: VUB Brussels University Press, 2002.

Cox, Robert. "Social Forces, States and World Orders: Beyond International Relations Theory." In *Neorealism and Its Critics*, edited by R. Keohane, 204-254. New York: Columbia University Press, 1985.

————. "Towards a Post-Hegemonic Conceptualization of World Order: Reflections on the Relevancy of Ibn Khaldun." In *Governance without Government: Order and Change in World Politics*, edited by James N. Rosenau and Ernst-Otto Czempiel, 132-159. Cambridge: Cambridge University Press, 1992.

Crawford, James. *The Creation of States in International Law*. Oxford: Clarendon Press, 1979.

Dahbour, Omar, and Micheline R. Ishay, eds. *The Nationalism Reader*. Atlantic Highlands, N.J.: Humanities Press, 1995.

Dante. *Monarchy*. Translated by Donald Nicholl. New York: The Noonday Press, 1947; Westport, Conn.: Hyperion Press, 1979.

Declaration of Independence and Sovereignty of Padania. 15 September 1996. Available from http://www.seveso.org/English_version/declaration_of_independence_of_padania. htm. Accessed 16 June 2003; on file with the author.

Del Rosso, Stephen J. Jr. "The Insecure State: Reflections on 'the State' and 'Security' in a Changing World." *Dædalus: Journal of the American Academy of Arts & Sciences* 124, no. 2 (1995): 175-207.

Der Derian, James. *Antidiplomacy: Spies, Terror, Speed, and War*. Cambridge, Mass.: Blackwell, 1992.

———, ed. *International Theory: Critical Investigations*. London: Macmillan, 1995.

Derrida, Jacques. *Specters of Marx: The State of the Debt, the Work of Mourning, and the New International*. Translated by Peggy Kamuf. New York: Routledge, 1994.

Donnan, Hastings, and Thomas Wilson, eds. *Border Approaches: Anthropological Perspectives on Frontiers*. Lanham, Md.: University Press of America, 1994.

Doty, Roxanne Lynn. "The Double-Writing of Statecraft: Exploring State Responses to Illegal Immigration." *Alternatives* 21 (1996): 171-189.

———. "Immigration and National Identity: Constructing the Nation." *Review of International Studies* 22 (1996): 235-255.

Dunne, Tim. *Inventing International Society: A History of the English School*. London: Macmillan, 1998.

Eriksen, Thomas Hylland. *Ethnicity & Nationalism: Anthropological Perspectives*. London: Pluto Press, 1993.

Ewin, R. E. "Peoples and Secession." *Journal of Applied Philosophy* 11, no. 2 (1994): 225-231.

Fawn, Rick, and Jeremy Larkins, eds. *International Society after the Cold War: Anarchy and Order Reconsidered*. London: Macmillan, 1996.

Fawn, Rick, and James Mayall. "Recognition, Self-Determination and Secession in Post-Cold War International Society." In *International Society after the Cold War: Anarchy and Order Reconsidered*, edited by Rick Fawn and Jeremy Larkins, 193-219. London: Macmillan, 1996.

Ferguson, Yale H., and Richard W. Mansbach. "Political Space and Westphalian States in a World of 'Polities': Beyond Inside/Outside." *Global Governance* 2, no. 2 (1996): 261-287.

Fighting for the Freedom of North-Italy. Available from http://www.seveso.org/English_version/Introduction_to_Lega_Nord.htm. Accessed 16 April 2003; on file with the author.

Foucault, Michel. "Nietzsche, Genealogy, History." In *Language, Counter-Memory, Practice*. Edited and with introduction by Donald F. Bouchard, translated by Donald F. Bouchard and Sherry Simon, 139-164. Oxford: Basil Blackwell, 1977.

Franck, Thomas M. "Tribe, Nation, World: Self-Identification in the Evolving International System." *Ethics & International Affairs* 11 (1997): 151-169.

Frankel, Lawrence M. "International Law of Secession: New Rules for a New Era." *Houston Journal of International Law* 14 (1992): 521-564.

Freeman, John. "A Model Territory: Enclosure in More's *Utopia*." In *The Territorial Rights of Nations and Peoples*, edited by John R. Jacobson, 241-267. Essays from the Basic Issues Forum, Studies in World Peace, vol. 2. Lewiston, N.Y.: Edwin Mellen Press, 1989.

Friedman, Jonathan. "The Past in the Future: History and the Politics of Identity." *American Anthropologist* 94, no. 4 (1992): 837-859.

Fussell, Paul. *The Great War and Modern Memory*. London: Oxford University Press, 1975.

Geertz, Clifford. *The Interpretation of Cultures*. New York: Fontana Press, 1973.

Gellner, Ernest. *Nations and Nationalism*. Oxford: Blackwell, 1983.

George, Jim. *Discourses of Global Politics: A Critical (Re)Introduction to International Relations*. Boulder: Lynne Rienner, 1994.

Giddens, Anthony. *The Nation-State and Violence*. Berkeley: University of California Press, 1987.

Giordano, Benito. "A Place Called Padania? The Lega Nord and the Political Representation of Northern Italy." *European Urban and Regional Studies* 6, no. 3 (1999): 215-230.

Gottlieb, Gidon. *Nation against State: A New Approach to Ethnic Conflicts and the Decline of Sovereignty*. New York: Council on Foreign Relations Press, 1993.

Greenfeld, Liah. *Nationalism: Five Roads to Modernity*. Cambridge: Harvard University Press, 1992.

Grosby, Steven. "Territoriality: The Transcendental, Primordial Feature of Modern Societies." *Nations and Nationalism* 1, no. 2 (July 1995): 143-162.

Gross, Hyman, and Ross Harrison, eds. *Jurisprudence: Cambridge Essays*. Oxford: Clarendon Press, 1992.

Grotius, Hugo. *De Jure Belli ac Pacis*. Translated by Francis W. Kelsey, edited by James Brown Scott. 1925. N.p.

Halász, Zoltán. *A Short History of Hungary*. Translated by Csaba Szabó. Budapest: Corvina Press, 1975.

Halperin, Morton H., and David J. Scheffer with Patricia L. Small. *Self-Determination in the New World Order*. Washington: Carnegie Endowment for International Peace, 1992.

Hannum, Hurst. *Autonomy, Sovereignty, and Self-Determination: The Accommodation of Conflicting Rights*. Philadelphia: University of Pennsylvania Press, 1990.

———. "The Specter of Secession: Responding to Claims for Ethnic Self-Determination." *Foreign Affairs* 77, no. 2 (1998): 13-18.

Hawai'i Constitution. 16 January 1995. Available from http://www.hawaii-nation.org/hawaii-nation.html/constitution.html. Accessed 16 June 2003; on file with the author.

Hayden, Robert M. "Constitutional Nationalism in the Former Yugoslav Republics." *Slavic Review* 51, no. 4 (1992): 654-673.

Heiberg, Marianne, ed. *Subduing Sovereignty: Sovereignty and the Right to Intervene*. London: Pinter, 1994.

Held, David. "Democracy and the New International Order." In *Cosmopolitan Democracy: An Agenda for a New World Order*, edited by Daniele Archibugi and David Held, 96-120. Cambridge: Polity Press, 1995.

Held, David, and Anthony McGrew. "The End of the Old Order? Globalization and the Prospects for World Order." *Review of International Studies* 24 (December 1998): 219-243.

Heraclides, Alexis. *The Self-Determination of Minorities in International Politics*. London: Frank Cass, 1991.

————. "Secession, Self-Determination and Nonintervention in Quest of a Normative Symbiosis." *Journal of International Affairs* 45, no. 2 (1992): 400-420.

————. "Secessionist Conflagration: What Is to Be Done?" *Security Dialogue* 25, no. 3 (1994): 283-293.

Herz, John H. *International Politics in the Atomic Age*. New York: Columbia University Press, 1959.

Hinsley, F. H. *Sovereignty*. 2d ed. Cambridge: Cambridge University Press, 1986.

Hobbes, Thomas. *Leviathan*. Edited by C. B. Macpherson. London: Penguin, 1985.

Hobsbawm, E. J. *Nations and Nationalism since 1780: Programme, Myth, Reality*. Cambridge: Cambridge University Press, 1990.

Hoffmann, Stanley. "An American Social Science: International Relations." In *International Theory: Critical Investigations*, edited by James Der Derian, 212-241. London: Macmillan, 1995. First published in *Dædalus* 106, no. 3 (1977): 41-60.

Honig, Bonnie. *Political Theory and the Displacement of Politics*. Ithaca: Cornell University Press, 1993.

————. "Difference, Dilemmas, and the Politics of Home." In *Democracy and Difference: Contesting the Boundaries of the Political*, edited by Seyla Benhabib, 257-277. Princeton: Princeton University Press, 1996.

Horowitz, Donald L. *Ethnic Groups in Conflict*. Berkeley: University of California Press, 1985.

Inayatullah, Naeem, and David L. Blaney. "Realizing Sovereignty." *Review of International Studies* 21 (1995): 3-20.

————. "Knowing Encounters: Beyond Parochialism in International Relations Theory." In *The Return of Culture and Identity in IR Theory*, edited by Yosef Lapid and Friedrich Kratochwil, 65-84. Boulder: Lynne Rienner, 1996.

Jackson, Robert H. *Quasi-States: Sovereignty, International Relations, and the Third World*. Cambridge: Cambridge University Press, 1990.

Jacobson, John R., ed. *The Territorial Rights of Nations and Peoples*. Essays from the Basic Issues Forum, Studies in World Peace, vol. 2. Lewiston, N.Y.: Edwin Mellen Press, 1989.

Kantorowicz, Ernst. *The King's Two Bodies: A Study in Mediaeval Political Theology*. Princeton: Princeton University Press, 1957.

Kaplan, Robert. *Empire Wilderness: Travels into America's Future*. New York: Random House, 1998.

————. "Travels into America's Future." *The Atlantic Monthly*, August 1998. Available from http://www.theatlantic.com/issues/98aug/amfuture.htm. Accessed 12 August 2003.

Kedourie, Elie. *Nationalism*. 4th ed. Oxford: Blackwell, 1993.

Keohane, Robert O., ed. *Neorealism and Its Critics*. New York: Columbia University Press, 1985.

Kofman, Daniel. "Rights of Secession." *Society* 35, no. 5 (1998): 30-38.

Koselleck, Reinhart. *Futures Past: On the Semantics of Historical Time*. Translated by Keith Tribe. Cambridge: MIT Press, 1985.

Koskenniemi, Martti. "National Self-Determination Today: Problems of Legal Theory and Practice." *International and Comparative Law Quarterly* 43 (1994): 241-269.

Kratochwil, Friedrich. "Of Systems, Boundaries, and Territoriality: An Inquiry into the Formation of the State System." *World Politics* 39, no. 1 (1986): 27-52.

Kristeva, Julia. "Strangers to Ourselves." In *The Portable Kristeva*, edited by Kelly Oliver, 264-294. European Perspectives Series. New York: Columbia University Press, 1997.

Kuehls, Thom. *Beyond Sovereign Territory: The Space of Ecopolitics.* Minneapolis: University of Minnesota Press, 1996.

Kundera, Milan. *Testaments Betrayed.* Translated by Linda Asher. London: Faber and Faber, 1995.

Kymlicka, Will. *Liberalism, Community, and Culture.* Oxford: Clarendon Press, 1989.

———. *Multicultural Citizenship: A Liberal Theory of Minority Rights.* Oxford: Clarendon Press, 1995.

———. "Modernity and Minority Nationalism: Commentary on Thomas Franck." *Ethics and International Affairs* 11 (1997): 171-176.

———, ed. *The Rights of Minority Cultures.* Oxford: Oxford University Press, 1995.

Lapid, Yosef. "Culture's Ship: Returns and Departures in International Relations Theory." In *The Return of Culture and Identity in IR Theory*, edited by Yosef Lapid and Friedrich Kratochwil, 3-20. Boulder: Lynne Rienner, 1996.

Lapid, Yosef, and Friedrich Kratochwil, eds. *The Return of Culture and Identity in IR Theory.* Boulder: Lynne Rienner, 1996.

Lask, Tomke. "'Baguette heads' and 'spiked helmets': Children's Constructions of Nationality on the German-French Border." In *Border Approaches: Anthropological Perspectives on Frontiers*, edited by Hastings Donnon and Thomas Wilson, 63-73. Lanham, Md.: University Press of America, 1994.

Lehning, Percy B., ed. *Theories of Secession.* London: Routledge, 1998.

Linklater, Andrew. "Citizenship and Sovereignty in the Post-Westphalian State." *European Journal of International Relations* 2, no. 1 (1996): 77-103.

———. "The Transformation of Political Community: E. H. Carr, Critical Theory and International Relations." *Review of International Studies* 23 (1997): 321-338.

Livingston, Donald W. "The Very Idea of Secession," *Society* 35, no. 5 (1998): 38-49.

Machiavelli, Niccolò. *The Prince.* Edited and translated by Robert Adams. New York: Norton: 1977.

Malley, R., J. Manas, and C. Nix. "Constructing the State Extraterritorially: Jurisdictional Discourse, the National Interest, and Transnational Norms." *Harvard Law Review* 103 (1990): 1273-1305.

Mansbridge, Jane. "Using Power/Fighting Power: The Polity." In *Democracy and Difference: Contesting the Boundaries of the Political*, edited by Seyla Benhabib, 46-66. Princeton: Princeton University Press, 1996.

Mayall, James. *Nationalism and International Society.* Cambridge: Cambridge University Press, 1990.

———. "Self-determination Reconsidered: Should There Be a Right to Secede?" *The Oxford International Review* 4, no. 1 (Winter 1993): 4-6.

Mayall, James, and Mark Simpson. "Ethnicity Is Not Enough: Reflections on Protracted Secessionism in the Third World." *International Journal of Comparative Sociology* 33, no. 1-2 (1992): 5-25.

McFarland, Philip. *The Brave Bostonians: Hutchinson, Quincy, Franklin, and the Coming of the American Revolution.* Oxford: Westview Press, 1998.

McGarry, John. "'Orphans of Secession': National Pluralism in Secessionist Regions and Post-Secession States." In *National Self-Determination and Secession*, edited by Margaret Moore, 215-232. Oxford: Oxford University Press, 1998.

McPherson, James. *Battle Cry of Freedom: The American Civil War.* London: Penguin Books Ltd., 1990.

Milliken, Jennifer, and David Sylvan. "Soft Bodies, Hard Targets, and Chic Theories: US Bombing Policy in Indochina." *Millennium: Journal of International Studies* 25, no. 2 (1996): 321-359.

Moore, Margaret, ed. *National Self-Determination and Secession.* Oxford: Oxford University Press, 1998.

More, Thomas, Sir. *Utopia.* Translated by Peter K. Marshall. New York: Washington Square Press, 1965.

Morgenthau, Hans. *Politics among Nations: The Struggle for Power and Peace.* Brief ed. Revised by Kenneth W. Thompson. New York: McGraw-Hill, 1993.

Mouffe, Chantal. "Democracy, Power, and the Political." In *Democracy and Difference: Contesting the Boundaries of the Political,* edited by Seyla Benhabib, 245-256. Princeton: Princeton University Press, 1996.

Moynihan, Daniel Patrick. *On the Law of Nations.* Cambridge: Harvard University Press, 1990.

Murray, Gilbert. "Revision of the Peace Treaties." In *The Intelligent Man's Way to Prevent War,* edited by Leonard Woolf. London: Victor Gollancz Ltd., 1933.

Neumann, Iver B., and Jennifer M. Welsh. "The Other in European Self-Definition: An Addendum to the Literature on International Society." *Review of International Studies* 17 (1991): 327-348.

Nielsen, Kai. "Secession: The Case of Quebec." *Journal of Applied Philosophy* 10, no. 1 (1993): 29-43.

Nietzsche, Friedrich. *Untimely Meditations.* Translated by R. J. Hollingdale. Cambridge: Cambridge University Press, 1983.

———. *On the Genealogy of Morality.* Translated by Carol Diethe. Cambridge: Cambridge University Press, 1994.

O'Brien, Conor Cruise. *God-Land: Reflections on Religion and Nationalism.* Cambridge: Harvard University Press, 1988.

O'Neill, Onora. "Justice and Boundaries." In *Political Restructuring in Europe: Ethical Perspectives,* edited by Chris Brown, 69-88. London: Routledge, 1994.

Padania: The Foundations of a Nation. N.d. Available from http://www.seveso.org /English_version/padania_the_foundations_of_a_nation.htm. Accessed 16 April 2003; on file with the author.

Parizeau, Jacques. "Who Are We? Where Are We Going?" Translated by P. Van de Wille. *The (Toronto) Globe and Mail,* 30 October 1996.

———. "The Objective Is Sovereignty, Not Partnership." Translated by P. Van de Wille. *The (Toronto) Globe and Mail,* 19 December 1996.

Patten, Alan. "Democratic Secession from a Multinational State." *Ethics* 112 (April 2002): 558-586.

Pavković, Aleksandar. "Recursive Secessions in Former Yugoslavia: Too Hard a Case for Theories of Secession?" *Political Studies* 48 (2000): 485-502.

Philpott, Daniel. "Sovereignty: An Introduction and Brief History." *Journal of International Affairs* 48, no. 2 (1995): 353-368.

Pocock, J. G. A. "Verbalizing a Political Act: Towards a Politics of Speech." In *Language and Politics,* edited by Michael Shapiro, 25-43. Oxford: Blackwell, 1984.

Premdas, Ralph. "Secessionist Movements in Comparative Perspective." In *Secessionist Movements in Comparative Perspective,* edited by Ralph Premdas, S.W.R. de A. Samarasinghe, and Alan Anderson, 12-25. London: Pinter, 1990.

Premdas, Ralph, S.W.R. de A. Samarasinghe, and Alan Anderson, eds. *Secessionist Movements in Comparative Perspective*. London: Pinter, 1990.

Proclamation of Restoration of the Independence of the Sovereign Nation State of Hawai ʻi. 16 January 1994. Available from http://www.hawaii-nation.org/proclamall.html. Accessed 16 April 2003; on file with the author.

Ringmar, Erik. "The Relevance of International Law: A Hegelian Interpretation of a Peculiar Seventeenth-Century Preoccupation." *Review of International Studies* 21 (1995): 87-103.

―――. "On the Ontological Status of the State." *European Journal of International Relations* 2, no. 4 (1996): 439-466.

Rosenau, James N., and Ernst-Otto Czempiel, eds. *Governance without Government: Order and Change in World Politics*. Cambridge: Cambridge University Press, 1992.

Ruggie, John Gerard. "Territoriality and Beyond: Problematizing Modernity in International Relations." *International Organization* 47, no. 1 (1993): 139-174.

Sack, Robert David. *Human Territoriality: Its Theory and History*. Cambridge: Cambridge University Press, 1986.

Said, Edward. *Orientalism*. New York: Vintage, 1979.

Schaeffer, Robert K. *Severed States: Dilemmas of Democracy in a Divided World*. Lanham, Md.: Rowman & Littlefield, 1999.

Schiesel, Seth, and Robert L. Turner. "Is Race Obsolete?" *The Boston Globe Magazine*, 22 September 1996, 13-20.

Schmitt, Carl. *Political Theology: Four Chapters on the Concept of Sovereignty*. Translated by George Schwab. Cambridge: MIT Press, 1985 [1932].

―――. *The Concept of the Political*. Translated with an introduction by George Schwab. Chicago: University of Chicago Press, 1996.

Sciortino, Giuseppe. "Just before the Fall: The Northern League and the Cultural Construction of a Secessionist Claim." *International Sociology* 14, no. 3 (1999): 321-336.

Shapiro, Michael, ed. *Language and Politics*. Oxford: Blackwell, 1984.

Shehadi, Kamal S. *Ethnic Self-Determination and the Break-up of States*. Adelphi Paper No. 283. The International Institute for Strategic Studies. London: Brassey's, 1993.

Sked, Alan. *The Decline and Fall of the Habsburg Empire 1815-1918*. London: Longman Group UK Limited, 1989.

Skinner, Quentin. *Machiavelli*. Oxford: Oxford University Press, 1981.

Smith, Steve. "The Self-Images of a Discipline: A Genealogy of International Relations Theory." In *International Relations Theory Today*, edited by Ken Booth and Steve Smith, 1-37. Cambridge: Polity Press, 1995.

Stille, Alexander. "The Fall of Rome?" *George*, September 1997, 102-108.

Strauss, Erwin S. *How to Start Your Own Country*. Port Townsend, Wash.: Loompanics Unlimited, 1984.

Tamir, Yael. *Liberal Nationalism*. Princeton: Princeton University Press, 1993.

Taylor, Charles. *Sources of the Self: The Making of the Modern Identity*. Cambridge: Cambridge University Press, 1989.

Tiryakian, Edward A. "Secession, Autonomy and Modernity," *Society* 35, no. 5 (1998): 49-59.

Tocqueville, Alexis de. *Democracy in America*. Everyman's Library. London: David Campbell Publishers Ltd., 1994.

Toolan, Michael J. *Narrative: A Critical Linguistic Introduction*. London: Routledge, 1988.

The Treaty of Westphalia. *Peace Treaty between the Holy Roman Emperor and the King of France and Their Respective Allies*, Munster, October 24, 1648. Translated by the British Foreign Office. Available from http://www.tufts.edu/fletcher/multi/texts/ historical/westphalia. txt. Accessed 25 April 2003.

Turack, Daniel C. *The Passport in International Law.* Lexington, Mass.: Lexington Books, 1972.

U.S. Immigration and Naturalization Service, *A Guide to Naturalization.* (M-476)(rev. 12/00). Available from http://www.immigration.gov/graphics/services/natz/English.pdf. Accessed 25 April 2003.

Virilio, Paul. *Speed & Politics: An Essay on Dromology.* Translated by Mark Polizzotti. New York: Semiotext(e), 1986.

Wæver, Ole, et al, eds. *Identity, Migration and the New Security Agenda in Europe.* London: Pinter, 1993.

Walker, R. B. J. "Security, Sovereignty, and the Challenge of World Politics." *Alternatives* 15, no. 1 (1990): 3-27.

———. "State Sovereignty and the Articulation of Political Space/Time." *Millennium: Journal of International Studies* 20, no. 3 (Winter 1991): 445-461.

———. *Inside/Outside: International Relations as Political Theory.* Cambridge: Cambridge University Press, 1993.

Walzer, Michael. *Just and Unjust Wars: A Moral Argument with Historical Illustrations.* New York: HarperCollins Publishers, 1977.

Watson, Adam. *The Evolution of International Society: A Comparative Historical Analysis.* London: Routledge, 1992.

Weber, Cynthia. *Simulating Sovereignty: Intervention, the State and Symbolic Exchange.* Cambridge: Cambridge University Press, 1995.

———. "Performative States." *Millennium: Journal of International Studies* 27, no. 1 (1998): 77-95.

Weber, Eugen. *Peasants into Frenchmen: The Modernization of Rural France, 1870-1914.* Stanford: Stanford University Press, 1976.

White, Hayden. *The Content of the Form: Narrative Discourse and Historical Representation.* Baltimore: The Johns Hopkins University Press, 1987.

Wilson, Woodrow. "Address to a Joint Session of Congress, January 1918." In *The Nationalism Reader*, edited by Omar Dahbour and Micheline R. Ishay, 309. Atlantic Highlands, N.J.: Humanities Press, 1995.

Woolf, Leonard. Introduction to *The Intelligent Man's Way to Prevent War*, edited by Leonard Woolf. London: Victor Gollancz Ltd., 1933.

———, ed. *The Intelligent Man's Way to Prevent War.* London: Victor Gollancz Ltd., 1933.

Wright, Lawrence. "One Drop of Blood." *The New Yorker*, 25 July 1994, 46-55.

Yaeger, Patricia, ed. *The Geography of Identity.* Ann Arbor: University of Michigan Press, 1996.

Young, Iris Marion. "Together in Difference: Transforming the Logic of Group Political Conflict." In *The Rights of Minority Cultures*, edited by Will Kymlicka, 155-176. Oxford: Oxford University Press, 1995.

Zalewski, Marysia, and Cynthia Enloe. "Questions about Identity in International Relations." In *International Relations Theory Today*, edited by Ken Booth and Steve Smith, 279-305. Cambridge: Polity Press, 1995.

Index

About the Author

Linda Bishai is Assistant Professor of International Relations at Towson University in Maryland, where she teaches courses on international law, force and aggression, and international relations. She has published articles on security and secession, minority rights and international law, and secession and liberal theory. Her current research interests concern the impact of American exceptionalism on the international legal system. In addition to her teaching, Dr. Bishai has been active in Towson University's Multicultural Institute and has taught in the Southeast Europe Youth Leadership Institute, a summer program for promising high school students from that part of Europe. She also serves as the university's media contact for international law and politics issues. During the 2003-2004 academic year, Dr. Bishai will serve as a Supreme Court Fellow at the Federal Judicial Center. Prior to teaching at Towson, Dr. Bishai was a research fellow on issues of intervention at the Swedish Institute for International Affairs. She holds a Ph.D. in International Relations from the London School of Economics and Political Science, an LL.M. in International Law from the University of Stockholm, a J.D. from Georgetown University Law Center, and a B.A. in history and literature from Harvard University.